Churchill and the Lion City
Shaping Modern Singapore

T0345564

Churchill and the Lion City
Shaping Modern Singapore

Edited by

Brian P. Farrell

NUS PRESS
SINGAPORE

© 2011 Brian P. Farrell

Published by:

NUS Press
National University of Singapore
AS3-01-02, 3 Arts Link
Singapore 117569

Fax: (65) 6774-0652
E-mail: nusbooks@nus.edu.sg
Website: http://www.nus.edu.sg/nuspress

ISBN 978-9971-69-552-1 (Paper)
ISBN 978-9971-69-565-1 (Case)

National Library Board, Singapore Cataloguing-in-Publication Data

Churchill and the lion city: shaping modern Singapore / edited by Brian P. Farrell. – Singapore: NUS Press, c2011.
   p. cm.
   Includes bibliographical references and index.
   ISBN: 978-9971-69-565-1
   ISBN: 978-9971-69-552-1 (pbk.)

   1. Churchill, Winston, 1874–1965 – Military leadership – Congresses.
   2. Imperialism – History – 20th century – Congresses. 3. World War,
   1939–1945 – Campaigns – Singapore – Congresses. 4. Singapore – History
   – Siege, 1942 – Congresses. 5. Singapore – History – 20th century
   – Congresses. 6. Great Britain – Colonies – Asia – Defenses – Congresses.
   I. Farrell, Brian P. (Brian Padair), 1960–

   DS610.4
   959.5705 — dc22   OCN705217676

Cover images:
Empire at bay: Churchill tames a lion, 10 September 1947; hand-drawn map in Churchill Papers outlining the Japanese conquest of Singapore, February 1942. (Supplied by the Churchill Archives Centre, with thanks to the Master, Fellows and scholars of Churchill College, Cambridge, and the Trustees of the Sir Winston Churchill Archive Trust.)

Typeset by: Scientifik Graphics
Printed by: C.O.S. Printers

CONTENTS

FOREWORD

This book has come about from a unique and very special collaboration between the National University of Singapore and Churchill College in the University of Cambridge. Its birth was a well attended one-day conference held at the NUS Cultural Centre on Friday 9 April 2010 — an event that deliberately brought together historians and experts from the United Kingdom, Singapore and Australia to discuss the role and impact of Sir Winston Churchill, Britain's most famous modern Prime Minister, and the man famously called upon to give the "lion's roar" in the Second World War, on the shaping of the Lion City.

With such a subject, the conference was always going to be large in scope. It had to seek to define Churchill's imperialism, to explain why Singapore mattered so much to someone who never set foot on its shores, and to show how Churchill's strategy and leadership, while motivated by the desire to preserve the Empire, led to the fall of Singapore to the Japanese, and to the island's rise as an independent power in the post-war world.

It was clear to all who attended the conference, and who engaged in the lively debate outside the formal sessions, that the proceedings deserved a longer life. We are therefore delighted that our partnership continues to live through this publication, and that the papers by our distinguished speakers will continue to inform further research and debate beyond the confines of our individual universities. Finally, we would like to thank the contributors to this volume, as well as Allen Packwood and Tan Tai Yong for their efforts to organise this project, and Brian Farrell for his role in coordinating the conference and editing the volume.

Professor Tan Chorh Chuan
President, National University of Singapore

Professor Sir David Wallace
Master, Churchill College, Cambridge

ACKNOWLEDGEMENTS

One of the more pleasant customs of scholarship is to acknowledge, with thanks, the many people who helped make it possible to publish this book. This is particularly true for a volume combining the efforts of several scholars, such as this one. The symposium which produced this volume, and the book itself, were the result of the initiative and generous support of Professor Tan Chorh Chuan, President of the National University of Singapore, and Sir David Wallace, Master of Churchill College of Cambridge University. Professor Barry Halliwell, Deputy President (Research and Technology) at NUS, kindly opened proceedings and lent his support. Allen Packwood, Director of the Churchill Archives Centre, and Tan Tai Yong, Vice-Provost (Student Life) at NUS and proud alumnus of Churchill College, launched the project and drove it forward. Ang Cheng Guan and Jonathan Haslam made welcome contributions to the symposium. Shirley Koh provided administrative support. The Centre for the Arts at NUS was an excellent venue for our proceedings. Volunteers, always essential for such a project, truly helped this one; to Angeline Chui, Pang Yang Huei, Tan Chye Guan and Tan Kia Lih, thank you. The book enjoyed strong support and careful reading from two anonymous peer reviewers, for which I am grateful. John Coates generously allowed me to use his outstanding maps from the atlas for which we are all in his debt. NUS Press, led by Paul Kratoska, did its usual excellent job producing the volume; Eunice Low pulled it all together very efficiently. I have been lucky in my projects over the years at NUS to enjoy strong support from my dean and head of department, and Brenda Yeoh and Yong Mun Cheong provided just that, which is much appreciated. I am even luckier to be working in the Department of History at NUS, with colleagues who, as always, were there to be counted on. But in a book such as this one, the editor is only one member of a team of scholars pursuing a common interest. The project and the book are only as strong as the team. This one was a pleasure from start to finish and my deepest gratitude is to my friends and fellow authors, who produced such strong and interesting work. On their behalf, I am pleased to direct whatever royalties this book generates to the good hands of the

The Straits Times School Pocket Money Fund for needy schoolchildren in Singapore. May it help some of the next generation to follow us to podium and print.

Brian P. Farrell
Singapore
18 February 2011

List of Illustrations

Note: Plates 3.1, 3.2, 3.5, 3.7 and 3.8 are reproduced with permission of Curtis Brown Ltd, on behalf of The Broadwater Collection and supplied by the Churchill Archives Centre, with thanks to the Master, Fellows and scholars of Churchill College, Cambridge, and the Trustees of the Sir Winston Churchill Archive Trust.

Plates 3.3, 3.4 and 3.6 are supplied by the Churchill Archives Centre, with thanks to the Master, Fellows and scholars of Churchill College, Cambridge, and the Trustees of the Sir Winston Churchill Archive Trust.

Maps

[†] Extracted from Brian Farrell and Garth Pratten, *Malaya* (Canberra: Australian Army History Unit, 2009), courtesy of the Australian Army History Unit.

* Extracted from John Coates, *An Atlas of Australia's Wars* (Melbourne: Oxford University Press, 2001), courtesy of John Coates.

Chapter 5

Last Lion and the Lion City: Churchill, Singapore and Empire

Brian P. Farrell

The British Empire had a profound influence on world history in the 20th century. So did Winston Spencer Churchill. The two also had a profound influence on each other. During an active public life that ran from 1900 to 1955, Churchill promoted the vision and reality of empire from a unique array of vantage points: statesman, politician, diplomat, orator, journalist, historian, national and world hero. As Prime Minister during the Second World War, Churchill became the icon of an empire waging total war, to prevent the destruction of a world order it did so much to build. Churchill squared up with conviction to profound forces challenging this British-centred world order, famously declaring in November 1942: "I have not become the King's First Minister in order to preside over the liquidation of the British Empire".[1] Fate had other ideas. The Empire over which he presided gave the United Kingdom the means to play an imperial role in world affairs. Both empire and role barely survived Churchill, crumbling visibly as he declined personally. This process began even as Churchill entered public life, defined his public career, and stemmed in part from challenges he helped to confront.

Perhaps the most dramatic single failure in Churchill's long association with the British Empire was his failure to defend it against Japanese attack in what the British called the "Far East", in 1941. Punctuated by the humiliating fall of "fortress" Singapore in February 1942, defeat by Japan seemed to shatter the prestige on which British power in Asia relied. Given the eastward trend in empire after the "loss" of the American colonies in 1783, the fall of Singapore suggested the empire's days were

1

numbered. The number turned out to be rather large, but the connection remained dramatic. After British power withdrew from India in 1947, post-war Singapore became the hub of British efforts to remain an imperial power in Asia — and therefore a mainstay of British efforts to preserve a wider role in world affairs. When, barely three years after Churchill died, a British government announced in January 1968 that it would rapidly withdraw British military garrison forces from Singapore, and all points "East of Suez", the number seemed called. Churchill himself never set foot in Singapore. But it played dramatic roles in the fortunes of the Empire, and the British world role, to which he devoted his public life.

This volume stems from a symposium jointly presented by Churchill College Cambridge University and the National University of Singapore (NUS), held on the NUS campus in April 2010. 2010 marked the 50th anniversary of the founding of Churchill College, supported by Sir Winston himself. Spurring the evolution of the College is the archive that has grown around its central collection, Churchill's own personal papers. Resting on the massive Winston Spencer Churchill Papers, the Churchill Archives Centre has become the principal archive holding private papers relating to British 20th-century history, including for example the Margaret Thatcher Papers. The Centre is an indispensable stop for serious researchers working on topics related to British policy in a wide range of areas, including three with which Churchill became so closely identified: defence, foreign relations, and the Empire/Commonwealth. NUS is the premier educational institution of the Southeast Asian island city-state which played such a significant role in the Empire/Commonwealth during Churchill's public life — and remained central to British efforts to manage Churchill's legacy for a generation after he retired. And the NUS main campus sits on the site of one of the last engagements in the February 1942 battle Churchill himself defined as "Britain's worst military disaster". Sir David Wallace, Master of Churchill College, and Professor Tan Chorh Chuan, President of NUS, decided to sponsor an academic symposium to explore the connections between Churchill, Empire, and Singapore, by bringing together the college that preserves so much of that story with the national university of a state so heavily shaped by it. The symposium of April 2010 was the result, and this volume is the outcome.

There is a very large literature indeed devoted to Winston Spencer Churchill, with no sign of the tap running dry. Even as this book goes to press, readers have been offered two fresh major monograph studies of Churchill as war leader and statesman of empire.[2] Nor is there any shortage of studies of the British Empire in the 20th century, a subject revived by the excitement surrounding the return of its final major overseas territory, Hong Kong, in 1997.[3] Studies of Singapore and the role it played in the British Empire experience do not lag behind.[4] The most dramatic event in Singapore's imperial experience was of course its surrender to the Japanese in February 1942, and all the many studies of that event evaluate Churchill's personal role.[5] There is nevertheless no single volume concentrating on the broader and longer interplay between three important factors: Churchill, Empire, and Singapore. Connecting the three is the question of empire as an instrument through which the UK played a wider role in world affairs, and thus influenced the evolution of a world political and economic order. Churchill, as First Lord of the Admiralty (twice), Colonial Secretary, Secretary of State for War, Chancellor of the Exchequer, and Prime Minister (twice), played a more extensive executive role in directing the affairs of the Empire, and shaping its legacy, than any other 20th-century figure. He augmented that role as a political journalist, widely-read historian and memoirist, Leader of the Opposition and Opposition MP, and elder statesman. This brings four issues to the fore: Churchill's understanding of empire; his perceptions of Singapore and its imperial role; his direction of affairs regarding Singapore and the Empire; and his influence on the subsequent relationship between them. This volume of collected essays will explore these issues, and the context in which they unfolded.

The essays range in focus from a close study of Churchill himself, his view of the empire, the wartime experience that forever linked Singapore and Churchill, to an examination of how British policy changed after Churchill retired. The discussion deliberately overlaps, while the focus varies from broad survey to tight scrutiny. The connecting thread is the interplay between Churchill, Empire/Commonwealth, and Singapore — particularly regarding problems of defence and foreign relations. Piers Brendon frames the volume in the first chapter by his penetrating study of Churchill's lifelong vision of empire, and how it influenced his conduct of British policy. Churchill saw the Empire as integral to what he viewed as British greatness, a view certainly influenced by his racial perceptions. Without the Empire, Britain would be nothing but "a glorified Belgium". But Churchill's vision of empire, while romantic, was never static. There were constants, even over such a long career: a dislike for sharing imperial power, the sense of the British as an imperial people, and of their empire as a civilising force. Yet this did not prevent Churchill from adjusting to changing conditions after the Second World War, to try to preserve what he saw as the essence of empire: Britain's ability to shape the turbulent world in which it lived. Empire was indeed "the grand theme" of Churchill's career.

Imperialism fostered arrogance in wielding power, a theme Churchill reflected very well. Directing the affairs of a global empire challenged British statesmen to diagnose regional conditions in very different parts of the world, not always effectively. But the metropolis faced its own regional conditions, imposing a tug of war between home and peripheries for attention from the top. How British statesmen understood this tug of war, and what personal characteristics they brought to bear to manage it, were important parts of the imperial story. Changing world conditions after the Great War prompted British statesmen to promote Singapore from busy commercial port to first-class naval base, as the hub of imperial defence in their Far East. Churchill played a key role in these decisions, but the outcome was dire. There was no more embarrassing failure to manage the tug of war that was imperial defence than defeat by Japan, east of India, in 1941–1942. Churchill played a leading role in that failure. This editor tightens the focus in the second chapter by examining how Churchill saw Singapore, against the larger backdrop of imperial defence. By analysing his understanding of the nature of imperial defence, his approach to the offices he held, and his self-image as a maker of grand strategy, this chapter explains the role Churchill played in compromising imperial defence in the Far East before 1941. But it concludes that, due to these same traits, Churchill ultimately kept Singapore in perspective within the larger canvas on which he had to paint, however painful the consequences — and that Churchill's impact underlines the importance of the individual in history.

Churchill's direct personal role in trying to defend Singapore against Japanese invasion, and squaring up to the consequences, is explored by Allen Packwood in Chapter 3. Drawing from the Churchill Papers now entrusted to his care, the Director of the Churchill Archives Centre vividly depicts a Prime Minister confounded by the stark revelation that British military power could not prevent humiliation in Asia. Well aware how overstretched Britain's global position really was, hard pressed by a run of painful military defeats, Churchill looked for a defiant and heroic stand by the men on the spot, to offset that weakness. The faster the position crumbled, the harder the Prime Minister pressed for what his forces could not do. The debacle left a lasting impression on Churchill, struggling to maintain Britain's place in the inner circle of the global war. Packwood's close examination leads him to identify one important reason why Churchill misread the situation in Singapore, and to connect that to the larger consequences of its fall: "To Churchill himself, however, Singapore was never a real place, so much as a symbol of British power and a centre of strategic interest".

Defeat at Singapore, humiliation notwithstanding, was only one campaign in a global total war. Churchill, Britain and the Empire had to determine how to relate this particular failure to this larger war. Geoffrey Till explores the first question in Chapter 4: how did Churchill relate the defence and then fall of Singapore to grand strategy for waging global war? In an overlapping and insightful exploration of how Churchill tried first to stop the Japanese onslaught, then to roll it back, Till argues the Prime Minister pursued four distinct objectives regarding Singapore and grand strategy: to deter or delay a Japanese attack; to draw the Americans into the war, using "a British sprat to catch an American mackerel"; to prevent the defence of Singapore from jeopardising what he saw as higher strategic priorities; and to restore and revive the territories and prestige the Empire lost in 1942. These objectives shaped Churchill's efforts to direct the war against Japan, which he rightly saw as less urgent than the war in Europe, but about which "there is room for questioning" how he proceeded. Imperial considerations decisively influenced Churchill's exchanges with Dominion governments, and with his own Chiefs of Staff (COS), regarding how to efface the loss of Singapore and restore imperial power in Asia. Churchill's determination to "recover lost ground, battered prestige and strategic advantage", ultimately expressed as the desire to retake Singapore by force, went beyond his advisers' desire to concentrate on defeating Japan, sparking the most acrimonious arguments of the war between them. Churchill understood the nature of the global war far better than his enemies, and his arguments did not derail Allied victory; they did, however, point towards problems bound to challenge, after the war, the "sense of shared Britishness" on which empire rested.

The fall of Singapore was not just a personal defeat for Churchill; it was also a painful exposé of imperial weakness. But was it seen as such by the general populations of Britain and the Empire? And did it affect their subsequent approach to global war? Richard Toye tackles these questions in Chapter 5, shifting the focus to explore how the fall of Singapore was seen and presented as a symbol of the British Empire — what it was and what it could become. Churchill naturally played a leading role in presenting the defeat, but could not necessarily define at the time how it should be seen. British public opinion saw it as a depressing military defeat, but was more exercised by an embarrassing naval failure in the English Channel that same month. Defeat by Japan did however raise questions about how the Empire was administered. Such questions spread across the Atlantic, prompting some leading American public men to portray failure at Singapore as "symbolic of the failure of the British colonial system as a whole". Asian residents of the Empire went further, tending to see it as the beginning of the end. Churchill had to respond to such criticism, prompting his defiant defence of the Empire in November 1942. Toye's careful evaluation of the general mood suggests that he had his work cut out for him.

That conclusion is supported by Peter Edwards' persuasive study, in Chapter 6, of the relationship between Churchill and Australia, and the impact of Singapore on that relationship. Ambivalence was the foremost common theme. There was the ambivalence with which Australians came to regard a statesman whose great achievements were admired there no less than elsewhere, but who came to be seen as symbolising a British tendency to be careless with Australian security, a tendency underlined by bloody defeats at Gallipoli in one war and Singapore in another. And there was the ambivalence with which Australians tended to regard their own defence imperatives, torn between working with "great and powerful friends" and looking out for themselves. National myths notwithstanding, failure at Singapore ultimately prompted Australians not to abandon but to redesign the imperial relationship, and their approach to defence. Churchill did not welcome, but could not prevent, Cold War Australia from striving to work with the Americans as well as the British, to secure itself. The turn towards the Americans was a deep flowing "great tide" which Churchill and Singapore only reinforced.

The fall of Singapore in 1942 certainly made an impact on the post-war fate of the British Empire, and thus on political change in Asia, but this can nevertheless be overstated. When imperial troops retreated onto Singapore Island on 31 January 1942 and army engineers tried to destroy the Causeway behind them, the explosion may well have provoked a teenage Lee Kuan Yew to declare that the sound marked "the end of the British Empire".[6] But its death rattle in Asia was protracted. The UK maintained strong military forces "East of Suez" through the 1960s, using them to support British overseas economic interests, wage the Cold War, and manage the transformation of Empire to Commonwealth — ultimately, to try to dismantle formal empire at its own pace, on its own terms. British Empire forces reclaimed Malaya and Singapore in 1945, then turned it into the hub of British military power in Asia after withdrawing from India in 1947. Forces based in or through Singapore waged war in Korea, fought off Communist insurgency in the 1950s and helped orchestrate independence for Malaya, and fought to enable the consummation of Malaysia in the 1960s. British power and policy made an impact on how Southeast Asia passed beyond European imperialism. Churchill made some contribution to this, first as Leader of the Opposition, then as Prime Minister from 1951–1955. Back in charge, he oversaw crucial decisions that helped defeat communism in Malaya and led to early independence. But by this time, he no longer fought to preserve the Empire just as he found it, accepting instead the broad consensus, expressed several years later by one of his successors, that it must bend to "the wind of change". Churchill now worked to reconcile British economic and defence requirements, the Cold War, and an evolving Commonwealth. While it fell to his successors to implement change in Asia, they worked from a legacy he helped to define. It can be expressed through two themes: to preserve as much British influence outside Europe as long as possible, and to use this to orchestrate the emergence of successor states friendly to British interests.

The final chapter addresses these themes. Malcolm Murfett's analysis in Chapter 7 reflects his deep grasp of subject and sources, as he explains the political battle in the UK over how to manage the withdrawal of British military power from "East of Suez", which became the issue of the day not long after Churchill died in January 1965. The 1968 decision to bring home the legions before 1972 provoked perhaps the last major British political battle over empire, a contest Churchill knew so well. It produced a controversy that challenged Churchill's own party of government, the Conservative Party, to define its worldview of British power and interests. But upon being elected to office in 1970, Edward Heath's Conservative government found it neither possible nor desirable to turn back the clock and remain an imperial military power. Profound global forces of economic and political change were too strong a current to resist. They had in fact forged a situation in which there was less latitude for real differences in British strategic foreign policy than the rhetoric of the day suggested — a Labour government first strove to prolong a British presence in Asia, and then its Conservative successor accepted the need to pack it in. The British left Singapore when they chose, but because they had no choice.

The final British imperial objective in Singapore and the region, to leave behind stable Commonwealth states willing and able to do business with Britain and the West and take its side in the Cold War, depended greatly on who stepped forward to exercise political power after the Union Jack was hauled down. In the case of Singapore, that turned out to be Lee Kuan Yew and his People's Action Party. Lee's Singapore remained in the Commonwealth and proved amenable to cooperation with Britain and the West, but declined to become a satellite and embraced change in the region.

One is tempted to think that Churchill would have seen the Singapore Lee Kuan Yew led from empire into independence as a successful outgrowth of the imperial experience. Singapore's colonial economic and social development displayed the drive and range of British imperialism, just as failure to defend it in 1942 exposed the relative decline of British power. Owing its very existence to the growth and evolution of the modern British Empire, the colonial city of Singapore spawned a post-colonial state that remains a model of economic development, social and political stability, and strategic engagement. Churchill's public life neatly spanned another theme that very much influenced British imperialism in Asia, and thus Singapore. As Churchill entered Parliament in 1900, British leaders were becoming concerned about the threat to the all-important balance of power in Europe posed by a rising Germany. When he retired in 1955, Britain's strategic priority had shifted squarely to the Cold War in Europe, notwithstanding the war it waged to midwife Malaya — while British leaders pondered whether to engage the diplomacy that, in the long run, led to European Union. Through its empire, Britain did much to shape the evolution of modern Asia, let alone Singapore. But British statesmen ultimately concluded the most they could do was influence the manner in which Asians determined their own postcolonial future, not least because they had to address more pressing matters closer to home. Lee Kuan Yew surely agreed.

Notes

1. Brian P. Farrell, *The Basis and Making of British Grand Strategy 1940–1943: Was There a Plan?* (Lewiston, NY: Edwin Mellen Press, 1998), p. 475.
2. Max Hastings, *Winston's War: Churchill 1940–1945* (New York: Alfred A. Knopf, 2010); Richard Toye, *Churchill's Empire: The World that Made Him and the World He Made* (London: Macmillan, 2010).
3. Examples include Piers Brendon, *The Decline and Fall of the British Empire* (London: Jonathan Cape, 2007); John Darwin, *The Empire Project: The Rise and Fall of the British World-System 1830–1970* (Cambridge: Cambridge University Press, 2009); Niall Ferguson, *Empire: The Rise and Demise of the British World Order and the Lessons for Global Power* (New York: Basic Books, 2004); Lawrence James, *The Rise and Fall of the British Empire* (New York: Little, Brown, 1994); Dennis Judd, *Empire: The British Imperial Experience from 1765 to the Present* (London: Phoenix, 2001).
4. Ernest C.T. Chew and Edwin Lee, eds., *Singapore: A History* (Singapore: Oxford University Press, 1991); Mark R. Frost and Yu-Mei Balasingamchow, *Singapore: A Biography* (Hong Kong: Hong Kong University Press, 2010); Karl Hack, *Defence and Decolonisation: Britain, Malaya and Singapore 1941–1967* (London: Routledge, 2001); Malcolm H. Murfett *et al.*, *Between Two Oceans: A Military History of Singapore: From First Settlement to Final*

British Withdrawal (Singapore: Marshall Cavendish Academic, 2004 [1999]); C.M. Turnbull, *A History of Modern Singapore 1819–2005* (Singapore: NUS Press, 2009 [1988]).

5.　Some do so very directly: Raymond Callahan, "Churchill and Singapore", in *Sixty Years On: The Fall of Singapore Revisited*, eds. Brian P. Farrell and Sandy Hunter (Singapore: Eastern Universities Press, 2006 [2002]); Karl Hack and Kevin Blackburn, *Did Singapore Have to Fall? Churchill and the Impregnable Fortress* (London: Routledge, 2004). Broader discussions include Brian P. Farrell, *The Defence and Fall of Singapore 1940–1942* (Stroud: Tempus, 2005); Ong Chit Chung, *Operation Matador: Britain's War Plans Against the Japanese 1918–1941* (Singapore: Times Academic Press, 1997); and Alan Warren, *Singapore 1942: Britain's Greatest Defeat* (Sydney: Talisman, 2002).

6.　Lee Kuan Yew, *The Singapore Story: Memoirs of Lee Kuan Yew* (Singapore: Singapore Press Holdings, 1998), pp. 50–3, 55.

CHAPTER 1

Churchill and Empire

Piers Brendon

From the beginning, Winston Churchill acted out his life on an imperial stage, which he valued for its own sake and because it enhanced the role he played. He was born in Blenheim Palace, a monument to his great ancestor's famous victory over Britain's hereditary foe and chief colonial rival. He spent much of his youth in the Viceregal Lodge in Dublin, a mimic prince in the shadow of Wellington's Obelisk and Nelson's Pillar. He "never forgot"[1] the unveiling of Field Marshal Lord Gough's equestrian statue in Phoenix Park, cast partly from guns captured from China in the Opium War.

Winston's father, Lord Randolph Churchill, became a formidable opponent of Home Rule as well as Secretary for India. Although not claiming to be an imperialist, he was quite capable of banging the rhetorical drum about imperial expansion and ruthlessly subordinating imperial matters to domestic considerations. In office, he annexed Upper Burma. In 1885, young Winston asked his father, "Are the Indians very funny?"[2] Lord Randolph seems to have thought so: he discovered that "any Hindoo whose ashes are thrown into the Ganges goes right bang up to heaven without stopping no matter how great a rascal he might have been", which suggested that Gladstone might adopt that religion.[3] Joking apart, Winston grew up to accept the Empire as the cornerstone of British greatness and India as — to employ what had been a cliché for at least a hundred years — the jewel in the imperial crown, and Singapore as the key bastion of British power in the Far East.

At Harrow, Churchill was stirred by the school songs and he wondered "how I could ever do something glorious for my country".[4] His headmaster, J.E.C. Welldon, who found Winston "troublesome" and birched him more than any other boy, asserted that Britain's special aptitude for "taking up the White Man's Burden" was attributable to "the spirit of organised games". Ironically, Kipling satirised Welldon in *Stalky & Co* as the embarrassingly over-patriotic "Jelly-Bellied Flag-flapper".[5] Aged 16, Winston printed verses in the school magazine asking God to "shield the Empire" from the "power of Hell" and "keep it ever in the hands" of those who "fought and conquered well".[6]

As a young subaltern, Churchill himself aimed to shield the Empire. Simultaneously and not incidentally, he would advance his own career. Yet even at the Empire's high noon, he and others were contemplating its dissolution. Returning from service in India in 1897, Churchill indulged in Gibbonian musings in the ruined Capitol of ancient Rome about whether the British Empire would suffer a similar decline and fall. Similarly, back in India in 1898, he speculated about future travellers visiting the subcontinent and seeing only a "few scraps of stone and iron"[7] to remind them of the raj. This was a familiar conceit. It was most famously expressed by Macaulay, whose peripatetic New Zealander stands on a broken arch of London Bridge to sketch the ruins of St Paul's.

The inevitability of imperial entropy was also to be found in Winwood Reade, whose influential book *The Martyrdom of Man* imbued Churchill with a mixture of evolutionary optimism and cosmic fatalism. A ruthless exponent of social Darwinism, Reade predicted the extinction of the black race, saying that it "illustrates the beneficent law of nature, that the weak must be devoured by the strong".[8] Churchill believed in the advance of his own race via "the combined influence of Rationalism and machine guns".[9] And he remarked in his first and only novel, the Ruritanian romance *Savrola* (1897), that "might is a form of fitness". Fitness entitled its possessors to survive provided they kept "faith with each other", and were loyal successively to clan, class, nation, English-speaking peoples and empire. But Savrola also took the view that life was finite and there could be only one outcome in the "old struggle between vitality and decay".[10]

Nevertheless, in his first political speech, Churchill denounced the "croakers" who prophesied that the empire, now at the height of its glory and power, would "begin to decline, as Babylon, Carthage and Rome had declined". We should, he said,

> give the lie to their dismal croaking by showing by our actions that the vigour and vitality of our race is unimpaired and that our determination is to uphold the Empire that we have inherited from our fathers as Englishmen, [*cheers*] that our flag shall fly high upon the sea, our

voice be heard in the councils of Europe, our Sovereign be supported
by the love of her subjects, then we shall continue to pursue that course
marked out for us by an all-wise hand and carry out our mission of
bearing peace, civilisation and good government to the uttermost ends
of the earth. [*Loud cheers.*]

This litany was a familiar one. But it was duly invested with Churchill's
eloquence and found classic expression during the Second World War
— "If the British Empire and its Commonwealth last for a thousand
years …"[11] For Churchill was the last and most declamatory of the Whig
historians, embroidering the theme of England's destiny, the nation's
climb to broad sunlit uplands with himself providentially in the van.

Churchill's early views about the Empire are enshrined in his first
book, *The Story of the Malakand Field Force* (1898). Here, he recounts
the tale of his initial campaign as a serving soldier in a small war fought
against the Pathans on the North West Frontier of India. Robert Baden-
Powell considered this region a God-given training ground for the British
army and Churchill rather agreed. But he also seemed to think of it as a
kind of adventure playground where he could win fame, glory, medals,
risking his life so that he could eventually, as he put it, beat his sword
into an iron dispatch box. What to modern eyes is most striking about
his vivid account of the conflict is its naked racial bias. Like Gibbon,
Churchill gives an account of the clash between barbarism and civilisation,
between savage tribesmen who "fight without passion and kill without
mercy"[12] and members of a superior race bearing the white man's burden.
Indeed, he made changes in the manuscript of the book to reinforce that
point. Thus, "the prestige of the dominant race enables them to ~~keep up
appearances~~ maintain their superiority over the native troops".[13]

It is clear — and this should not shock or surprise us today — that
Churchill shared many (but not all) of the racial prejudices that were
current when he was a young man. Moreover, *pace* such authorities as
Martin Gilbert, Paul Addison and Ronald Hyam, he largely retained these
prejudices, especially where Indians were concerned, into mature years.
To take one of many examples: in February 1945, Jock Colville records,
Churchill described Hindus as a "foul race 'protected by their mere
pullulation from the doom that is their due' and he wished Bert Harris
could send some of his surplus bombers to destroy them".[14] It was
when he talked of India or China, Churchill's doctor later recorded, that
"you remember he is a Victorian".[15] He could even criticise Australians
— whom he deemed "second-class citizens"[16] — on grounds of race, attri-
buting the unusually poor performance of their troops at Singapore to the
"bad stock"[17] (convict, Irish) from which they sprang.

So, in *The Story of the Malakand Field Force*, Churchill summed up his views thus: "As the sun of civilisation rose above the hills the fair flowers of commerce unfolded, and the streams of supply and demand, hitherto congealed by the frost of barbarism, were thawed".[18] This was a Kiplingesque view very much current, particularly among soldiers, in the Empress of India's Diamond Jubilee year. Kipling, incidentally, though he shared many of Churchill's imperial views and admired the clarity of his history, deplored his use of "that infamous non-Aryan, cinema-caption-epithet 'vibrant', which is as base as 'glimpse', 'sense', 'grip', 'urge', 'glamourous', [sic] and the rest of the thieves-kitchen dictionary that Judaea has decanted upon us".[19] Ironically, Churchill loved Kipling's poetry, which he used to recite in his bath. And according to David Gilmour, the cadences of Churchill's "we shall fight them on the beaches" speech may even have owed something to the seals in the *Jungle Book* who "fought in the breakers, they fought on the sand, and they fought on the smooth-worn basalt rocks of the nurseries".[20] Churchill did not doubt that Britain's civilising mission involved having, and if necessary using, military strength. He said that from the technical point of view, the dum-dum bullet was a beautiful machine. And he prided himself in shunning the usual contemporary circumlocutions: he did not write of "punishing" villages but of "burning" them.[21]

Churchill, however, was primarily interested in the welfare of subject peoples. He did not favour Christian missions — they were, he said, "attempts to annoy the heathen".[22] But he disagreed with British philan-thropists who wished to leave the natives alone, in a state of what he called "degraded barbarism".[23] East of Suez, he said, democracy was impossible and India "must be governed on the old principles".[24] The "Imperial Democracy of England" must cultivate its "great estates that lie beyond the seas". Britons would thus be fulfilling the higher destinies of their race and seizing the opportunity afforded by that "mysterious Power" which regulated "the rise and fall of Empires", as he put it, in order to add to the "happiness, the learning and the liberties of mankind".[25]

Now what is interesting about this viewpoint is not so much that Churchill held it in 1897 but that he continued to hold it throughout the 1930s and into the 1940s and 1950s. Churchill's views fluctuated, as will be seen, sometimes in response to alluring rhetorical opportunities. Nothing captured his imagination more than words. Sir Robert Menzies later said, "his real tyrant is the glittering phrase"[26] and Leo Amery said that the only way to get home to Churchill was to formulate "equally striking counter-phrases".[27] Here are a few of the phrases that fired him: "The Garden of England" (Kent), "The Pearl of the Antilles" (Cuba),

"The hooligan of the Empire" (Natal), "The Harlot of Europe" (Italy), "The Light of Asia" (India), "The Soft Under-belly of Europe" (a dangerously misleading formulation), "The Olive of the North"[28] (the buckthorn shrub — its alias literally put Churchill off his stroke while he was playing golf with Asquith and while turning it over in his mind, he lost a game he had been winning).

Inspired by a hard gem-like phrase, Churchill could vow to "devote my life"[29] to the maintenance of the empire one minute, and the next, he could deplore the fact that "Imperialism sinks into jingoism".[30] Still, he was as tenacious as he was impetuous and he clung doggedly to many of his convictions about the empire, particularly about the Indian empire within the empire. For example, he always saw Gandhi as a kind of fake fakir or Mad Mullah, a hopeless but dangerous obscurantist of the kind he lampooned in his first book.

In 1898, Churchill fought in Sudan, taking part in the cavalry charge at Omdurman. He regretted that there had not been enough casualties to make it a truly historic engagement but he also evinced a rare humanity, which was the obverse of his capacity for aggression. He blamed Kitchener for leading his soldiers to "believe that it was quite correct to regard their enemy as vermin — unfit to live"[31] and for "the inhuman slaughter of the wounded at Omdurman".[32] Even so, the aim of the campaign was imperial improvement. In *The River War* (1899), Churchill wrote: "What enterprise that an enlightened community may attempt is more noble and more profitable than the reclamation from barbarism of fertile regions and large populations?" However, perhaps as a result of seeing what George Orwell called the dirty work of empire at close quarters, Churchill was becoming more suspicious of selfish imperial entrepreneurs: "The inevitable gap between conquest and dominion becomes filled with the figures of the greedy trader, the inopportune missionary, the ambitious soldier, and the lying speculator".[33]

At home, too, Churchill was beginning to enter his liberal phase. Before the end of the Victorian age, he said: "To keep our Empire we must have a free people, an educated and well-fed people. That is why we are in favour of social reform. That is why we long for Old Age Pensions and the like".[34] By contrast, Lord Rosebery thought Old Age Pensions "a scheme so prodigal of expenditure" that it would deal "a blow at the Empire which might be almost mortal".[35] Churchill, though, was already anticipating the Edwardian anxiety about national inefficiency and deterioration: "To keep the Empire we must have an imperial stock".[36]

Churchill had long thought that sooner or later, Britain would have to fight the Boers "for the sake of the Empire".[37] And he famously played his part in the South African war. But as early 1900, he was advocating a "generous and forgiving policy"[38] towards the Afrikaners, though he railed against the "indolent Kaffir" enjoying the bounty of South Africa "while Englishmen choke and fester in crowded cities". Instead, he dreamt of "a brave system of State-aided — almost State-compelled — emigration".[39] It was a contention that went back to Seeley, Froude, Carlyle, Edward Gibbon Wakefield and beyond, one to which Churchill often returned. During the 1920s, he supported schemes to transfer "our surplus unproductive population from here to other parts of the Empire".[40] During the 1930s, he urged emigration to the Empire as a "blessed remedy"[41] for unemployment.

In December 1900, Churchill's views on the connection between empire and social reform were reinforced by the publication of the Seebohm Rowntree Report on poverty. "I see little glory in an Empire which can rule the waves and is unable to flush its sewers", he said. And he was moved to a characteristic flight of oratory: "Although the British Empire is so large [the poor] cannot find room to live in it; although it is so magnificent, they would have had a better chance of happiness if they had been born cannibal islanders of the Southern seas; although its science is so profound, they would have been more healthy if they had been the subjects of Hardicanute". He concluded: "This festering life at home makes world-wide power a mockery".[42]

This was an idea Churchill harped on frequently during the Edwardian age. He opposed tariff reform because it would end the era of cheap food and raw materials, and thus worsen poverty, increase international tension and "shut the British Empire up in a ringed fence". Protection would create "inside our planet a smaller planet called the British Empire, cut off by impenetrable space from everything else".[43] Most colonials disliked his policy on tariff reform and Alfred Deakin, the Australian Prime Minister, said that one of his speeches on the subject (in 1906) suggested "the indulgence of a riotous imagination".[44]

As Churchill grew more progressive at home, crossing the floor to join the Liberals in 1904 and gaining office as Under-Secretary for the Colonies in 1906, he became more generous abroad. He favoured Home Rule for Ireland and a conciliatory South African settlement within "true and indissoluble union of Empire".[45] He described this settlement as stepping forward "into the sunshine of a more gentle and generous age".[46] It was a fulfilment of the liberal dream of the Empire as "a great moral force on the side of progress";[47] though for the "African aboriginal", he declared, "civilisation has no chance".[48] He favoured the Empire (at this stage) as an instrument of peace, progress and trade. If it held together,

Churchill said, this would not be because of its expensive army but "because it is based upon the assent of free peoples, united with each other by noble and progressive principles; because it is animated by respect for right and justice".[49]

Many were now beginning to prefer the term "Commonwealth" to Empire and the Colonial Conference of 1907 rejected imperial unity in favour of Dominion autonomy and freedom under the Crown. This promised an eventual disintegration of the British Empire. But Churchill himself did not advocate imperial federation in the manner of Joseph Chamberlain, or his cousin, the Duke of Marlborough. Where the dependent Empire was concerned, he championed trusteeship as against the "bastard imperialism" of the Tories, condemning the harsh methods of Frederick Lugard and Lord Milner — whom Churchill dubbed "the disconsolate pro-consul".

Lugard, who favoured use of the pillory and the stocks in Nigeria, wanted to mount a punitive expedition to "pacify" the north. Churchill said that the "enterprise is liable to be misrepresented by persons unacquainted with Imperial terminology as the murdering of natives and stealing of their lands". Full of youthful idealism, he was a benevolent paternalist to his fingertips. Churchill protested against reprisals in East Africa: "It looks like butchery". He insisted on righting injustice even when colonial governors objected that it would be inconvenient to do so: "The inconvenience inseparable from the reparation of injustice or irregularity is one of the safeguards against their recurrence".[50] It was this sort of radicalism that caused organs of colonial opinion such as the *Sydney Bulletin* to pronounce that "The so-called British Empire is a nigger empire, run by Jews".[51]

On his East African expedition — 1907–1908, when he coined the term "Sofari so goody"[52] — Churchill was much exercised about the "primordial nakedness" of the natives. He wanted them to wear "civilised attire", preferably manufactured by his Manchester constituents, who would receive raw cotton from Uganda produced by the native population "organised and directed by superior intelligence and external capital".[53] Just as he dreamt of turning West Africa, via cotton and capital and railways, into "a second India",[54] so Churchill, mulling over his schemes of social reform at home, saw Uganda as ripe for "a practical experiment in State Socialism".[55] The Africans should not be under the control of businessmen working "only for profits"; they should be disciplined, educated, and brought to a higher social level by the state. "It will be an ill day for these native races when their fortunes are removed from the impartial and august administration of the Crown and abandoned to the fierce self-interest of a small white population".[56]

Even then, however, Churchill was by no means consistent and there were indications that the aggressive imperialist in him was merely dormant. For example, he told the Governor of Kenya to expand across the Tana River, bringing 150,000 more Africans under British control, and commented: "Thus the Empire grows under Radical Administration".[57] On the other hand in 1908, according to Wilfrid Scawen Blunt, Churchill was almost converted to his view that the Empire would ruin England. "We get no advantage from it," he said, "and it's a lot of bother. The only thing one can say for it is it is justified if it is undertaken in an altruistic spirit for the good of the subject races".[58] In much the same vein, Churchill criticised Tories in 1910 for demanding "patriotism and imperialism by the Imperial pint".[59] Yet by 1911, Churchill had returned to his earlier theme, bracketing imperialism and social reform. He declared that the seeds of imperial ruin and national decay lay in "the unnatural gap between rich and poor, the divorce of the people from the land, the want of proper discipline and training in our youth, the exploitation of boy labour, the physical degeneration" and so on. These were "the enemies of Britain. Beware lest they shatter the foundations of her power".[60] Churchill was back in the "ultra-Imperialist groove," said Blunt, who could well believe the common Conservative opinion "that Winston will one day return to the Tory fold".[61]

Meanwhile, Churchill denounced Tory behaviour over Ulster as treason and for a time before the Great War, as First Lord of the Admiralty, he seemed willing to use the fleet to coerce the "Loyalists". But here and elsewhere, his real aim was conciliation from a position of strength. And in general, he wanted Peace, Retrenchment, Reform, based on a supreme navy. In March 1914, he justified naval estimates in the House of Commons with mordant candour: "our claim to be left in undisputed enjoyment of vast and splendid possessions, mainly acquired by violence and largely maintained by force, often seems less reasonable to others than to us".[62] However, he also acknowledged that the German threat in the North Sea meant that Australia and New Zealand could not count on the Royal Navy. In the worst case, "the only course for the five million white men in the Pacific would be to seek the protection of the United States".[63]

No one had better cause than Churchill to appreciate the imperial, and particularly the Antipodean, contribution to Allied victory in the First World War. In March 1940, he invoked the sacrifice Australia's sons had made through "the red, leaden-footed years of war" and their "ultimate triumph".[64] Less robust empires were liquidated. On Turkey's surrender in October 1918, Churchill noted, "A drizzle of empires falling through the air".[65] And Lord Rothermere even proposed selling Jamaica and other colonies to pay off the national debt. Churchill himself was all the more intent on propping up the British Empire, particularly in view of the new international threat of Bolshevism.

Obsessed by this menace, Churchill moved to the right: witness his dinner-time suggestion to Edwin Montagu, Secretary of State for India, that Gandhi "ought to be laid, bound hand and foot, at the gates of Delhi and then trampled on by an enormous elephant with the new Viceroy seated on its back".[66] But Churchill was still wedded to conciliation, particularly when he could clothe it in magniloquence. Thus, in July 1920, he memorably condemned the Amritsar massacre: "Frightfulness is not a remedy known to the British pharmacopoeia". Frightfulness was the essence of Bolshevism and there was no place for it in the "august and venerable structure" of the Empire. Not for the first time, he quoted Macaulay's dictum that "the most frightful of all spectacles [was] the strength of civilisation without its mercy".[67] The British Empire, Churchill said, rested on cooperation, not coercion.

At the same time, as Sinn Fein violently challenged British rule in Ireland, Churchill once more allowed himself to be provoked. Despite his reluctance to use Prussian methods, he did recommend bombing and machine-gunning Sinn Fein meetings from the air, and raising the temperature of the conflict until it became a real "trial of strength". His wife Clementine urged him to avoid "the rough, iron-fisted, 'Hunnish' way".[68] And once Churchill became convinced repression was merely breeding terror, he favoured a truce, accomplished in June 1921. He played a major role in getting an agreement, on a par with his conciliatory endeavours after the Boer War, whereby Ireland remained within the Empire. Churchill maintained that the magnanimity of British genius triumphed over the mediaeval hatreds pervading John Bull's Other Island.

In February 1921, Churchill became Colonial Secretary. He faced a series of problems, many created or exacerbated by the war, notably revolt in India and Egypt (as well as Ireland) against the background of the Communist world revolution. While shoring up the Empire wherever possible, he needed urgently to reduce British military expenditure, particularly in the Middle East. There were also problems in the Far East where, said Churchill, Japan represented a danger to the Empire, which made an alliance with the USA necessary. Thanks to Greater Britain beyond the seas, it would be an equal alliance. Without the Empire, he wrote — in what would become a constant theme — "we could never meet our great sister nation, who speaks our language, who are our kith and kin, on those terms of perfect equality which alone can be the foundation for a still higher synthesis and a still more important destiny".[69] Yet so serious was the danger of overstretch that in December 1921, Churchill went so far as to talk about "The passing of the British Empire".[70]

Palestine was a particularly intractable problem. As early as 1908, Churchill had thought that a Jewish state in the Middle East could be a bridge between Europe and Asia and an immense advantage to the British Empire. This argument became even more compelling in 1917 and one reason Churchill supported the Balfour Declaration was to thwart Trotsky's schemes of a "world-wide communistic state under Jewish domination".[71] Churchill told Lloyd George that Jews (i.e., Bolsheviks) were "the main instigators of the ruin of the Empire".[72] But Zionist Jews would help to preserve it. Churchill informed Chaim Weizmann that Britain did not mind gun-running to protect Jewish settlements, "but don't speak about it".[73] On the other hand, Churchill worried about the £6 million annual cost of running Palestine. In the White Paper of 1922, he tried to restrict the Jewish National Home to part of Palestine, to place economic limits on Jewish immigration, and to ensure that Arab rights were maintained. His plan to establish gradually a joint Arab-Jewish government was the first of many attempts to square the circle in the Holy Land.

Elsewhere in the Middle East, Churchill tried to divide and rule, creating out of the mandated territories an indirectly ruled Transjordan with the Hashemite emir Abdullah on the throne, and doing the same for Mesopotamia. He wanted to run Iraq (to give the country its Arabic, nationalist name) through King Feisal, "like an Indian native State".[74] Economy was Churchill's main aim — he cut expenditure on Iraq from £45m to £11m in two years — and in pursuit of it, he advocated the use of cheap control from the air. He was also "strongly in favour of using poisonous GAS against uncivilised tribes".[75] In the event only gas shells and high explosive bombs seem to have been used, though Churchill said gas bombs were "a scientific expedient for sparing life which should not be prevented by the prejudices of those who do not think clearly".[76] At the Cairo Conference in March 1921, he spoke sharply to Arab deputations protesting about the injustice of permitting a national home for the Jews on Arab lands. He still considered democracy unsuitable for African or Asiatic people. But somehow Churchill avoided succumbing to the temptation, which Curzon said he would find irresistible, "to declare himself King in Babylon".[77]

In 1921, Churchill tried to effect a compromise in Kenya — the first of eight put forward between the wars — similar to that proposed in Palestine. In Kenya, European settlers desired white dominion; Indian immigrants had ambitions to make East Africa a "second India"[78] or the "America of the Hindu";[79] and Africans wanted native interests to be paramount. Churchill offended everyone. He agreed to Cecil Rhodes's formula of "votes for civilised men", reserved the highlands for Europeans, and made a vague promise of future "responsible self-government".[80] But he did not propose to limit Indian immigration, or inflict urban segregation, or have a separate electoral roll for Indians (ten per cent of whom would be enfranchised). This provoked talk of a settler revolt, a revival of the "old Bostonian spirit" and an Ulster-style loyalism which expressed itself in the cry "For King and Kenya".[81] Churchill responded in characteristic fashion, intimating that he would send a cruiser to Mombasa to blockade the settlers. Nothing was resolved by the time he left the Colonial Office.

In 1922, Churchill — with Lloyd George, Curzon and others — considered that the Turks must be kept on the Asiatic side of the Bosphorus, "the most important strategic position in the world". Churchill, previously Turkophile, told the cabinet that however fatigued the British Empire was, he thought it "would put up some force to preserve Gallipoli with the graves of so many of its soldiers".[82] But the Dominions, especially Canada and Australia, resented being dragooned into another war, which Churchill seemed prepared to countenance. Some also resented Churchill's statement, made in an effort to achieve closer imperial cooperation, that "possibly for generations the title deeds of the British Empire will be deposited at Westminster".[83] This, though, was another indication that Churchill's imperialism was hardening by the 1920s. He often took the opportunity to express confidence in the greatness and strength of the British Empire; and he criticised those who said it was falling to pieces after the Great War.

Churchill was thus incensed when the Conservatives, to whom he had "re-ratted" with such spectacular success, started to go liberal on the Empire. After the Tory election defeat of 1929, Lord Irwin announced that the "natural issue of India's constitutional development was the attainment of Dominion status". According to Samuel Hoare, Churchill was "almost demented with fury".[84] In the *Daily Mail* on 16 November 1929, Churchill wrote that Irwin's statement was "criminally mischievous", issued as it was before the Simon Report had been published, and at a time when India was riven by social, religious and racial tensions.[85] Leo Amery stated that "the key to Winston is to understand that he is a mid-Victorian". This was only concealed by his "verbal exuberance",[86] said Amery, with whom he disagreed on the subject of Empire Free Trade — when a slight move was made towards it at the Imperial Economic Conference at Ottawa in 1932, Churchill damned it as "Rottawa".[87] Baldwin shared Amery's view of Churchill. At the time of the Round Table Conference of 1930, Baldwin said that Churchill wished the Tory party to "go back to pre-war and govern with a strong hand. He has become once more the subaltern of hussars of '96".[88] This was his default position. Imbued with the romance of equestrian gallantry, Churchill told the House of Commons in December 1940 that the Australian Light Horse Regiment had made a "dashing cavalry charge"[89] in North Africa when in fact it was mechanised. And in 1946, Ernest Bevin tellingly rebuked Churchill for his "Poona mentality",[90] which did not suit modern conditions.

Churchill certainly lived up to that stereotype in the decade before the war. He thought 1930 a year of miserable imperial retreat: "My only interest in politics is to see the position retrieved".[91] He criticised defeatist, weak-minded policies and advocated in India the crushing of "Gandhi-ism".[92] He wanted the Tories to identify themselves aggressively against Labour and with "the majesty of Britain as under Lord Salisbury and Lord Beaconsfield".[93] And he let fly many a "thrilling peroration about the Empire".[94] Churchill told Baldwin that he cared more about the Indian issue than anything else in public life, a clear instance of his making a priority of an imperial matter out of the line of official duty.

Churchill resigned from the Shadow Cabinet in January 1931. To Clementine, he lamented the fact that Baldwin felt "the times were too far gone for any robust assertion of imperial greatness",[95] and he embarked on a public speaking campaign to promote that cause and perhaps to promote himself. In February, Churchill famously denounced the "nauseating" spectacle of "a seditious Middle Temple lawyer, now posing as a fakir of a type well-known in the East, striding half-naked up the steps of the Vice-regal palace, while he is still organising and conducting a campaign of civil disobedience, to parley on equal terms with the representative of the King-Emperor".[96] He described British policy in India as "a hideous act of self-mutilation".[97] Making concessions to Gandhi was like feeding cat's meat to a tiger — a bizarre analogy in view of the Mahatma's vegetarianism. Churchill's championship of Untouchables was seen as "divide and rule" opportunism. And he himself admitted later that he "regarded the Hindu-Moslem feud as a bulwark of British rule in India".[98]

After the Gandhi outburst, Irwin told J.C.C. Davidson that Churchill's attitude was "completely and utterly hopeless". "The day is past," he said, "when Winston's possessive instinct can be applied to Empires and the like. That conception of Empire is finished."[99] Churchill gave as good as he got, writing in 1933 that the plan to give India local autonomy was the thin end of the wedge, and that "Irwinism has rotted the soul of the Tory party".[100] Hoare thought Churchill wanted to rule India as Mussolini ruled North Africa. Baldwin said that on the subject of India, Churchill was like George III "endowed with the tongue of Edmund Burke".[101]

Certainly, Churchill waxed eloquent and passionate on the subject. On 21 July 1934, he wrote in *Answers*: "Our continued existence as a great power is at stake. The loss of India would mark and consummate the downfall of the British Empire. That great organism would pass at a stroke out of life into history. From such a catastrophe, there could be no recovery". Without empire, Britain would be nothing but a "glorified Belgium". In 1935, Churchill famously denounced the India Bill as "a monstrous monument of sham built by pygmies".[102] In his final campaign against it, he insisted that the British "are there for ever" and "honoured partners with our Indian fellow-subjects" for the good of both.[103] In the cheers for the Bill, Churchill prayed that "there may not mingle the knell of the British Empire in the East".[104]

Of course, Churchill was a romantic about the empire. In 1937, he wrote sadly: "my ideal is narrow and limited. I want to see the British Empire preserved for a few more generations in its strength and splendour".[105] But he also saw the Empire as increasingly vulnerable. In 1938, he wrote in the *News of the World*: "the wide open spaces of the British Empire are a standing temptation to imperialist adventure by foreign powers". He urged that the British should fill them by their own exertions and with their own stock, adding that South Europeans could not mix with such stock because they went in for "blood feud and vendetta". To defend the Empire, any tactic was legitimate, even an alliance with Bolshevik Russia. "The shores of History are strewn with the wrecks of Empires. They perished because they were found unworthy".[106]

When war broke out in 1939, Churchill strained every sinew to ensure that the British Empire should prove worthy. It should stand together. Individual units should make sacrifices for the whole. Churchill regarded the Empire as a support to British power first and British power a support to the Empire second. So he was dismissive about Antipodean wishes to deploy their own troops in their own region, reckoning that they should go where London directed them. As Stafford Cripps noted after an interview in October 1939, Churchill evinced the "utmost determination to support and maintain the most full-blooded British imperialism".[107] When he became Prime Minister, the Empire was once again central to his rhetoric: "What is our aim … victory … for without victory there is no survival. Let that be realised; no survival for the British Empire; no survival for all that the British Empire has stood for ..."[108] But America was central to his strategy. Churchill's first message to Roosevelt, on 15 May 1940, included the words: "We are looking to you to keep that Japanese dog quiet in the Pacific, using Singapore in any way convenient".[109]

As if to prove that his 1930s campaign over India had been genuine, Churchill seemed almost as passionate about preserving the subcontinent in the summer of 1940 as about saving Britain. Of course he was keen to gain Indian cooperation in the war effort and to that end he was prepared to allow a few "representative Indians" — by which, of course, he meant a few *un*representative Indians — to sit on the Viceroy's Council. But he refused to permit any substantive moves towards independence that would satisfy Congress. Churchill told Leo Amery on 26 July that "he would sooner give up political life at once, or rather go out into the wilderness and fight, than to admit a revolution which meant the end of the Imperial Crown in India".[110] As Amery said: "India, or any form of self-government for coloured peoples, raises in him a wholly uncontrollable complex".[111] Certainly, Nehru regarded Churchill's vague statements about eventual Dominion status as "fantastic and absurd".[112]

The following year, Churchill was equally implacable over the Atlantic Charter, a vague, sententious affirmation of Anglo-American principles. On 9 September 1941, he specifically told the House of Commons that the Charter's promises about self-determination did not apply to the Empire, further inflaming nationalist sentiment in India. To counter tales of his "reactionary, Old World outlook" which had supposedly given such pain to Roosevelt, Churchill claimed in his *History of the Second World War* that the Charter had been "cast in my own words".[113] In fact, the President had edited his draft. Privately, Churchill thought it was "pretty good cheek" for the Americans to try "to school-marm us into proper behaviour" in the Empire.[114] But Roosevelt treated Churchill on India in the same way as he treated southern senators on the subject of black Americans. According to Norman Angell, he thought the British people decent, law-abiding and freedom-loving; but their government, ruled by caste, had imposed "a world tyranny compounded of imperialism, colonialism and power politics which violates all political morals and in particular, denies the elementary human rights of all peoples to be independent like the United States".[115]

Churchill's strategy in 1941 hinged first on defending the British Isles, then on the security of the Middle East; it extended to assisting Russia after Operation Barbarossa, and to resisting Japan after Pearl Harbor. But Churchill had already assured the Prime Ministers of Australia and New Zealand, on cabinet authority, that if they were invaded by Japan, "we should then cut our losses in the Mediterranean and proceed to your aid, sacrificing every interest except only the defence and feeding of this Island on which all depends".[116] Churchill thought, however, that the Japanese would go for the Dutch East Indies, and that the United States would enter the war if they did. He also thought that the Japanese had not "the inclination or the capacity to invade Australia".[117]

After Pearl Harbor, Australian Prime Minister John Curtin worried about Singapore and said he would "gladly accept United States command in Pacific". Churchill — having on 12 December 1941 assured Curtin that American involvement made eventual victory certain — replied that he did not agree about "the danger of early reduction of Singapore".[118] He said that air support was on its way and tanks would be sent when the situation in Libya permitted — they were too late. Curtin suspected the Lion City was far from being the "Gibraltar of the East".[119] On 27 December, he wrote a signed article in the *Melbourne Herald* saying that the Pacific must not be treated as a subordinate theatre of war, and that Australia looked to the USA "free of any pangs as to our traditional links or kinship with the United Kingdom".[120] He feared that Australia might "go" while Britain held on.

Churchill had indeed treated Antipodean troops as British — though some Australians themselves, Richard Casey for example, considered them all part of one imperial force — and had starved the Far East of resources in favour of Middle East and Russia. And he was unapologetic: "I would do exactly the same again". Unified command in an ABDA (American, British, Dutch, Australian forces) headquarters under Wavell should have improved cooperation with the Australians in the Far East. But on 8 January 1942, Curtin again demanded reinforcements. Churchill replied, "We are doing our utmost in the Mother Country to meet living perils and onslaughts … [and had suffered the shocking loss of two of the finest ships in Far East, *Prince of Wales* and *Repulse*]. I hope therefore you will be considerate in the judgement which you pass upon those to whom Australian lives and fortunes are so dear".

Only at this stage did Churchill discover that Singapore was so weak, having previously assumed that it could withstand a long blockade, like the fortresses besieged by the Duke of Marlborough. Embattled at home as well as abroad, he responded vehemently but fitfully. First, he demanded total resistance. Then, on 21 January 1942, he suggested that Singapore should be wrecked and evacuated to defend Burma. But when the Australian government cabled that evacuation would be an "inexcusable betrayal", [121] Churchill allowed 18th Division to go to Singapore, where it proved no more able to stem the Japanese tide than did 44th Indian

Brigade. On 10 February, he signalled that the "battle must be fought to the bitter end at all costs", and that senior officers "should die with their troops" to preserve the honour of the British Empire.[122] Eventually and reluctantly, an anguished Churchill sanctioned surrender, which occurred on 15 February. The fall of Singapore has been well described as "another Yorktown".[123]

The debacle was intensely humiliating for a number of reasons. It cast doubt on Churchill's judgement in general, and revealed in particular what one historian has called his "long-standing blind spot to Far-Eastern dangers".[124] As Chancellor, he opposed spending on the naval base at Singapore; as First Lord of the Admiralty, he argued that an aerial assault on armoured British warships would "not prevent the full exercise of their superior sea power";[125] as Prime Minister, he assumed that Singapore was well defended on the landward side and derided the Japanese will and capacity to fight. Instead, to his shame, the European would-be master race, softened by imperial self-indulgence — servants, curry tiffins at the club requiring two-hour siestas, lazy afternoons of golf, cricket or sailing, cocktail parties and fancy dress balls — proved to be almost grotesquely incompetent and ill-prepared.

After the Royal Navy's disastrous failure to exert "a paralysing effect on the Japanese",[126] the RAF sent up a menagerie of Buffaloes, Wildebeestes and Walruses, obsolete aircraft aptly known as "flying coffins",[127] which were quickly shot down by Mitsubishi Zeros. Over 130,000 British and imperial troops surrendered to General Yamashita's three outnumbered divisions, which had badly strained their supply lines during the last battle on Singapore Island. Churchill famously acknowledged that this was "the worst disaster and largest capitulation in British history".[128] To his intense chagrin, British prestige plummeted in both West and East, where colonial people — the young Lee Kuan Yew among them — noted how decisively Japanese bayonets had cut through the flimsy and often rotten fabric of its oriental Empire. The leader of the Japanese-sponsored Indian National Army, Subhas Chandra Bose, described Singapore as "the graveyard of the British Empire".[129]

Furthermore, the Japanese had smashed the lock on the gateway to India. They attacked Burma, capturing Rangoon on 8 March 1942, forcing the evacuation of Mandalay by the end of the following month. Curtin having withheld the I Australian Corps, Churchill urgently needed to mobilise support in the subcontinent and elsewhere by reaching an accord with the Congress Party. Amery noted in his report to King George VI: Winston "hated the idea of giving up all his most deeply ingrained prejudices merely to secure more American, Chinese and Left Wing support.

He was undergoing all the conflicting emotions of a virtuous maiden selling herself for really handy ready money".[130] The King was amused and riposted with an unprintably improper story of his own. Anyway, the Cripps Mission went ahead. Churchill's attitude was summed up in his wry remark to Mackenzie King on 18 March: "We have resigned ourselves to fighting our utmost to defend India in order, if successful, to be turned out".[131]

On 23 March 1942, Cripps — said to be so humourless that he saw jokes by appointment only — arrived in Delhi. He offered progress towards representative self-government, including an immediate Indian role in running the defence of the subcontinent. But he could not give enough and anyway Gandhi refused to accept "a post-dated cheque" from — a journalist added — "a failing bank".[132] Congress rejected the plan and the Cripps Mission failed. Linlithgow echoed a newspaper headline, "Goodbye, Mr Cripps".[133] Churchill quieted the United States by warning that an independent India would come to terms with the Japanese and threaten the Middle East. On 9 August 1942, Gandhi and Nationalist leaders were arrested on suspicion of preparing a Nationalist revolt. Repression was the effective British response to the "Quit India" campaign. According to Amery, Churchill himself got into a "frantic passion on the whole subject of the humiliation of being kicked out of India by the beastliest people in the world next to the Germans".[134]

In the autumn of 1942, Wendell Willkie asserted that the war was being fought to end the imperial domination of one nation by another, a view confirmed by Roosevelt in a press conference at which he said that the Atlantic Charter applied to all. On 10 November 1942, Churchill famously riposted: "We mean to hold our own. I have not become the King's First Minister in order to preside over the liquidation of the British Empire".[135] American opinion was appalled by the declaration. Lugard, in a letter to *The Times*, explained it as a refusal to surrender trusteeship. But Churchill remained bellicose on the subject of the empire. At the Teheran Conference in November 1943, he said that nothing — he was especially thinking of Hong Kong and Singapore — would be taken from Britain's empire "without a war", though Britain might later voluntarily relinquish portions of the Empire.

Churchill also refused to give way to Gandhi's fasting during the early part of 1943. In an undelivered broadcast, he described it as a "fast or farce — because I understand there is some doubt about whether he kept to his own rules",[136] and he suggested to Linlithgow that Gandhi's doctors were slipping glucose into his drink. Although Gandhi was almost certainly unaware of it, this may well have been the case, since he actually "gained one pound"[137] in weight during the last week of his fast. Churchill remained convinced that Gandhi was a fraud and a menace. The Prime Minister elaborated on his imperial views in a speech which, in the event, he never gave to the House of Commons. He acknowledged there had been a time of "wicked and brazen exploitation of colonies and conquests. But the broad, shining, liberating and liberalizing tides of the Victorian era flowed across this scene. The exploitation of weaker and less well-armed peoples became odious, together with the idea of subject races". For at least 80 years, Britain had simply served India, bringing peace, trade and progress. "Our stewardship and our mission may come to an end but to India it may well be the age of the Antonines".[138] This high-minded statement did not comport well with Churchill's refusal in 1943 to divert scarce shipping to help relieve the Bengal famine; he stated that "the starvation of anyhow under-fed Bengalis is less serious [than that of] sturdy Greeks".[139] Despite the famine, Churchill said, Indians would continue to breed "like rabbits".[140]

In November 1944, Churchill was shaken by the murder of his friend Lord Moyne at the hands of Jewish terrorists. He told Weizmann that gangster tactics were killing the noble dream he had always supported. He would never meet Weizmann again and now seemed to wash his hands of the Zionist cause in Palestine. Supporting it, he wrote in a secret minute, had been a "painful and thankless task" which had never brought the "slightest advantage" to Great Britain. Churchill evidently concluded that Zionists were unreliable colonial clients, and he later mocked Attlee for giving up "mighty India" while holding on to "tiny Palestine".[141]

Elsewhere, though, Churchill remained adamantly imperialistic. On 31 December, he told the Colonial Secretary (who was on a pre-Yalta visit to Roosevelt): "'Hands off the British Empire' is our maxim and it must not be weakened or smirched to please sob-stuff merchants at home or foreigners of any hue".[142] This position he adhered to resolutely. At Yalta in February 1945, he declared that Britain would not permit the Empire to be placed in the dock and subjected to international examination. Assured that UN trusteeship of mandated territories did not concern the British Empire — though in practice it might — he agreed to it, having been "bamboozled" by the Americans. In March, he fiercely resisted pressure from the United States to hand back Hong Kong to the Chinese. To the American ambassador in China, Patrick Hurley, he spoke "with violence about Hong Kong and said that never would we yield an inch of the territory that was under the British flag".[143] At Bretton Woods, it was possible to see the USA preparing to supersede Britain's formal political empire with an informal economic empire of its own. In August 1945, after Churchill's defeat at the polls, he was reduced to begging Wavell to "Keep a bit of India for the Empire".[144]

Despite the unfavourable auguries in 1946, Churchill stressed "the abiding power of the British Empire and Commonwealth". In his "Iron Curtain" speech at Fulton, Missouri, he talked of a "fraternal association" with the USA, which stood "at the highest point of majesty and power ever attained by any community since the fall of the Roman Empire".[145] He also extolled the "special relationship" with the United States: "do not suppose that we shall not come through these dark years of privation as we have come through the glorious years of agony". The State Department told Truman that Churchill was using the "special relationship to buttress Britain's waning prestige and influence".[146]

It was all too true. India gained its freedom in 1947, soon followed by Burma and Ceylon. Churchill famously lamented, "It is with deep grief that I watch the clattering down of the British Empire … Many have defended Britain against her foes. None can defend her against herself".[147] Yet with some part of himself Churchill recognised that imperial attitudes were obsolescent or unfashionable, at least where the Italians were concerned. He wrote that Mussolini's designs on Ethiopia were "unsuited to the ethics of the twentieth century. They belonged to those dark ages when white men felt themselves entitled to conquer yellow, brown, black or red men, and subjugate them by their superior strength and weapons".[148]

In April 1949, Lord Simon wrote to Churchill gloomily: "The truth is that Nehru and Cripps have won. The agreement [whereby India became a republic within the Commonwealth, which Churchill supported] may be the best way out but the fact remains that Cripps has attained his ambition to 'dissolve the British Empire.'"[149] Moreover, Simon added, Nehru got advantages without responsibilities. But Churchill was reconciled to Nehru, hailing India under his leadership as "The Light of Asia",[150] and accepted independence with as good a grace as he could muster. He even found a precedent in Roman times for the presence of a republic in the Commonwealth. As he told Indira Gandhi in 1953, he had once hated India but did not now. Nevertheless, he seemed to feel some residual bitterness over the loss of this magnificent imperial possession, which he thought a great blunder.

Once back in Downing Street in 1951, Churchill focussed his remaining energies on ending the Cold War, rather than on sustaining the Empire. He acquiesced at the independence of colonies, though he fought hard to keep the Simonstown naval base, "more important to the British Commonwealth of Nations than Gibraltar or Malta",[151] because Suez was less significant and Egypt was precarious. He was conciliatory and prag-matic over the Gold Coast and Kenya. He was even conciliatory towards the Mahdi, who arrived when he was holding a cabinet meeting, telling his Private Secretary: "Well, he must wait ... unless you think he will go off and make another revolt".[152] Moreover, Churchill made light of distur-bances in Bechuanaland in 1952, remarking ironically: "Indeed a terrible position. An angry mob, armed with staves and stones, inflamed with alcohol, and inspired by liberal principles".[153]

Churchill was more combative over the riots in Egypt in January 1952. He said that they proved the Egyptians were uncivilised and that Britain should hold fast to the Canal Zone, if possible with American help (though this was not forthcoming). But in 1953, though still pug-nacious, he became conscious of the cost of the Suez base (£56m per annum) and its obsolescence. Jordan was a better bet and in 1954, it was thought, thermo-nuclear weapons made occupation of the Canal Zone unnecessary. Churchill concluded that there must be a settlement with Egypt that did not involve "scuttle". But he was still sad, saying on 24 April: "We have thrown away our glorious empire...."[154] He was also unhappy to be playing second fiddle to the USA. On 7 January 1952, Lord Moran wrote in his diary: "Once more he spoke of the feeling of inequality; it was a canker in his mind, he grieves that England in her fallen state can no longer address America as an equal, but must come, cap in hand, to do her bidding".[155]

The mood of gloom persisted. After he left office, Churchill told his cousin, Clare Sheridan, that his life had "all been for nothing ... The Empire I believed in has gone".[156] Perhaps he exaggerated. Ronald Hyam concluded that for all his pronouncements Churchill proved by his actions that he was not much interested in the empire, except "when he had to be by virtue of office".[157] Hyam argued that Churchill was a pragmatist and conciliator, and an improver of great estates. Where possible, he wanted the Empire to serve British interests, and where this did not happen, it should be merely controlled informally. This author hesitates to disagree with such a distinguished authority, especially as he learnt so much from Hyam ever since sitting at his feet as an undergraduate. But as indicated in this chronological survey, this author argues that the British Empire was the grand theme informing Churchill's existence and his worldview. It was a talisman that captured his imagination and informed his rhetoric. It was a field of adventure and Churchill himself learnt the kind of ruthlessness that stood the Empire in good stead when it fought alone against the Third Reich.

Churchill believed in the Empire because it was integral to the greatness — one might say to the racial superiority — of Britain and, to a lesser
extent, because it provided a theatre of power in which he could perform
in a suitably splendid and dramatic manner. As Mackenzie King said,
Churchill spoke of Communism as being a religion to some people and "the
British Empire and Commonwealth is a religion to him".[158] Of course, he
was keener on the Empire than the Commonwealth — defined by Smuts
as "the widest example of organized human freedom which has ever existed
in human history"[159] — but as he once leeringly said to Senator Arthur
Vandenburg when citing both, "we keep trade labels to suit all tastes".[160]
Essentially, Churchill identified himself with the British Empire. And he
was not alone. On 8 February 1942, Harry Hopkins told Churchill that
he heard one workman say to another as the PM passed, "There goes the
bloody British Empire". Churchill smiled with relish: "*Very* nice".[161]

Notes

1.   P.W. Fay, *The Opium War 1840–1842* (Chapel Hill, NC: UNC Press, 1975),
     p. 369. Gough's statue was later vandalised and removed to England. It is now
     located at Chillingham Castle.
2.   Randolph S. Churchill, *Winston S. Churchill*, I (London: Heinemann, 1966),
     p. 64.
3.   R.F. Foster, *Lord Randolph Churchill* (Oxford: Clarendon Press, 1981),
     p. 168.
4.   Churchill, *Churchill*, I, p. 113.
5.   D. Gilmour, *The Long Recessional: The Imperial Life of Rudyard Kipling*
     (London: Farrar, Strous & Giroux, 2002), p. 164.
6.   Martin Gilbert, *Churchill* (London: Heinemann, 1991), p. 26.
7.   Winston S. Churchill, *The Story of the Malakand Field Force* (London: Library
     of Imperial History, 1974), p. 95.
8.   S. Lindquist, *Exterminate All the Brutes* (London: Granta, 1997), p. 131.
9.   Piers Brendon, *Winston Churchill* (New York: Harper & Row, 1984), p. 23.
10. Winston S. Churchill, *Savrola* (London: Random House, 1974), pp. 78–81.
11. Winston S. Churchill, ed., *Never Give In! The Best of Winston Churchill's
     Speeches* (London: Hyperion, 2003), pp. 4, 229.
12. Churchill, *Malakand*, p. 5.
13. CAC, Churchill Papers, CHAR 8/2/7.
14. John Colville, *The Fringes of Power: Downing Street Diaries, 1939–1955*
     (London: Hodder & Stoughton, 1985), p. 563. For a more positive view of
     Churchill's racial attitudes, see R. Quinault, "Churchill and Black Africa",
     History Today 55, 6 (2005): 31–6.
15. Lord Moran, *Winston Churchill: The Struggle for Survival 1940–1965*
     (Boston: Constable, 1966), pp. 131, 464.

16. William R. Louis, *In the Name of God, Go! Leo Amery and the British Empire in the Age of Churchill* (London: W.W. Norton, 1992), p. 45. The words are Louis'.

17. David Day, *The Great Betrayal: Britain, Australia & the Onset of the Pacific War 1939–42* (London: Angus & Robertson, 1988), p. 355.

18. Churchill, *Malakand*, p. 25.

19. CAC, Churchill Papers, CHAR 8/487/72, Kipling to Churchill, 26 October 1934.

20. Gilmour, *Recessional*, p. 196.

21. Churchill, *Malakand*, p. 167.

22. Churchill, *Churchill*, I, p. 325.

23. Churchill, *Malakand*, p. 88.

24. Churchill, *Churchill*, Companion I, pp. ii, 751.

25. Churchill, *Malakand*, pp. 9, 217.

26. Robert Menzies, *Afternoon Light* (London: Cassell, 1967), p. 66.

27. R.W. Thompson, *The Yankee Marlborough* (London: Allen & Unwin, 1963), p. 251.

28. T. Morgan, *Churchill 1874–1915* (London: Triad/Panther, 1983), p. 288.

29. A. Leslie, *Jennie: The Life of Lady Randolph Churchill* (London: Hutchinson, 1969), p. 211.

30. Gilbert, *Churchill*, p. 89.

31. Winston S. Churchill, *The River War*, II (London: Longmans, Green & Co, 1902), p. 195.

32. Churchill, *Churchill*, I, p. 425.

33. Churchill, *River War*, I (London: Longmans, Green & Co, 1899), pp. 9–10.

34. Henry Pelling, *Winston Churchill* (London: Macmillan, 1974), p. 70.

35. Viola Bonham Carter, *Winston Churchill as I Knew Him* (London: Harcourt, Brace & World, 1965), p. 166.

36. Pelling, *Winston Churchill*, p. 73.

37. Churchill, *Churchill*, I, pp. 449–50.

38. Ibid., p. 521.

39. Winston S. Churchill, *London to Ladysmith via Pretoria* (London: Library of Imperial History, 1974) p. 19.

40. CAC, Churchill Papers, CHAR 2/134/15-16.

41. *Pictorial Weekly*, 14 April 1933.

42. Gilbert, *Churchill*, p. 146.

43. Ibid., p. 153.

44. Pelling, *Winston Churchill*, p. 101.

45. Randolph S. Churchill, *Winston S. Churchill*, II (London: Heinemann, 1967), p. 446.

46. Ronald Hyam, *Elgin and Churchill at the Colonial Office* (London: Macmillan, 1968), p. 152.

47. Ibid., p. 49.

48. Churchill, *Churchill*, II, p. 164.

49.   Gilbert, *Churchill*, p. 172.

50.   Hyam, *Elgin and Churchill*, pp. 183, 208, 215, 227.

51.   *United Empire* I (1910): 283.

52.   Churchill, *Churchill*, II, p. 235.

53.   Winston S. Churchill, *My African Journey* (London: Icon Books, 1964), pp. 4, 21, 142.

54.   R. Hyam, "Churchill and the British Empire", in *Churchill*, eds. R. Blake and W.R. Louis (Oxford: Oxford University Press, 1994), p. 170.

55.   Churchill, *African Journey*, p. 83.

56.   Ibid., p. 25.

57.   Churchill, *Churchill*, II, p. 232.

58.   W.S. Blunt, *My Diaries*, II, *1900–1914* (London: M. Secker, 1920), p. 284.

59.   T. Paterson, *A Seat for Life* (Dundee: David Winter, 1981), p. 68.

60.   Ronald Hyam, "Winston Churchill before 1914", *Historical Journal* XII 1 (1969): 169.

61.   Blunt, *Diaries*, II, p. 400.

62.   Arthur J. Marder, *From Dreadnought to Scapa Flow*, I (London: Oxford University Press, 1961), p. 322.

63.   Quoted in H.G. Gelber, *Nations out of Empires* (Basingstoke: Palgrave, 2001), p. 147.

64.   *Sunday Dispatch*, 17 March 1940.

65.   M. Gilbert, *Winston S. Churchill*, IV (London: Heineman, 1975), p. 158.

66.   Brendon, *Churchill*, p. 95.

67.   Gilbert, *Churchill*, IV, pp. 405–8.

68.   Ibid., pp. 448–60.

69.   *Times*, 3 November 1921.

70.   Hyam in *Churchill*, eds. Blake and Louis, p. 169.

71.   Gilbert, *Churchill*, IV, p. 484.

72.   N. Rose, "Churchill and Zionism", in *Churchill*, eds. Blake and Louis, p. 150.

73.   Gilbert, *Churchill*, IV, p. 621.

74.   Ibid., p. 799.

75.   *Times*, 29 November 1998.

76.   Gilbert, *Churchill*, IV, p. 810.

77.   Pelling, *Winston Churchill*, p. 263.

78.   E. Huxley, *White Man's Country 1914–1931*, II (London: Chatto & Windus, 1935), p. 121.

79.   Hyam in *Churchill*, eds. Blake and Louis, p. 175.

80.   Huxley, *White Man's Country*, II, p. 126.

81.   Ibid., p. 135.

82.   Gilbert, *Churchill*, IV, pp. 821, 826.

83.   CAC, Churchill Papers, CHAR 2/121/37; Cf. CHAR 2/120/61-2ff, Professor G. Wrong to Churchill, 6 December 1921.

84.   Gilbert, *Winston S. Churchill*, V (London: Heineman, 1979), p. 354.

85.   Ibid., p. 356.

86. A.J.P. Taylor *et al.*, *Churchill: Four Faces and the Man* (London: Allen Lane, 1967), p. 89.

87. Louis, *Name of God*, p. 106.

88. Gilbert, *Churchill*, V, p. 375.

89. A. Cooper, *Cairo in the War 1939–1945* (London: H. Hamilton, 1989), p. 58.

90. William R. Louis, *The British Empire in the Middle East* (London: Oxford University Press, 1984), p. 241.

91. Gilbert, *Churchill*, V, p. 366.

92. Ibid., p. 376.

93. Winston S. Churchill, *The Second World War*, 6 vols, I (London: Cassel, 1948–1954), p. 26.

94. CAC, Churchill Papers, CHAR 2/169/60, Sir Abe Bailey to Churchill, 17 September 1930.

95. Raymond A. Callahan, *Churchill: Retreat from Empire* (Wilmington, DE, Scholarly Resources, 1984), p. 35.

96. Gilbert, *Churchill*, pp. 499–500.

97. S. Gopal, "Churchill and India", in *Churchill*, eds. Blake and Louis, p. 460.

98. Paul Addison, *The Road to 1945* (London: Cape, 1975), p. 84.

99. Geoffrey Best, *Churchill: A Study in Greatness* (London: Hambledon, 2001), p. 135.

100. Gilbert, *Churchill*, V, p. 467.

101. Pelling, *Winston Churchill*, p. 352. Churchill would say that Roosevelt's conception of the British Empire dated back to the time of George III.

102. Richard Toye, *Churchill's Empire: The World that Made Him and the World He Made* (London: Macmillan, 2010), p. 187.

103. Gilbert, *Churchill*, V, p. 603.

104. CAC, Churchill Papers, CHAR 9/113.

105. Gilbert, *Churchill*, V, p. 886.

106. *News of the World*, 22 May 1938.

107. P. Clarke, *The Cripps Version: The Life of Sir Stafford Cripps* (London: Allen Lane, 2002), p. 111.

108. Gilbert, *Churchill*, p. 646.

109. Warren F. Kimball, ed., *Churchill & Roosevelt: The Complete Correspondence* I (New York: Collins, 1984), pp. 37–8.

110. J. Barnes and D. Nicholson, eds., *The Empire at Bay: The Leo Amery Diaries 1929–1945* (London: Hutchinson, 1988), p. 637.

111. Louis, *Name of God*, p. 20.

112. Ibid., p. 135.

113. Churchill, *Second World War*, II, p. 386.

114. Hyam in *Churchill*, eds. Blake and Louis, p. 180.

115. Norman Angell, "A Re-Interpretation of Empire", *United Empire* 43 (Sept–Oct 1952): 255.

116. NA, PREM4/43B/1, 11 August 1940.

117. Day, *Great Betrayal*, p. 216. See p. 354 where Day, having criticised Churchill for taking this view, adopts it himself.

118. Richard Lamb, *Churchill as War Leader — Right or Wrong* (London: Bloomsbury, 1991), p. 189.

119. *Sydney Morning Herald*, 14 February 1938.

120. *Melbourne Herald*, 27 December 1941.

121. Lamb, *Churchill*, pp. 190–1, 194.

122. Martin Gilbert, *Winston S. Churchill*, VII (London: Heineman, 1986), p. 54.

123. Nicholas Tarling, *The Fall of Imperial Britain in Southeast Asia* (Singapore: Oxford University Press, 1993), p. 140.

124. Christopher Bell, "The 'Singapore Strategy' and the Deterrence of Japan: Winston Churchill, the Admiralty and the Dispatch of Force Z", *English Historical Review* 116 (2001): 619.

125. David Reynolds, *In Command of History: Churchill Fighting and Writing the Second World War* (London: Allen Lane, 2004), p. 115.

126. Max Hastings, *Finest Years: Churchill as Warlord 1940–45* (London: HarperPress, 2009), p. 205.

127. Piers Brendon, *The Decline and Fall of the British Empire* (London: Jonathan Cape, 2007), p. 420.

128. Churchill, *Second World War*, IV, p. 81.

129. C.M. Turnbull, *A History of Singapore* (Singapore: Oxford University Press, 1977), p. 215.

130. Barnes and Nicholson, eds., *Empire at Bay*, p. 783.

131. Nicholas Mansergh *et al.*, eds, *The Transfer of Power 1942–47*, I (London: HMSO, 1970), p. 440.

132. Clarke, *Cripps*, p. 305.

133. Mansergh *et al.*, eds, *Transfer of Power*, p. 634.

134. Barnes and Nicholson, eds., *Empire at Bay*, p. 842.

135. *The Observer*, eds., *Churchill by His Contemporaries: An Observer Appreciation* (London: Hodder and Stoughton, 1965), p. 97.

136. CAC, Churchill Papers, CHAR 9/191/33 ff.

137. Y. Chadha, *Rediscovering Gandhi* (London: Century, 1997), p. 392.

138. CAC, Churchill Papers, CHAR 9/191A/3-12.

139. Barnes and Nicholson, eds., *Empire at Bay*, p. 943.

140. Louis, *Name of God*, p. 173.

141. M.J. Cohen, *Churchill and the Jews* (London: Frank Cass, 1985), pp. 326–7.

142. W.R. Louis, *Imperialism at Bay: The United States and the Decolonization of the British Empire 1941–1945* (London: Oxford University Press, 1977), p. 433.

143. Ibid., pp. 458, 460, 548.

144. Penderell Moon, ed., *Wavell: The Viceroy's Journal* (London: Oxford University Press, 1973), p. 168.

145. Martin Gilbert, *Winston S. Churchill*, VIII (London: Heineman, 1988), pp. 203, 216.

146. Callahan, *Churchill*, pp. 256, 258, 260.

147. A. Seldon, *Churchill's Indian Summer* (London: Faber & Faber Limited, 1981), p. 15.
148. Churchill, *Second World War*, I, p. 129.
149. J.M. Brown, "Gandhi — A Victorian Gentleman: An Essay in Imperial Encounter", *Journal of Imperial and Commonwealth History* XXVII (May 1999): 107.
150. Gopal in *Churchill*, eds. Blake and Louis, p. 470.
151. Hyam in *Churchill*, eds. Blake and Louis, p. 180.
152. George Mallaby, *From My Level: Unwritten Minutes* (London: Hutchinson of London, 1965), p. 44.
153. Harold Macmillan, *Tides of Fortune 1945–1955* (London: Macmillan, 1969), p. 391.
154. Evelyn Schuckburgh, *Descent to Suez: Diaries 1951–56* (London: Weidenfeld & Nicolson, 1986), p. 173.
155. Moran, p. 381.
156. Callahan, *Retreat from Empire*, p. 265.
157. Hyam in *Churchill*, eds. Blake and Louis, p. 183. But for illuminating further comments on this topic, see Ronald Hyam, *Understanding the British Empire* (Cambridge: Cambridge University Press, 2010), p. 39.
158. J.W. Pickersgill, *The Mackenzie King Record*, I (Toronto: Toronto University Press, 1960), p. 679.
159. *Life*, 28 December 1942.
160. Lord Halifax, *Fulness of Days* (London: Collins, 1957), p. 273.
161. Colville, *Fringes of Power*, p. 341.

CHAPTER 2

Churchill and Imperial Defence 1926–1940: Putting Singapore in Perspective

Brian P. Farrell

Few people left behind as many quotable quotes as Winston Spencer Churchill. Many defined him. Some stigmatised him. But some cast more shadow than light. One of the most celebrated came from a speech at the Mansion House in London on 10 November 1942: "Let me, however, make this clear, in case there should be any mistake about it in any quarter. I have not become the King's First Minister in order to preside over the liquidation of the British Empire".[1] Such rhetoric followed the long political career of a statesman who made a name adventuring in South Africa, introduced the Black and Tans to Ireland, unleashed the Royal Air Force (RAF) to bomb rebel forces into submission in Iraq, and nearly destroyed his career by denouncing constitutional reform for India. It certainly produced a strong impression. The picture is of a statesman for whom Britain's overseas empire ranked first when it came to economic policy, foreign relations, and especially defence. But this picture is dangerously simplistic. For Churchill, the Empire, and the larger system which rested on it, was fundamental to his understanding of Britain, past, present, future. But it was also never more than a means to an end. That end was British prosperity, security and influence. Empire made the United Kingdom (UK) a global power of the first rank, with all that entailed for the British nation. But, and this is the big but, the UK made the Empire.

Churchill's vision of Empire, so ably discussed by Piers Brendon,[2] never strayed far from the late 19th-century notion of the expansion of

England and Englishness. The relationship flowed more than one way, but the metropolis defined, drove and underpinned. What mattered most moved outwards: modernity, represented by investment capital, technology, manufactured goods, expertise, and settlers who knew how to use them all to develop modern societies overseas. The metropolis was literally heart and brain, the muscle that drove the system, the acumen that directed it. Without the Empire, the UK would decline; but without the UK, the Empire would die instantly. And this relationship rested on a prerequisite: a stable balance of power in Europe. The British Isles were rooted by geography 40 kilometres north of continental Europe. The only thing that allowed any British government to assume colonial burdens all over the world, deploy nearly all the nation's naval and military power away from home, and encourage the investment of most of its capital overseas, was the absence of any grave threat to British security in Europe. This is the first of three key points to grasp in order to understand Churchill's approach to imperial defence, and how he placed Singapore in perspective within that approach.

The first point derived from Churchill the historian and military strategist. The second point derived from Churchill the dynamic politician. From 1901 to 1955, Churchill held nearly every senior office the British government had to offer: Home Secretary, First Lord of the Admiralty, Secretary for War, Colonial Secretary, Chancellor of the Exchequer, and especially, twice, Prime Minister. Churchill threw himself into these offices with the zeal, ambition, self-confidence, and sheer drive that so marked his character. In so doing, he defined a clear pattern: whatever appeared to be the most pressing challenge facing that particular office defined Churchill's agenda. The social reformer who joined Lloyd George to condemn an expensive naval arms race gave way to the naval strategist who ran his reputation aground on the shores of Gallipoli. The Secretary for War who tried to destroy the Russian Revolution gave way to the Chancellor of the Exchequer who placed the Ten Year Rule on a new clock every day, to keep defence spending as low as possible. Churchill's diagnosis of any problem in imperial defence was always influenced by whatever office he held, or did not hold, at the time. As Robert Rhodes James said so well, the only way to focus Churchill's full attention on the broadest issues was for him to take on the broadest responsibilities.[3]

The third key point will therefore appear to contradict. Churchill, as statesman, student of war and history, romantic champion of England and Empire, fancied himself, at all times, as a maker of grand strategy. Grand strategy may be defined as the art of relating the organisation and application of all available power to the pursuit of the largest, most important objective. That meant either the central direction of war if nation and Empire were at war, or the central direction of defence policy if they were not. But Churchill also, whether as First Lord, Secretary for War, or backbench Member of Parliament, time and again threw himself into specific plans or campaigns with such zeal that he seemed to lose sight of any broader context. Many saw this as revealing a fatal flaw in his character: lack of judgement and perspective. Churchill rationalised the contradiction to himself by arguing that the plans he championed were in fact the best way to achieve the larger ends of grand strategy, rather than erratic departures from it. But this was not always the case. The ability to connect a broad appreciation for grand strategy to the prosecution of a specific plan rests, fundamentally, on the ability to make sure each are sound and practical in their own right — and both are realistically connected to each other. This most demanding requirement often eluded Churchill, the maker of grand strategy.[4]

Let us combine these three key points. First, for Churchill, imperial defence rested, always, on a stable balance of power in Europe. British physical security was the basis for imperial defence. Second, Churchill pursued with determination whatever appeared to be the most pressing problem facing the office he held at any given time. Finally, while Churchill fancied himself as a strategic planner on the grand scale, his tendency to miss the devil in the detail made him vulnerable when it came to connecting ultimate ends to particular means. These three points provide a framework for analysis within which we may shed light on how Churchill treated Singapore, within the larger problem of imperial defence. This chapter shall zoom in on three episodes. The first is his decision as Chancellor of the Exchequer, in 1926, to oppose the completion of a new naval base at Singapore. The second is his decision, as First Lord of the Admiralty, to assure the Australian government in autumn 1939 that it could rely on British guarantees regarding defence against Japan and dispatch an expeditionary force to Europe. The third is his decision as Prime Minister to oppose plans by the Chiefs of Staff (COS), in late 1940, to send stronger reinforcements to the Far East. It shall argue that Churchill's decisions demonstrate three important things. First, for British decision-makers, the Far East was indeed a region whose defence problems "were going to be, in the last resort and the worst case, insoluble".[5] Second, for students of the higher direction of defence, individuals always matter; answers cannot be found by ignoring them. Finally, Churchill's actions underlined a universal fact for any military coalition: it is always about homeland security.

Winston Churchill was not suited by training or experience to become the nation's finance minister. He was not an economist, did not read widely or critically on the subject before becoming Chancellor of the Exchequer in 1924, and his previous offices involved spending as much money as possible.[6] But there was one exception, directly relevant to our concern regarding Singapore and imperial defence. Driven by the tendency to champion what he saw as the legacy of his father, Churchill temperamentally sympathised with the principle that the nation should not spend any more on defence than it truly must. He called it retrenchment. Churchill spent most of his time dealing with matters in which he struggled to hold his own: the Gold Standard, unemployment, overseas trade. Defence spending, especially the naval programme and naval strategy, was another matter. The son of retrenchment met the confident maker of grand strategy in the person of the former political boss of the navy, and they all agreed: this was one matter on which they could lead, and one area in which there could be cuts.

Churchill provoked the navy by objecting to their shipbuilding programme of cruisers and destroyers on the grounds they did not need so many, rather than just insisting the nation could not afford them. He compounded this trespass across department lines by submitting vigorously argued papers on grand strategy to reinforce his financial point. This poisoned the atmosphere in a debate that climaxed over a matter for which Churchill shared earlier responsibility: the plan to defend the Far East against any threat from Japan, a plan known now as the "Singapore Strategy". Adopted in 1921 by the coalition government in which Churchill served as Colonial Secretary, the plan called for constructing a modern main base in Singapore, complete with all the support facilities the main fleet would require to sustain operations in that part of the world. This was a second best compromise, to compensate for the fact the nation could not afford to maintain a strong battle fleet in Asia permanently, as a deterrent. Driven by the need to reduce public spending, confirmed by the decision to accept the Washington Treaties as a basis for security in Asia, the British government reduced the size of the Royal Navy (RN) to a level too small to allow it to maintain powerful fleets both at home and in Asia. The idea was that a fully equipped main base facility in Singapore, close enough to the interests to be protected, far enough from the threat to allow time to respond, would allow the main fleet to charge to the rescue should the need arise.[7] This was not necessarily an unworkable strategy, in principle. The Empire faced no serious or imminent military threat in the 1920s. Japan was not overtly hostile, and the Treaties capped its fleet at a strength below the RN. But there were two prerequisites for the plan. First, the facilities must be completed as planned. Second, they must be sufficient to support the plan. Churchill inherited the first issue, but did much to disrupt the second.

The "Singapore Strategy" became a political football when a Labour government came into office, as a minority administration led by Ramsay Macdonald, in 1923. Macdonald attacked the policy of naval deterrence, arguing that the nation should instead pursue the policy of general disarmament pledged in the 1919 peace treaties. This forced the Admiralty to trim its plans to try to save its strategy, and proved to be the slippery slope. The original plan, the "Green scheme", envisaged a massive facility able to support the entire main fleet. This was the crucial point. If deterrence failed and war with Japan broke out, the fleet would bear the brunt of the conflict. It would face an enemy whose home economy and bases were much closer to the theatre of operations than the British Isles. To prevail, the British would have to concentrate the main power of their battle fleet. That would depend on the facilities available in Singapore to sustain it. The "Singapore Strategy" was in fact an insurance policy, but unless a sufficient premium was paid, the coverage could never meet the requirement. To preserve their plan, the Admiralty offered a revised "Red scheme" which greatly reduced the overall facility. Macdonald's government vetoed the plan anyway, but everyone skipped past the main point. Such a facility, even if it did materialise, could only support less than half of the main fleet. That would never be enough to promise a good chance of success in any war against Japan. Despite the price tag of £25 million, by far the biggest defence expenditure proposed since the end of the Great War, the insurance premium would be too low.[8]

Churchill inherited this issue in 1924 when a new government led by Stanley Baldwin revived the deterrence policy. The Admiralty tried to make up for lost time by pressing forward with the reduced scheme, hoping contracts for construction could at last be tendered. Churchill pounced on this proposal from the start, treating it as justification for the shipbuilding programme he opposed. In December, he insisted even the reduced base was larger and more expensive than required, and the crux of his argument was grand strategy:

> The only war it would be worth our while to fight would be to prevent an invasion of Australia, and that I am certain will never happen in any period even the most remote, which we or our children need foresee. I am therefore convinced that war with Japan is not a reasonable policy any reasonable government need take into account.

We should not condemn Churchill for failing to foresee that Japanese ambitions in China, rather than any "drive to the south", would in fact set the two empires on a collision course. But we must note his reasoning and arguments. Churchill did not just say he could not find the money, which in fact he wanted to spend on "many social schemes" — he also said there was no strategic need to spend it. The COS fought back hard. Baldwin had to intervene personally when the entire Board of Admiralty threatened to resign if Churchill's refusal to fund shipbuilding was allowed to "ruin the navy". Churchill retorted by urging the Cabinet to declare that "no naval war against a first class navy is likely to take place in the next twenty years". The dispute was not resolved until November 1926 when a contract for constructing the naval base in Singapore was finally approved — but this contract removed all major repair capacity, leaving only docking and petrol storage facilities in a "truncated Red scheme". Churchill carried on the argument until he finally wore down his colleagues and persuaded them to amend the Ten Year Rule, to begin anew every day, in 1928.[9]

The reduced naval base in Singapore was completed in time for the test of war in 1941, and Churchill returned to publicly supporting re-armament during the more dangerous circumstances of the 1930s. But much damage was done, no small amount by him. During his campaign to cut the navy's plans down to size, he complained that had he known the "Singapore Strategy" would cost so much when he supported it in 1921, he would have reconsidered. This was revealing. Churchill the Colonial Secretary arguing "what we have we hold" had no qualms about balancing guns and butter. Churchill the Chancellor suddenly found stra-tegic arguments against the need for guns. The reduction in shipbuilding delayed plans to modernise the navy. This contributed to a long-term decline in the structural capacity of British heavy industry that made it much harder to rearm when it became necessary to do so. Lord Hankey, serving then as Secretary to the Committee of Imperial Defence, opposed Churchill at the time and complained bitterly about his influence many years later. He argued that Churchill made a real impact on the final Cabinet decisions, persuading his colleagues there was no great danger in paring down capabilities. Churchill did this by vigorous and sustained pressure, expressed through confident arguments that connected strategic to financial considerations. The chickens came home to roost the next decade.[10] That included the "Singapore Strategy".

The truncation of the naval base meant the British did not have a viable military strategy to defend their Empire against Japan by relying in the end on their own strength, come what may. This was the point on which Churchill's advocacy made the most impact. Churchill was not the only one to fail to see the inherent danger in proceeding with a strategic plan that could never be realistic, but he was the most persuasive when it mattered. This can only be explained by two assumptions which guided his thoughts. One is not unreasonable: the British Empire was never likely to have to fight Japan by itself. That assumption was written into British grand strategy by the Washington Treaties. The other is more problematic: it was not likely to have to fight Japan at all. Is not the whole point of insurance to guard against not just the unwanted but also the unexpected?

There are two points of contact we can identify to connect the 1926 decisions to the situation Churchill addressed in 1939. The first was his evaluation of Japan. The second was his perception of Australia. Connecting both were his perceptions of the strategic situation in Asia and British grand strategy. We should examine them from a certain vantage point: the relationship between circumstances, intentions and capabilities. Circumstances can change very rapidly. They did, when the Great Depression destroyed the optimism of the 1920s and war clouds darkened the sky in both Europe and Asia. Intentions can change almost as rapidly. They did, when a militarist Japan and a Nazi Germany launched fundamental challenges to the status quo. No power stood to lose more from violent changes to the status quo than the British Empire. Churchill did more than any other public figure to respond, courageously and with crucial insight, to changing circumstances, particularly in Europe. But his was then a voice in the wilderness, message diluted if not discredited by the tarnished reputation of the messenger.[11] The grave problem is that capabilities can only be changed much more slowly than circumstances and intentions. Here, the bitter harvest had to be reaped, for which Churchill had to face his share of the reckoning. Churchill's perceptions of threats in Europe and Asia reflected, to some extent influenced, the rethinking of British grand strategy. Asia was a concern, but Europe was the threat. From 1934, Japan pursued an imperial policy in China that threatened to provoke war with the Western Powers over the future of Asia. But Nazi Germany, the "ultimate enemy", threatened the balance of power in Europe. Churchill did everything he could to champion, and nothing to impede, a rearmament policy that concentrated on air defence at home, at the expense of sea power in general. But by the time the British nation agreed with Churchill that Nazi Germany was a menace that must be confronted, it was 1939 and time was desperately short.[12]

The circumstances in which war broke out in Europe in September 1939 and Churchill returned to office as First Lord of the Admiralty influenced what he did next. The Japanese government was as surprised as everyone else by the bargain between Adolf Hitler and Joseph Stalin that cleared the way for the German attack on Poland, which provoked the Allied declaration of war on Germany. Japanese-British relations were now very poor, but the confused Japanese government sat still to wait on events. This gave the British a stay of execution in the Far East. It was reinforced by Mussolini's decision to wait and see before jumping into Hitler's war. From 1935, the COS most feared having to fight Germany, Italy and Japan at the same time. Their grand strategy became to play for time in Asia, resurrect the Western Front in France, and "go after" Italy in the Mediterranean, to knock out what appeared to be the weakest link. But the British Empire now found itself at war with Germany alone, at least for the moment. The First Lord strode once more unto the breech with his usual vigour, demanding plans to take the war to Germany and build up a strong position in the Mediterranean. But what about Japan? On 31 October, the COS advised that while it posed no immediate threat, it would surely exploit any opportunity opened up by developments in Europe, and could not be expected to sit still for long. On the other hand, they told the Australian government the Japanese posed no immediate threat, and urged them to send the expeditionary force now being raised in Australia to the European theatre of war as soon as possible.[13] This provoked an Australian inquiry that dropped the problem squarely in Churchill's lap.

From 1937, Australian officials grew increasingly concerned about the "Singapore Strategy". This was not surprising, given that Australian security rested in practice upon this British guarantee. Australia would contribute, as before, to any general war that jeopardised the imperial system on which it ultimately depended. But in the Great War, Australian forces were able to reinforce Allied campaigns in the Middle East and Europe because Japan was an ally, and there was no direct threat to Australia itself. This was no longer the case, which made any decision to commit Australian power to war in Europe contingent on homeland security. Australia was not strong enough to pursue any alternative, so Australian governments rested their defence policy on the general reinforcement of British power. The connecting link between that and the security of Australia was the "Singapore Strategy".

By autumn 1939, Singapore boasted an incomplete base, but no fleet, and inadequate defences. Attention focused on the so-called "period before relief", the time that must elapse between the beginning of a crisis and the arrival of a British fleet in Singapore. The original stipulated time was 42 days. It was increased in 1938 to 70 days, then in 1939 to first 90 and then 180 days. This fundamentally changed the entire strategy.

Plans to defend the Empire in Asia rested on sending a battle fleet to
Singapore. Those plans thus now rested on protecting its base for as long
as six months against Japanese attack. This called for much stronger forces
to defend Malaya and Singapore. But British rearmament struggled to
catch up to the German threat, and the navy came last in line. From
1938, the Australians asked somewhat tougher questions and pressed a bit
harder for answers. In response, the British warned that the situation in
Europe would determine what could be done to respond to any crisis, but
also reaffirmed their promise to send a strong fleet to meet any Japanese
attack on the Empire.[14] When crisis became war, Australian Prime Minister
Robert Menzies sent R.G. Casey to London to put the issue categorically
to the British government: before Australia could send military forces
to war in Europe, it must know how the British would respond to any
attack by Japan.

No one man could have quickly changed the hard facts of time,
space and capabilities in November 1939. It would take time to build
up a credible defence against Japan, whatever the British and Australian
governments decided to do to balance the war in Europe against the
threat in Asia. But margins always matter. And individuals can influence
margins. Churchill did so. And as usual, he did so with confidence and
emphasis. Casey made the Australian position crystal clear: "If Australia
were to put in the full war effort of which she was capable, his Government would require a most comprehensive undertaking regarding the
security of Singapore". Churchill gave one, in person and in writing,
in a memorandum for the record on 17 November. Singapore was now
a "powerful and well-defended fortress", one the Japanese could only
subdue if they besieged it for four or five months with an army of at least
60,000 troops, escorted by the bulk of their fleet. Ignoring the fact that
this time span lay within the "period before relief", Churchill argued that
the distances were so great the Japanese must assume the British would
intervene before they could overrun the base. Given that they were already
bogged down by a major war in China, and that they must be wary of
any American reaction, they were not likely to attack Singapore. But
they could not attack Australia itself unless they first took Singapore. No
enemy would launch such a rash invasion so far from home before first
reducing a base on the flank, from which a strong foe could counter-
attack. Based on this reasoning, Churchill repeated the assurance that if
the Japanese nevertheless directly attacked Australia, the RN would set
aside all other concerns and charge to the rescue. So reassured, Menzies'
government committed Australian forces to the war in Europe.[15]

Churchill's reassurance demands careful reassessment. It rested on assumptions stretching far back in time, as well as on a premise the two parties did not interpret the same way. A generation earlier, Churchill provoked Australian ire by recalling the capital ships of the China Squadron to Europe, to concentrate against the German threat. He justified this in 1912 by underlining the gravity of that threat to the balance of power in Europe, as well as pointing towards a remote worst case scenario: "If the power of Britain were shattered upon the sea, the only course open to the 5 millions of white men [sic] in the Pacific would be to seek the protection of the United States".[16] The Great War only seemed to vindicate the argument. It took the combined might of the British Empire, as well as its allies, to defeat the German threat to the balance of power in Europe. Should that balance ever be shattered, British power and security would shatter with it. This would render the Empire overseas so vulnerable that only American power could fill the breech. When the issue was the balance of power in Europe, the Empire must concentrate. The 1925 discussions provided another insight. Churchill argued then that the only threat he saw as grave enough to justify a change in British grand strategy was a Japanese attack on Australia itself. Because such an attack seemed so remote, it did not make sense to build such an expensive deterrent against it. The circumstances of 1939 were of course drastically different, but still Churchill focused on the scenario of a direct invasion of Australia. Here, crucially, the parties disconnected.

In November 1939, Churchill combined longstanding assumptions with strategic priorities of the moment. War raged again in Europe, threatening the all-important balance of power. This, not the security of Poland, was the cardinal threat to which the Empire must again respond. The enemy had a weakness: the junior partner not yet engaged in the fight. When Italy did intervene, the navy expected to knock it out quickly — which would change the trajectory of the war. Should Japan be rash enough to attack Australia in the meantime, it could not prevail before success in the Mediterranean "would liberate very powerful naval forces to cut the invaders from their base". Nor would the Americans stand idly by while Australia fought off invasion. The Dominions should therefore reinforce the main front at the point of decision: the war in Europe. The Australians did not point out the most obvious hole in this argument: if they sent most of their rapidly mobilising military forces to reinforce the war in Europe, and Japan did attack after all, what would be left of "Australian manhood" to hold the Japanese at bay long enough to buy time for "great and powerful friends" to intervene?[17] They focused not on

Churchill's stipulation regarding an invasion of Australia itself but rather on his evaluation of the security and importance of Singapore. He said in effect: "Japan will not dare attack you as long as we hold Singapore, and we can hold Singapore with what is already there, but if Japan attacks you directly nonetheless then we will send a battle fleet". They chose to hear "we will hold Singapore and if necessary we will send a battle fleet to do so". This was far from a minor disconnection. For Churchill, the promise to be redeemed *in extremis* was to defend Australia itself against invasion. For the Australian government, the promise that allowed them to join the war in Europe was the assurance Singapore would be held come what may. Both failed to make sure each clearly understood the other. This planted a time bomb in grand strategy, imperial defence and British-Australian relations. The fuse would start ticking if the war in Europe did not go well and Japan did not sit still.

Churchill's evaluation of Japan not only did much to shape his fateful 1939 promise, it also connected it to even more fateful 1940 decisions. His view of Japan influenced his view of the problem that most directly linked Australian concerns to British grand strategy: how to defend Singapore before the fleet could charge to the rescue. Churchill simply did not believe Japan would be rash enough to attack the British Empire or, at the very least, could not do crippling damage even if it did. He was certainly not alone in being complacent about Japanese intentions and capabilities. But from May 1940, he became the most important person to feel this way when he became Prime Minister. And he did so amid circumstances so dire they compelled everyone to rethink everything.

Churchill climbed to the top of the greasy pole just as the Germans invaded Western Europe. In six weeks, they drove the British Army off the continent, forced France to surrender, destroyed Allied grand strategy, and stood poised to invade the British Isles. Italy jumped in, to share the spoils. German victories were the nail in the coffin that made Singapore indefensible. Instead of being a buffer between the Japanese and Malaya, French Indochina now became a staging base for Japanese invasion. German victories opened up prospects for Japanese exploitation. The British could do little to deter them because they now faced a mortal threat to the very survival of the metropolis, menaced by a much stronger enemy. British grand strategy had to be redesigned in circumstances for which there was no contingency plan. When Churchill asked the COS at the end of May how final victory might still be won, they produced a chilling reply: the British Isles must first survive onslaught from the air and invasion from the sea. Home defence now became the only priority.[18] Churchill made his reputation immortal by his leadership in responding to this mortal threat. The Prime Minister defined the war for a bewildered nation waiting to be led, inspiring it to survive "their finest hour". He sounded a clarion call to arms defined by absolute certainty that Nazi Germany was a mortal threat to civilisation itself, not just to the balance of power in Europe. That left little room for anything else. Churchill adopted two fundamental policies that shaped the central direction of the war from summer 1940: nothing could be done that might jeopardise home defence; in order to win the war, the British must bring the Americans in on their side, as soon as possible.[19]

Such drastic changes in circumstances and policy naturally affected grand strategy regarding the Far East. On 19 June, the Australians were told that for the "foreseeable future ... we see no hope of being able to dispatch a fleet to Singapore". On 28 June, the COS admitted that as a result, it was necessary to strengthen the ground and air defences of Malaya. On 15 August, they produced a report titled *The Situation in the Far East in the Event of Japanese Intervention Against Us*. This document noted that until survival at home was assured, there could be no promise to implement the "Singapore Strategy". The conclusion was stark:

> In the absence of a fleet, we cannot prevent damage to our interests in the Far East. Our object must, therefore, be to limit the extent of the damage and in the last resort to retain a footing from which we could eventually retrieve the position when stronger forces become available.[20]

Fighting the Battle of Britain at home, expecting invasion any day, British grand strategy in the Far East was reduced to little more than to rely on American protection. Churchill had already told President Franklin Roosevelt: "In the Pacific I look to you to keep the Japanese dog quiet".[21]

Churchill was of course right to prosecute total war against Nazi Germany. He was also right to concentrate ruthlessly on home defence. And above all, he was right to see American intervention as the only hope for ultimate salvation. On the other hand he also decided the war could only be won by throwing the combined power of the Empire into the struggle and refused to give way anywhere: what we have, we hold. He also agreed with the COS that even in these new circumstances, the previous plan still made sense: "Our best hope of being able to supply naval forces for the Far East in the near future lies in the possibility of early and successful naval action against Italian naval forces in the Mediterranean".[22] The Prime Minster focused on the war at hand. This made it even more important that what arrangements could be made for the Far East were as effective as possible. It was the old problem: both grand strategy and specific plans must be sound and practical in their own right, and the connection between them must be realistic. Here, on the margin of grand strategy, Churchill once again made a difference by the way he put Singapore in perspective.

From 1938, theatre commanders in Singapore correctly assumed that the only way to carry out their mission to hold the naval base was to defend all of Malaya. If the Japanese approached within striking distance, they could either suppress the base or isolate it. Airpower gave them the means to do this from some distance. The only way to keep them at bay was to keep them out of Malaya. By autumn 1940, the three armed forces in the Far East were nowhere near strong enough to defend all of Malaya. The COS appreciation in August accepted the premise that all Malaya must be held in order to hold Singapore and agreed the air force should play the lead role in keeping the Japanese at bay. To do this, RAF Far East needed 22 squadrons, some 336 first line combat aircraft. At that time, it had eight, with 88 aircraft, most of them obsolete. The army's Malaya Command must play the lead role until air reinforcements arrived, but to do this, it required at least 27 battalions. At that time, it had nine. Rather than direct theatre commanders to improvise to the best of their ability until help could be spared, the COS confirmed the strategy to defend all of Malaya in order to preserve the naval base. This rested on nothing more than the hope that the Japanese would not strike before the British could respond.[23]

At least one member of the COS did try to address this dilemma. General Sir John Dill, Chief of the Imperial General Staff, took note of the warnings that Malaya Command could not spread out to defend all of Malaya with so few battalions. From September, he pressed for reinforcements for the Far East, including lobbying Churchill to ask the Australians to divert their 7th Division, scheduled to go to the Middle East, to Malaya instead. But on the other hand, Dill declined to authorise Malaya Command to concentrate its strength in a smaller more defensible area, covering the immediate approaches to Singapore. That would allow the Japanese to isolate Singapore by seizing central Malaya. That would prevent the RN from sending a fleet to Singapore even if it decided to do so in spite of the war in Europe. This would be tantamount to admitting the British would not hold Singapore after all. That would mean reneging on the promise to Australia — and confessing to the Americans the British could not support any common front against Japan. Dill did not contest the overriding emergency at home, but saw the potentially fatal disconnection in the Far East: if ground and air forces were compelled to fight according to a strategy they were not strong enough to prosecute, in order to try to preserve a grand strategy the navy was too weak to implement, the result might not just be defeat. It might be humiliation and disaster, inviting defeat in detail. But if there were objections to changing strategy and grand strategy, then reinforcements must somehow be found.[24]

Churchill rejected Dill's persistent lobbying. He argued the risk was acceptable. After weeks of discussion, he put his foot down to define a policy. As long as the "garrison" was strong enough to hold the "fortress" of Singapore, and given that the Americans could intervene, there was no need to defend all of Malaya. It was more important to press the offensive now underway in the Mediterranean. Strongly defending "the approaches to Singapore" would be enough to allow the fleet to intervene if necessary. When the worried Australians did offer in December to send a brigade of their 8th Division to Malaya, Churchill accepted with thanks but argued that would suffice: "it would be unwise to spare aircraft to lay idle in Malaya on the remote chance of an attack by Japan when they should be playing their part in Europe".[25]

In January 1941, the COS proposed to accelerate reinforcements to the Far East, especially fighter aircraft. The Battle of Britain was won but the Blitz continued, and home defence remained paramount. The COS tried to anticipate their Prime Minister by qualifying the proposal "taking into account the demands of theatres already the scene of war". Churchill put both feet down this time, declaring on 13 January:

> I do not remember to have given my approval to these very large diversions of forces. On the contrary, if my minutes are collected they will be seen to have an opposite tendency. The political situation in the Far East does not seem to require, and the strength of our Air Forces by no means warrants, the maintenance of such large forces in the Far East at this time.[26]

Reinforcements were in fact sent to Malaya throughout 1941. And there is no reason to condemn Churchill for being preoccupied with the war in Europe in autumn 1940. But the reinforcement argument was conditioned by something important: the connection between grand strategy and the defence of Singapore.

The cold hard fact of the matter is that Churchill was wrong and Dill was right regarding defence plans for Malaya and Singapore. If the aim was to hold the base in order to preserve it for the fleet, thus reassuring Empire and ally, then the defenders must defend all of Malaya. If they could not do so without serious reinforcement, then either the aim must be changed or reinforcements found. Churchill would not accept either point. He had one understandable reason: the conviction the Americans would not stand aside and the strength of their Pacific Fleet. No one, it must be remembered, expected it to be knocked out of the fight on the first morning of the war. But relentless efforts to woo the Americans had not, by January 1941, produced any realistic expectation that they would intervene quickly enough to prevent a Japanese attack on Singapore. At that point, Churchill could not see the American factor as anything more than a fail-safe backstop. There was another reason. Brazening it out by insisting Singapore would not be allowed to fall enabled the British to claim they acted in good faith, summoning Australian forces to Europe. As Australian ground troops spearheaded the counterattack that drove the Italians out of Egypt while Churchill and Dill argued about defending Singapore, this was not irrelevant. Changing the defence plan in a manner that made it obvious Singapore would be cut off would amount to cancelling the 1939 promise to Australia. Churchill would not do this. Rather than face certain political consequences, he opted to face possible military consequences. He justified this on the very point that divided him and the COS: defence plans for Malaya and Singapore.

Churchill never went to Singapore. Nor did he visit Australia, or anywhere in the Far East. He did not venture further east than India, and there not after 1897. Singapore and the region were abstractions to him. This mattered when the issue of defence plans reached the level of fine detail. Churchill regarded the island of Singapore, home of the naval and air bases on which British grand strategy rested, as a true fortress. By this, he meant a strongpoint able to defend itself effectively against attack from any direction. It was nothing of the kind. Coastal artillery defences were strong enough to make direct invasion from the sea very risky. But only an understrength army and air force, plus a narrow strait barely a kilometre wide, stood before any attack through mainland Malaya from the north. Singapore sat in the shadow of Malaya. The mainland was its defensive shield. To make matters worse, the naval base was on the north coast. If an enemy overran the mainland, no one could use the naval base — or hope to stand fast on the island. The COS understood these cardinal military realities. They knew that if the aim must be to hold the naval base, then the battle must be fought as far north as possible. It would make no sense to concentrate in the south and allow the enemy to isolate Singapore, which must then fall in due course. They also knew the air force was too weak to defeat any invasion, the army too small and spread out to contain any advance. Their bounden duty, to provide professional military advice to the government on the direction of the war, pointed only one way: they must make sure the Prime Minister understood that his perception of defence plans for Singapore was not realistic, and therefore did not connect to higher strategy.

Sadly, the COS did nothing of the kind. The discussion petered out as other problems came to the fore. The COS found Churchill a handful, to say the least. Dill in particular was not up to the challenge to establish effective rapport. Repeated disagreements between the two compromised their working relationship. Every issue great and small could become an ordeal of persuasion and debate with this supremely confident maker of grand strategy. This was one of several occasions on which the COS decided to leave the issue to lie quiet for the moment, while they turned to other problems.[27] Not only did that delay reinforcements for Singapore, it also meant no effort was made to realign theatre defence plans and grand strategy to make sure they connected realistically. This left open a gap the Japanese exploited ruthlessly when they invaded in December 1941. Churchill and the COS resumed the argument in far more dire circumstances in January 1942, when the Prime Minister at last realised how completely he failed to understand the defence position on the ground in Malaya and Singapore. By then, it was far too late to avert military humiliation, imperial acrimony, and political disaster.[28] Churchill and the COS must share the blame for failing to argue the issue through to clarity and conclusions in December 1940 and January 1941, failure both consequential and inexcusable.

Neither clarity nor conclusions in January 1941 would have kept the Japanese from taking Singapore a year later, but that is not the point. Churchill did not condemn Singapore to defeat. Profound forces, the defeat of France, and the attack on Pearl Harbor did that. But he helped push defeat towards disaster. In 1926, he made a major contribution both to ensuring British defence capabilities would decline to a dangerously low level, and the naval base in Singapore could never be sufficient to support the strategy resting on it. This helped make British plans for imperial defence against Japan dangerously unrealistic from the start. In 1939, Churchill made the promise to Australia that became a hostage to fortune when the war in Europe went disastrously wrong in 1940. That promise was a major reason why British defence plans became even more unrealistic and inflexible as the strategic situation worsened. And in 1940, Churchill prevented a proper review of the connections between grand strategy and the defence of Singapore. Because the Japanese invaded before any such review could be conducted, they were able to turn pre-dictable British defeat into avoidable British disaster. Churchill was never the only reason for these outcomes. But he was on these three occasions a very powerful reason. His self-confidence, determination, persistence and advocacy dominated debates and shaped decisions — decisions that suffered from failure to focus and clarify essential details and points of connection. The British Empire could not hold Singapore in 1941. But it need not have been humiliated in the attempt. Churchill must share responsibility for the fact that it was.

This must not however be the last word in this evaluation. Great men make great mistakes, but Churchill did not mistake the greatest issue of all. There is little to mitigate the 1926 arguments. Churchill dismissed the Turks and the Japanese for not much more than ethnocentric prejudice, and paid for it. There is no point in buying insurance to cover a broken arm when you need to insure against being crippled, and there is no real excuse for Churchill going along with this. But we can present different verdicts for 1939 and 1940. Churchill was surely right to see the balance of power in Europe as the prerequisite for British security. The descendant and biographer of Marlborough felt this in his bones, understood it viscerally. He was also surely right to see Nazi Germany as a threat even more dire than the one defeated by his great ancestor, a threat to be destroyed at any cost. We must remember that Hitler expressly denied any desire to challenge the British Empire overseas, but Churchill defied him anyway. Only after the tide began to turn did Churchill start talking about preserving the Empire. Nothing, ever, came before winning the war. Becoming Prime Minister actually made Churchill more effective, because he finally assumed an office that required him to make the biggest decisions. His allies endorsed the one that mattered most: making "Germany first" the basis of Allied grand strategy. This can at least put in context his desire to secure Australian support for the war in Europe in 1939, and determination to prosecute that war defiantly in 1940. The hardest coldest fact was that the British Empire could lose Singapore and still win the war — but the home islands must hold, whatever the cost. Churchill tipped margins and shifted directions in debates and decisions. When he was wrong, there were consequences. But on the biggest issue, he was not wrong. Churchill put Singapore in perspective when he made decisions about imperial defence. It suffered accordingly, but the Allies won the world war. That, surely, is the last word.

Notes

1. Brian P. Farrell, *The Basis and Making of British Grand Strategy 1940–1943: Was There a Plan?* (Lewiston, NY: Edwin Mellen Press, 1998), p. 475.
2. Piers Brendon, *Churchill: A Short Life* (New York: Harper & Row, 1984); see also Chapter 1 in this volume.

3. Robert Rhodes James, *Churchill: A Study in Failure 1900–1939* (London: Penguin, 1981).

4. Farrell, *The Basis and Making of British Grand Strategy 1940*, *passim*; Max Hastings, *Winston's War: Churchill 1940–1945* (New York: Alfred A. Knopf, 2010); Raymond A. Callahan, *Churchill and His Generals* (Lawrence, KS: University Press of Kansas, 2007).

5. Geoffrey Best, *Churchill: A Study in Greatness* (London: Hambledon, 2001), p. 127.

6. Paul Addison, *Churchill on the Home Front 1900–1955* (London: Jonathan Cape, 1992); James, *A Study in Failure*.

7. Brian P. Farrell, *The Defence and Fall of Singapore 1940–1942* (Stroud: Tempus, 2005), Chapter 1; David McIntyre, *The Rise and Fall of the Singapore Naval Base 1919–1942* (London: Macmillan, 1979); Martin Gilbert, *Winston S. Churchill: The Exchequer Years, 1922–1929* (Documents companion) (London: Heineman, 1979).

8. NA, CAB4/15, minutes, Imperial Conference of 1926; Farrell, *Defence and Fall*, Chapters 1–2; James Neidpath, *The Singapore Naval Base and the Defence of Britain's Eastern Empire 1918–1941* (Oxford: Clarendon Press, 1981).

9. Ian Hamill, *The Strategic Illusion: The Singapore Strategy and the Defence of Australia and New Zealand 1919–1942* (Singapore: Singapore University Press, 1981), pp. 99–101; Stephen W. Roskill, *Naval Policy Between the Wars*, Vol. 1 (London: Collins, 1968), p. 464; Malcolm H. Murfett *et al.*, *Between Two Oceans: A Military History of Singapore* (Singapore: Marshall Cavendish Academic, 2004 [1999]), Chapter 6; John R. Ferris, *Men, Money and Diplomacy: The Evolution of British Strategic Policy 1919–1926* (Ithaca, NY: Cornell University Press, 1989).

10. CAC, Hankey Papers, 4/34, Correspondence regarding Churchill and strategy. Series 1/7 contains the Hankey Diary, also useful.

11. Winston S. Churchill, *The Second World War*, Vol. 1 (London: Cassell, 1948); Piers Brendon, *The Dark Valley: A Panorama of the 1930s* (New York: Viking Books, 2000 [2002]).

12. Martin Gilbert, *Winston S. Churchill*, Vol. V, *The Prophet of Truth 1922–1939* (London: Heineman, 1976); William Manchester, *The Last Lion: Winston Spencer Churchill: Alone, 1932–1940* (New York: Bantam, 1989); John H. Maurer, ed., *Churchill and Strategic Dilemmas before the World Wars: Essays in Honour of Michael I. Handel* (London: Frank Cass, 2003).

13. NA, CAB80/21, COS(40)21(O), 8 November, Dill to Joint Planning Staff, 9 November 1941; Farrell, *The Basis and Making of British Grand Strategy*, pp. 77–8.

14. Peter Dennis, "Australia and the Singapore Strategy", in *Sixty Years On: The Fall of Singapore Revisited*, eds. Brian P. Farrell and Sandy Hunter (Singapore: Eastern Universities Press, 2002); John McCarthy, *Australia and Imperial Defence 1918–39: A Study in Air and Sea Power* (St Lucia, Queensland: University of Queensland Press, 1976); Hamill, *The Strategic Illusion*, pp. 304–6.

15. NA, CAB66/3, WP(39)125, 17 November 1939; CAB99/1, War Cabinet minutes, Visit of Dominions Ministers, 20 November 1939; David Horner, *High Command: Australia and Allied Strategy 1939–1945* (Sydney: George Allen & Unwin, 1982), pp. 28–31; Farrell, *The Defence and Fall of Singapore*, pp. 47–8.

16. Raymond Callahan, "Churchill and Singapore", in *Sixty Years On*, eds. Farrell and Hunter, p. 156.

17. Horner, *High Command*; Hamill, *The Strategic Illusion*; Robert Menzies, *Afternoon Light* (London: Cassell, 1967).

18. NA, CAB80/11, COS(40)390, 25 May 1940; CAB80/12, COS(40)397, 26 May 1940.

19. Farrell, *The Basis and Making of British Grand Strategy*, Part 1; Hastings, *Winston's War, passim*.

20. NA, WO106/5158, DMO & P to DP etc., 17 June 1940; CAB80/15, COS(40)592 (Revise), *The Situation in the Far East in the Event of Japanese Intervention Against Us*, 15 August 1940; R.G. Neale, ed., *Documents on Australian Foreign Policy*, Vol. III (Canberra: Australian Government Publications Service, 1976), p. 459; Horner, pp. 35–7.

21. Warren F. Kimball, ed., *Churchill and Roosevelt: The Complete Correspondence*, Vol. 1 (Princeton, NJ: Princeton University Press, 1984); C-9x, Churchill to Roosevelt, 15 May 1940.

22. NA, CAB80/15, COS(40)592(Revise), *The Situation in the Far East in the Event of Japanese Intervention Against Us*, 15 August 1940.

23. NA, CAB80/15, COS(40)592(Revise), *The Situation in the Far East in the Event of Japanese Intervention Against Us*, 15 August 1940; Farrell, *The Defence and Fall of Singapore*, Chapters 3–6; Ong Chit Chung, *Operation Matador: Britain's War Plans Against the Japanese 1918–1941* (Singapore: Times Academic Press, 1997); Henry Probert, *The Forgotten Air Force: The Royal Air Force in the War Against Japan 1941–1945* (London: Brasseys, 1995).

24. NA, CAB79/11, COS minutes, April 1941; CAB79/12, COS minutes, June–July 1941; CAB79/13, COS minutes, August 1941; CAB69/2, Defence Committee (Operations) minutes, April 1941; Horner, pp. 58–64.

25. NA, CAB79/6, COS minutes, September 1940; CAB80/18, COS(40)732, 10 September 1940; CAB79/8, COS minutes, December 1940; CAB120/615, Secretariat Files, Churchill to Menzies, 23 December 1940; *Documents on Australian Foreign Policy*, Vol. IV, pp. 282–9.

26. NA, CAB79/8, COS minutes, January 1941; CAB120/521, COS to Brooke-Popham, 10 January 1941; CAB120/521, Churchill to COS, 13 January 1941.

27. Farrell, *The Defence and Fall of Singapore*, Chapters 3, 4, 9, 13; Hastings, *Winston's War*; Alex Danchev, *Very Special Relationship: Field Marshal Sir John Dill and the Anglo-American Alliance 1941–1944* (London: Brasseys, 1986).

28. NA, CAB79/17, COS minutes, 19 January 1942; CAB65/29, War Cabinet minutes, Confidential Annex, 19 January 1942; CAB106/38, *Despatch on Operations in Southwest Pacific*, 15 January–25 February 1942 (Wavell Despatch); Cabinet Office (UK), *Principal War Telegrams and Memoranda 1940–1943*, Vol. 1 (Nandeln, Lichtenstein: KTO Press, 1976), telegrams exchanged between Wavell and Churchill, 16 through 21 January 1942; Farrell, *The Defence and Fall of Singapore*, Chapter 13; Brian P. Farrell, "The Dice were Rather Heavily Loaded: Wavell and the Fall of Singapore", in *Leadership and Responsibility in the Second World War*, ed. Brian P. Farrell (Montreal: McGill-Queen's University Press, 2004).

CHAPTER 3

Heart versus Head: Churchill Comes to Terms with the Fall of Singapore?

Allen Packwood

In October 1988, Denis Kelly, a former literary assistant to Sir Winston Churchill, wrote to Martin Gilbert, the historian and Churchill biographer. A copy of the letter survives in the small collection of Kelly's papers at the Churchill Archives Centre. He began:

> My dear Martin, You tell me you are writing a book about the Second World War. Here is what Churchill told me about it. I have been careful to distinguish between what he said and my now subsequent comments. All that he told me was in private conversation, with no-one else present, at lunch or dinner. I can give you no dates except that it took place at Chartwell between 1947 and 1957.

Kelly then relates how he put the question to Churchill: "What were the biggest mistakes in the Second World War? Immediate answer. 'Losing Singapore and letting the Russians into Europe.'"[1]

Of course, this letter is problematic. It was written years after Kelly's relationship with Churchill ended, and years after the supposed dinner conversations took place. Moreover, as Kelly admits, there were no witnesses, and as Duff Cooper so memorably put it in the title of his memoirs, "Old Men Forget". Old men can also exaggerate, and here there was scope for invention or exaggeration by both Churchill, who was talking to Kelly with the benefit of hindsight after the war ended, and by Kelly, who was remembering a conversation that took place 30 or 40 years previously. Yet, if we accept that some such comment was made to Kelly by Churchill at some point, it hints at the significance that Churchill put on the loss of Singapore. This chapter will look inside the Churchill despatch box and try to analyse why it might have mattered so much to him.

Fortunately, there is no shortage of sources at the Churchill Archives Centre. Churchill's own copies of his Prime Ministerial telegrams and minutes allow us to see both the information that he was receiving about Singapore throughout the crisis, and the subsequent decisions he was conveying to allies, Commonwealth leaders, politicians, diplomats and the military commanders. Add to these the handwritten drafts of key discussions that were kept, against all the rules, by Assistant Secretary to the War Cabinet, Lawrence Burgis, and a picture starts to emerge of the policy being formulated at the centre — particularly when these contemporary official records can be juxtaposed with the private diaries and letters of some key observers and protagonists. Duff Cooper served in Singapore as Minister Resident from September through December 1941; the Centre holds Cooper's annotated typescript of his Singapore diary, which survives among his papers, along with his letter to the Prime Minister of 18–20 December 1941. It also holds the diary of Sir Alexander Cadogan, Under Secretary of State at the Foreign Office, a Far East expert — having been British Ambassador to China — and a participant in some of the key Whitehall meetings on Singapore.

And then of course, there are the memoirs; accounts written after the event, by Churchill, Duff Cooper, Kelly and others. Certainly, all of these sources must be carefully and critically analysed. For while the contemporary sources are often powerful in conveying a sense of immediacy and in revealing responses to the evolving crisis, they may be based on partial or incorrect evidence; and where the later accounts benefit from reflection, they may also be distorted by hindsight and the need for self-justification. Documents are often presented as evidence. Indeed, this is how Churchill uses them in the appendices of his six-volume *History of the Second World War*. But they are evidence that must be used critically. The truth, if it can be found, lies in analysing the body of material, identifying the political agendas, and reconciling the different perspectives — the public, the personal, the contemporary and the retrospective.

So what do the documents tell us? In the first place, there is no doubt that in his contemporary telegram correspondence, Churchill urged the defence of Singapore, and urged it almost to the very last moment. The Centre holds his personal copy of his celebrated telegram to General Wavell of 20 January 1942. Churchill informs Wavell that, now he is

Supreme Commander of the ABDA (American-British-Dutch-Australian) forces operating in Southeast Asia, Churchill could not send him any direct instructions, as Wavell's orders were to come through the Combined Chiefs of Staff Committee in Washington. But, and there is a big "but", "Nevertheless I propose to continue our correspondence whenever I have suggestions to make or questions to ask". Wavell would already have known the British Prime Minister for long enough never to have doubted it. And then Churchill goes on, "This will be especially the case where the local defence of a fortress like Singapore is involved". The ending is unambiguous and typically Churchillian:

> ... I want to make it absolutely clear that I expect every inch of ground to be defended, every scrap of material or defences to be blown to pieces to prevent capture by the enemy and no question of surrender to be entertained until after protracted fighting among the ruins of Singapore City.[2]

Churchill's telegram was sent partly in response to this gloomy but accurate telegram sent by Wavell the previous day, 19 January 1942, in which the general reported that, "I have ordered Percival to fight out the battle in Johore but to work out plans to prolong resistance on island as long as possible should he lose Johore battle. I must warn you however that I doubt whether island can be held for long once Johore is lost. Fortress guns have been cited for use against ships and have mostly (?ammunition) for that purpose only, many can only fire sea-wards". Wavell ends, "I am sorry to give you depressing picture, but I do not want you to have false picture of island Fortress. Singapore defences were constructed entirely to meet seaward attack".[3] Churchill dictated a minute, added to the bottom of this telegram, addressed to General Alan Brooke as the Chief of the Imperial General Staff, instructing him to consult the Admiralty "about ammunition for fortress guns". This belated action, along with his reference to "fortress guns" here, and to a "fortress like Singapore" in his reply to Wavell, suggest that he had not or could not grasp the full extent of what Wavell was telling him about the weakness of Singapore's defences, and their vulnerability to attack from the peninsula. Indeed, as the situation rapidly deteriorated and the defences of Johore and then Singapore Island were breached, Churchill remained bullish. On 11 February, he cabled President Roosevelt, stating, "We have 106,000 men in Singapore Island, of which nearly 60,000 are British or Australian, 40,000 being British. I am very glad Wavell is there today. The battle must be fought to the bitter end, regardless of consequences to the city or its inhabitants".[4] The following day, he informed the American leader that "A fierce battle is raging at Singapore and orders have been given to fight it out".[5]

We also know how Churchill reacted to the loss of Singapore. The Churchill Archives Centre holds the final text of his speech to the House of Commons of 24 February 1942, set out in the blank verse format that his office called speech form and others "psalm form". The wording, as delivered, is rather simple and statesmanlike. Churchill now acknowledged that "Singapore was of course a naval base rather than a fortress", and that "the field works constructed upon the island itself were not sufficiently large scale", and he concludes that, "I shall certainly not attempt at this stage to pass any judgement upon our troops or their Commanders ... we have more urgent tasks to do".[6]

Yet it is a final text that differed markedly in tone from the first draft, which also survived. This then is what Churchill had wanted to say:

> 100,000 men in the island at the time of the Japanese landings. In spite of the absence of Air support, it might have been thought that this garrison which was merely equal to all the Japanese forces in the Malay Peninsula and incomparably more numerous than those who effected landings on the island, would have been able to throw the enemy back into the sea on several occasions and to maintain a protracted defence, similar to that maintained at Tobruk without air support.[7]

So much for not passing judgement on the troops and their commanders. Churchill was effectively forced to take this passage out by his key advisers. On one draft, someone pointed out that "the defence might well have been prolonged had it not been for the presence of a population of one million civilians",[8] while Sir James Grigg, the Secretary of State for War, wrote a note beginning, "Prime Minister, I hope that you will modify materially the end of the passage about Singapore. We do not know all the reasons for the collapse of the defence though we can assign a good many besides cowardice and bad leadership".[9] Grigg's view was that even if Churchill believed these were the causes, implying he clearly thought the Prime Minister did, it would do enormous harm to morale and to the war effort to say so publicly. On this occasion at least, Churchill allowed himself to be overruled, but the drafts reveal something of his true feelings.

True feelings also surface in his drafts about the loss of Singapore in volume four of his post-war history of the Second World War. This was written in 1948–1949, at around about the time he was discussing Singapore over lunch or dinner with Denis Kelly. The final published version deliberately, indeed perhaps too deliberately, often held back from giving Churchill's own views. The chapter on "The Fall of Singapore" opens, "I judged it impossible to hold an inquiry by Royal Commission into the circumstances of the fall of Singapore while the war was raging … I confined myself to recording the salient facts as I believe them, and to documents written at the time. From these the reader must form his own opinion".[10] The drafts are often less forgiving. The chapter entitled "Penalties in Malaya" which leads up to the loss of Singapore was originally entitled "Shock at Singapore", and among sheaves of annotated drafts and typescripts, perhaps indicating the difficulties posed by this section, are some typescript notes by Churchill setting out his early thinking for these chapters. He writes, "I did not intend to pass judgement on the behaviour of generals or troops at Singapore. Forgive us our trespasses". But the clear inference is that he did wish to pass judgement, for while he admits that he did not turn his mind to the situation in Singapore until "after the Japanese had declared war and the Americans were our Allies", when it was already too late, it did not matter because — as he added so forcibly in his own hand at the bottom of the page — "The major dispositions were right".[11] In other words, the grand strategy was correct; it was the local execution before and during the war that was flawed. He is dismissive of the Japanese advance: "The Japanese became possessed of a fleet of small nondescript vessels and ran up all the creeks and rivers to turn every fighting position we tried to hold. Three or four destroyers or sloops could have cut this trash to pieces, but they were not there";[12] and on the lack of preparedness for war, he states that:

> Of course the reason was that the people we sent out were an inferior troop of military and naval men. None of them thought of any of these things. It may be said that I deliberately neglected this aspect of the war because I had no other steps in my mind for dealing with this problem. If it had been studied with the intensity with which we examined the European and African operations, these disasters could not have been prevented, but they might at least have been foreseen.[13]

In the drafts and proofs, you can see this robust Churchillian line being progressively toned down. This time, the chief architect of this rearguard action was Lieutenant General Sir Henry Pownall, one of Churchill's team of expert advisers, but also the man who was briefly Commander-in-Chief Designate of the British Far East Command at Singapore in late 1941, before becoming Wavell's deputy, and a soldier with a good overview of what happened at Singapore, and why. Pownall cleverly bombarded Churchill with further reading: a summary of Percival's despatch; a note on the changes in defence policy and estimated defence requirements in

Malaya between 1921 and 1941; a summary history of the defence works of Singapore; and a note on the military operations in early 1942.[14] Ultimately, Churchill gave in to his military expert and even printed Pownall's memorandum on Singapore defences as Appendix D in his final published volume. In the end, he was prepared to let sleeping dogs lie, noting to Pownall and others, "One must avoid all squabbles with the Australians and their beastly general (Bennett) about it".[15]

So why did Churchill feel so strongly about Singapore? In this author's view, the records show that the loss of the naval base came at the worst possible time for Churchill personally, politically and strategically, and challenged some of his deepest assumptions about British Imperial power.

Churchill never visited Singapore. Indeed, he never travelled east of India. His parents, Lord and Lady Randolph Churchill, did visit the island, on their world tour of 1894, but before the building of the naval base. Photographs of Government House and Travellers Tree in Singapore survived among papers inherited by Churchill from his mother.[16] She wrote later that,

> Sir John and Lady Mitchell invited us to Government House, where we stayed a week. I found the heat for the first time nearly unbearable; it was like a vapour bath, and so enervating one felt absolutely incapable of doing anything. The beauty of the tropical plants, however, delighted me, especially the traveller's palm, its height and symmetry being quite a revelation.[17]

To Churchill himself, however, Singapore was never a real place, so much as a symbol of British power and a centre of strategic interest.

This comes over in his writings. In March 1924, he wrote a newspaper article vigorously defending the decision to build a naval base at Singapore, and attacking socialist Prime Minister Ramsay MacDonald's attempts to abandon or defer the project. The article carried the subtitle "Abandonment a Long Step towards Imperial Disintegration". In it, the former First Lord of the Admiralty made the case that the dawn of the oil age in naval construction necessitated the building and maintaining of refuelling stations around the globe if British dominance of the high seas was to be retained. Unless such a base was built at Singapore, it would be impossible for Britain to send a strong fleet into the Pacific Ocean, and if Britain cannot do this, then it has sacrificed the power to come to the aid of Australia and New Zealand, "two great democratic communities … united to us by the strongest ties of sentiment and interest".[18] Churchill was prepared to leave the final decision of the siting of this base to the experts, who had recommended Singapore. He was not interested in the geography or in the detail; he was interested in the principles of keeping a global navy, maintaining a presence in the Pacific Ocean, and binding together the Empire and Commonwealth, and particularly the English-speaking democracies.

And did this view change? Well, there was a second article, written by Churchill in March 1934, ten years later, entitled "Singapore — Key to the Pacific". And what do we notice? The text is almost exactly the same as that of the earlier article. Churchill simply reissued his older piece, with its identically worded conclusion:

> But the unity of the British Empire is directly involved and if, listening to specious but misguided counsels, the British people placed it beyond their power to come to the rescue of their own flesh and blood at the Antipodes, they would be taking a long step downwards upon the path of Imperial disintegration.[19]

Such evidence suggests that Churchill did not take a strong interest in the nature of the defences at Singapore, or the implications of the growth of Japanese air power. According to Denis Kelly, in his letter to Martin Gilbert, Churchill admitted that once the war had begun, "There was a veil over my mind about the Japanese War. All the proportions were hidden in the mist".[20] Certainly, the telegrams and official papers show how much else Churchill was wrestling with by the end of 1941: the need to coordinate grand strategy with the Americans; the continuing war in the Atlantic; the aftermath of defeat in Greece and heavy fighting in the Middle East; growing restlessness in his war leadership in the Commons; the opening up of a whole new theatre in the Far East, and the unexpected speed and dominance of the Japanese advance throughout the area. Burgis' handwritten minutes for the end of January and early February 1942 show the War Cabinet concerned not just with Singapore, but also with the escape of the German capital ships Scharnhorst and Gneisenau from France to Germany, with convoys to Russia, the defence of Malta and the struggle in Burma.[21] The truth is that the loss of Singapore could not have come at a worse time for Churchill.

It was bad personally because at the end of January 1942, he faced a vote of No Confidence in his government in the House of Commons. The debate of 27–29 January 1942 added much to the Prime Minister's already considerable burdens. Taking place as it did, against the unfolding crisis on the Malay Peninsula, Churchill faced many awkward criticisms of British policy in the Pacific, and in Singapore in particular. A note prepared for the Prime Minister summarising the questions raised in the debate identified a selection of them: Mr. Pethick-Lawrence for the Labour Party, demanding further information on the loss of *HMS Prince of Wales* and *HMS Repulse*; stating that the Malays and Chinese had been "pushed to one side and 'told that this is a white man's business'"; criticising the scorched earth policy in Penang; reporting that the Australians had wanted a different disposal of their forces; and attacking the delay in coming to the aid of Singapore.[22] Although Churchill comfortably won the debate, by 464 votes to 1, these attacks must have stung, putting him very much on the defensive over Singapore.

Defeat was bad politically because it came just at the moment when Churchill needed to demonstrate British determination to fight to his political allies. He had just returned from his first wartime visit to the United States, where he had addressed the Joint Houses of Congress, and publicly pledged his determination to fight the Japanese with the statement, "What kind of people do they think we are?"[23] Neither Australia nor New Zealand was prepared for the suddenness of the British collapse. On 23 January 1942, the Australian government cabled that the evacuation of Singapore would be an "inexcusable betrayal".[24]

Defeat was bad strategically because Britain lost its one supposedly strong naval base in the Pacific theatre. Churchill was now faced with the unravelling of the policy of Imperial naval defence he had advocated since 1924, just at the moment when the English-speaking Dominions were directly threatened. But for Churchill, it seemed even worse than that.

It has been suggested that Churchill felt guilt about Singapore: guilt about ordering *Prince of Wales* and *Repulse* to their destruction in the South China Sea, and guilt about sending additional British and Indian troops to reinforce Singapore when it was already too late for them to affect the outcome, thereby condemning them to Japanese captivity. It would have been inhuman for him not to feel sadness, particularly as only a few months before, he had crossed the Atlantic aboard *Prince of Wales* to meet President Roosevelt, and so would have been able to put faces to many of the lost company and crew. Yet all the evidence we have seen suggests that, while Churchill was certainly prepared to accept that he was not sufficiently informed about the inadequacies of Singapore's defences, he was also prepared to argue that this was because he had been too preoccupied with the war in other theatres: first in Europe and then in the Middle East. Moreover, Churchill could point to the fact that he was not being given better advice by the civilian and military experts on the spot.

Duff Cooper had been sent out to Singapore as the Cabinet's representative, the Minister Resident in the Far East. On 18 December 1941, Duff Cooper wrote a letter for the Prime Minister, summarising the situation as he saw it. It concluded that "Unless the unforeseen happens — such as a successful enemy landing on the island itself — I have no doubt of our ability to hold out for three or four months, or even indefinitely provided we can get reinforcements and, later, food supplies".[25] The despatch of this letter was delayed, and Duff Cooper was able to add a codicil on 20 December, in which he stated that,

> So long as we hold Singapore it will be easy to rectify the set-backs we have hitherto experienced. But if we lose it, owing to our attaching excessive importance to North Africa, we may find that we have won the war in Europe only to start it all over again in Asia with all the cards in the hands of the enemy.[26]

In other words, he urged on Churchill the very policy that the Prime Minister was to pursue, namely the reinforcement of Singapore from the Mediterranean theatre. At the same time, the Australian Government was urging the continued defence of Singapore, and even General Wavell failed to appreciate the full enormity of the deficiencies in Singapore's defences until it was too late. It was only in his telegram of 21 January 1942 that Wavell wrote, "I did not realise myself until lately how entirely defences were planned against seaward attack only".[27] This perplexed Churchill, who struggled with this issue when it came to writing his history. In one of his unpublished notes to his literary team, he posed the question, "How can we explain them not fortifying the Gorge. Nobody thought of it in time. In Wavell's telegrams he only just found out how it had been neglected. He had been Commander-in-Chief India for a year".[28] His use of the word "Gorge" is of course revealing, and clearly demonstrates his lack of personal knowledge of conditions on the ground in Malaya; the banks of the Straits of Johore being relatively flat.

Yet you can feel the exasperation in Churchill's writings. The inference is clear. If Churchill's key political and military experts in the Far East did not foresee this crisis, then how could the Prime Minister have been expected to? This author believes that Churchill's real concern about Singapore was not about the lack of preparation. It was about the fear that the campaign highlighted a fundamental inability of British troops to stand their ground and fight. In this respect, what he labelled "the worst disaster and largest capitulation in British history"[29] was the culmination of a series of retreats and defeats that had begun in Norway and France in 1940, and continued in Greece and the Middle East in 1941. It was a view shared by other members of his inner circle. Alexander Cadogan's diary entry for Saturday 31 January 1942 reads: "We've retreated into Singapore island. That must surely be indefensible against the air. Coming on top of our loss of Benghazi, most depressing. I'm afraid our soldiers seem very incapable". By Monday 9 February, he was prepared to be even more scathing, "Our generals are no use and do our men fight? ... As P.M. says, what will happen if Germans get a footing here? ... Poor Winston v. desperate".[30]

Churchill's view is perhaps best articulated by his broadcast just a few months earlier after the fall of Crete in April 1941. His heavily annotated speech notes reveal his engagement with this particular text:

> Military defeat or miscalculations can be redeemed. The fortunes of war are fickle and changing. But an act of shame would sap the vitals of our strength and deprive us of the respect which we now enjoy throughout the world, and would especially rob us of the immense potent hold we have, during the last year gained by our bearing, a potent hold upon the sentiments of the people of the United States.[31]

All of the evidence, in his telegrams and in the drafts for his speech and for his memoirs, indicates that Churchill saw the inability to defend Singapore as just such an act of shame. Moreover, it came at the worst possible moment, just as he wanted to exert a potent hold on his new American allies, just as he needed to demonstrate his commitment to imperial defence, and just as he was desperate to strengthen the image of his war premiership at home. It is in this vein, seen through this lens, that Churchill's telegram to Wavell of 10 February makes sense. All was already lost, but Churchill wrote:

> The 18th Division [e.g. the newly arrived British Division] has a chance to make its name in history. Commanders and Senior Officers should die with their troops. The honour of the British Empire and of the British Army is at stake. I rely on you to show no mercy to weakness in any form. With the Russians fighting as they are and the Americans so stubborn at Luzon, the whole reputation of our country and our race is involved. It is expected that every unit will be brought into close contact with the enemy and fight it out.[32]

Churchill's head may have understood all the reasons for the loss of Singapore; perhaps partially in 1942, but surely completely by 1948. The truth would seem to be that his heart could not accept them.

Notes

1. CAC, Kelly Papers, DEKE 1, Denis Kelly to Sir Martin Gilbert, 11 October 1988.
2. CAC, Churchill Papers, CHAR 20/68B/124, telegram from Churchill to Wavell, 20 January 1942.
3. CAC, Churchill Papers, CHAR 20/68B/ 120, telegram from Wavell to Churchill, 19 January 1942.
4. CAC, Churchill Papers, CHAR 20/70/12, telegram from Churchill to Roosevelt, 11 February 1942.
5. CAC, Churchill Papers, CHAR 20/70/30, telegram from Churchill to Roosevelt, 12 February 1942.
6. CAC, Churchill Papers, CHAR 9/183B/200, notes for speech by Churchill, 24 February 1942.
7. CAC, Churchill Papers, CHAR 9/183C/246, draft notes for speech by Churchill, 24 February 1942.
8. CAC, Churchill Papers, CHAR 9/183C/226, annotated draft of speech notes, February 1942.
9. CAC, Churchill Papers, CHAR 9/183C/237, letter from Grigg to Churchill, February 1942.
10. Winston S Churchill, *The Second World War*, Vol. IV (London: Cassell, 1951), p. 81.
11. CAC, Churchill Papers, CHUR 4/255A/118, note by Churchill, c1948.
12. CAC, Churchill Papers, CHUR 4/255A/120-121, note by Churchill, c1948.
13. CAC, Churchill Papers, CHUR 4/255A/122, note by Churchill, c1948.
14. For reports and notes by Pownall, see CAC, Churchill Papers, CHUR 4/255A/, pp. 99, 102–10.
15. CAC, Churchill Papers, CHUR 4/255A/119, note by Churchill, c1948.
16. CAC, Churchill Papers, CHAR 28/87A/2, photograph of Government House, Singapore, 1894; CHAR 28/87A/30, photograph of travellers tree, Singapore, 1894. See Plates 3.3 and 3.4.
17. Mrs George Cornwallis West, *The Reminiscences of Lady Randolph Churchill* (London: Edward Arnold, 1908), p. 270.
18. CAC, Churchill Papers, CHAR 8/200B, "The Case for Singapore" by Winston Churchill, newspaper cutting, March 1924.
19. CAC, Churchill Papers, CHAR 8/501, "Singapore — Key to the Pacific" by Winston Churchill, newspaper cutting, March 1934. See Plate 3.5.
20. CAC, Kelly Papers, DEKE 1, Kelly to Gilbert, 11 October 1988.
21. CAC, Burgis Papers, BRGS 2/11, handwritten minutes of War Cabinet meetings by Lawrence Burgis, January–February 1942.
22. CAC, Churchill Papers, CHAR 9/183A/43, typescript note of some points made in Debate, 27 January 1942.
23. CAC, Churchill Papers, CHAR 9/153/ 42, annotated typescript for address to Joint Houses of Congress, 26 December 1941.

24. CAC, Churchill Papers, CHAR 20/69A/6-8, telegram from Curtin to Churchill, 23 January 1942.

25. CAC, Norwich Papers, DUFC 3/7, Duff Cooper to Churchill, 18 December 1941.

26. CAC, Norwich Papers, DUFC 3/7, Duff Cooper to Churchill, 20 December 1941.

27. CAC, Churchill Papers, CHAR 20/68B/138, telegram from Wavell to Churchill, 21 January 1942.

28. CAC, Churchill Papers, CHUR 4/255A/119, note by Churchill, c1948.

29. Winston S Churchill, *The Second World War*, Vol. VI (London: Cassell, 1953), p. 81.

30. David Dilks, ed., *The Diaries of Sir Alexander Cadogan* (London: Putnam, 1971), pp. 430, 432–3.

31. CAC, Churchill Papers, CHAR 9/181B/180, annotated notes for broadcast by Churchill, 27 April 1941.

32. CAC, Churchill Papers, CHAR 20/70/9, telegram from Churchill to Wavell, 10 February 1942.

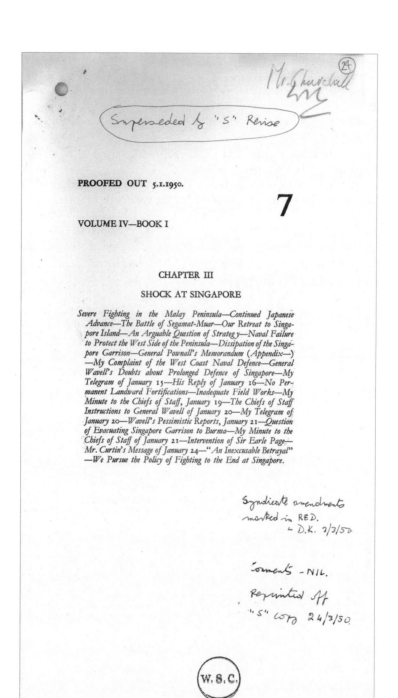

PROOFED OUT 5.1.1950.

7

VOLUME IV—BOOK I

CHAPTER III

SHOCK AT SINGAPORE

Severe Fighting in the Malay Peninsula—Continued Japanese Advance—The Battle of Segamat-Muar—Our Retreat to Singapore Island—An Arguable Question of Strategy—Naval Failure to Protect the West Side of the Peninsula—Dissipation of the Singapore Garrison—General Pownall's Memorandum (Appendix—) —My Complaint of the West Coast Naval Defence—General Wavell's Doubts about Prolonged Defence of Singapore—My Telegram of January 15—His Reply of January 16—No Permanent Landward Fortifications—Inadequate Field Works—My Minute to the Chiefs of Staff, January 19—The Chiefs of Staff Instructions to General Wavell of January 20—My Telegram of January 20—Wavell's Pessimistic Reports, January 21—Question of Evacuating Singapore Garrison to Burma—My Minute to the Chiefs of Staff of January 21—Intervention of Sir Earle Page—Mr. Curtin's Message of January 24—"An Inexcusable Betrayal" —We Pursue the Policy of Fighting to the End at Singapore.

Syndicate amendments
marked in RED.
↳ D.K. 2/3/50

'omments - NIL.
Reprinted off
"S" copy 24/3/50

W.S.C.

Plate 3.1 First Impressions: Churchill suggested the title "Shock at Singapore" for the first draft of the chapter in his memoirs, before being dissuaded.

NOTE.

I did not intend to pass judgment on the behaviour of generals or troops at Singapore. Forgive us our trespasses. I considered that an enquiry during the war was impossible for reasons of public safely. I always intended to have one into Singapore and Tobruk after the war was over. This is still my opinion. I am not going to go into details at all on this subject. There will be sufficient for one Chapter of five or six thousand words on the fall of Singapore. This dates from the blowing up of the causeway to the actual surrender. Still it must be admitted I did not attempt to turn my mind on to the situation until after the Japanese had declared war and the Americans were our Allies. Then I did, and it was too late, but even if it had not been too late, it would have been right not to do it. *The major dispositions were right.* *for minor adjustments.*

W.S.C.

Plate 3.2 Margin Notes: A defensive Churchill amended a first draft, to present a more defiant justification of his grand strategy regarding the Far East.

Plate 3.3 Sight Unseen: Photo of the Istana lawn in Singapore, 1894, acquired by Lord Randolph and Lady Churchill, Winston Churchill's parents.

Plate 3.4 The Exotic East: Photo of striking tropical tree at the Istana Lawn in Singapore, 1894, acquired by Lord Randolph and Lady Churchill.

SINGAPORE—

Key to the Pacific

By the Rt. Hon. WINSTON S. CHURCHILL, M.P.

Shall Britain spend £9,000,000 on a naval base at Singapore? There are arguments for and against the project. Our famous contributor crystallises the case for the plan in his own masterly style

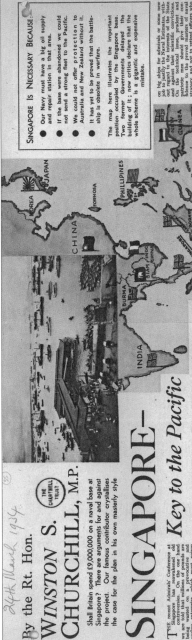

THE recent Admirals' Conference at Singapore has aroused an old controversy anew. On the one hand we are told that millions of pounds are being wasted upon a profitless and useless enterprise, which must poison our relations with a great and friendly Oriental Power, and throw doubt upon the sincerity of our desire for disarmament. On the other, it is urged that the completion of this great naval base is vitally and urgently necessary to the safeguarding of British commercial interests in the Far East.

It is only fitting that in exploring the question of Singapore should be examined coolly, fairly, and without prejudice. This base must be so simple that anyone can understand them.

An Oil-Age Problem

Such was the state of affairs until a very few years before the War. Suddenly we were confronted, in the building construction. It was found impossible to build the best and fastest kind of warship, as rapid as oil, with a liquid fuel.

From the end of the Great War the transition was complete and none of the modern navies of the world relied upon coal. Coal had become obsolete, whereas we had coaling stations in every part of this world, we had hardly any oil stations outside the Fleet had theretofore for the time being abandoned.

At the same time the size and complications of modern ships had become so great that they could not remain long at sea in any part of the world unless they had within reasonable distance of their bases docks capable of receiving them and of repairing them if damaged in action. This meant that the largest vessels and of repairing them if damaged in action. This meant the batteries of large guns and a certain number of aeroplanes and submarines.

Unless we have such a base at Singapore, or somewhere in that neighbourhood, we could not make up our mind that we could never send a strong Fleet into the Pacific Ocean no matter how great the need.

In the Pacific Ocean dwell two of our democratic communities—the Australian Commonwealth and the Dominion of New Zealand. These dominions came to our aid spontaneously in the Great War. They gained everywhere across the seas. They have the battlefields of Gallipoli and Flanders left behind them on the battlefields of Gallipoli and Flanders their share of their manhood. Great Britain freely offered sacrifice that Great Britain and that for the first time in her history the British Navy was unable to protect the Mother Country had deliberately resolved to put it out of her power to do their best, and, whatever their need might be.

Arguments That Only Confuse

Such a declaration must excite unmisgivings even in the coldest heart. It constituted an act of desertion, of abnegation of duty of imperialism both and fatal. Yet it was made when the first Socialist government took office and proceeded with the scheme for the Singapore base.

Fortunately this administration was abolished... the decision which followed it, and of which I was a member, reversed the decision. From the international standpoint in 1929, when the Socialists returned to power for two disastrous years. And upon its depletion of this vital link in the chain of Imperial defence are again marshalling their forces...

"That to turn the second cheek is the lesson of the Cross."
"To be proved by calculation of the profit and the loss."

Battleships, we are told, are obsolete, and therefore the construction of a dock to receive them can quite safely be abandoned. The capital ship counts no more. Such are the tales. The naval authorities ought at least to weigh against them by submarines and cruisers. No decision was taken, men who were not the bound bureaucrats of tranquil years. We had instead, the proved War leaders of the Navy in all its branches and in every rank.

We had the men who in person led our Fleet; who solved the problem of the German submarine attack, and who had lived in the closest association with every development of naval science as it emerged from the crucible of war...

Supremacy Of The Japanese Navy

Some years ago, a committee of the Cabinet held a prolonged inquiry upon this subject... The capital ship would for many years remain the dominating factor in naval war.

It is indeed unworthy to suggest that simply trying to find comfortable berths Such a danger is no doubt remote and speculative...

Another Striking Article By MR. **WINSTON CHURCHILL**

16   17

Plate 3.5 Imperial Defence: A newspaper column published by Churchill on 24 March 1934, stressing the importance of Singapore to British defence strategy.

Some points made in Debate, January 27, 1942.

References are to columns in Hansard.

Mr. Pethick-Lawrence.

620. "The smoke screen put over events in the Pacific
to hide them from the British public". A request
for further information about "Prince of Wales" and
"Repulse". (See also Mander, 650) (Admiralty
have been asked to supply brief)

621/2. Malays and Chinese pushed to one side and "told
that this is a white man's business". (Also
Haden Guest 666/7) (Colonial Office asked to
supply brief)

622. Penang and the scorched earth policy. (Colonial
Office asked to supply brief)

622. Further information wanted about the Australian
desire for some different disposal of the Forces.

623. Delay in coming to the aid of Singapore.

623. India.

624. Production - representations by Shop Stewards.

Mr. Erskine-Hill.

626/7. Over-confidence about Malaya. (See also
Sir Herbert Williams 646)

628/9. Conduct of administrative affairs and
bureaucratic working of various Departmental
administrations. Need for fewer forms.

Plate 3.6 Under Pressure: Briefing notes arising from the tough House of
Commons discussion as enemy forces closed on Singapore, 27 January 1942.

How can we explain them not fortifying the Gorge.
Nobody thought of it in time.   In Wavell's telegrams he
only just found out how it had been neglected. He had been Commander-
in-Chief in India for a year.

Read Percival.

The Secret Session speech on Singapore is most
important.

One must avoid all squabbles with the Australians
and their beastly general (Bennett) about it.

W. S. C.

Plate 3.7 Family Feud: A Churchill memo regarding how to describe the fall of Singapore in his memoirs, urging his assistants to steer clear of Australian recriminations.

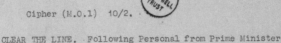

MOST SECRET
CIPHER TELEGRAM

SERIAL No. T 206/2
MOST SECRET.

From:- The War Office.

To:- C.-in-C., S.W. Pacific.

Desp. 0130. 10/2/42.

MOST IMMEDIATE.

69733   Cipher (M.0.1) 10/2.

CLEAR THE LINE. Following Personal from Prime Minister
to General Wavell.

I think you ought to realise the way we view the
situation in Singapore. It was reported to the Cabinet by the
C.I.G.S. that Percival has over 100,000 men of whom 33,000 are
British and 17,000 Australian. It is doubtful whether the
Japanese have as many in the whole Malay Peninsula, namely
five divisions forward and a sixth coming up. In these
circumstances defenders must greatly outnumber Japanese forces
who have crossed the Straits and in a well-contested battle they
should destroy them. There must at this stage be no thought of
saving the troops or sparing the population. The battle must be
fought to the bitter end at all costs. The 18th Division has a
chance to make its name in history. Commanders and Senior Officers
should die with their troops. The honour of the British Empire
and of the British Army is at stake. I rely on you to show no
mercy to weakness in any form. With the Russians fighting as
they are and the Americans so stubborn at Luzon, the whole
reputation of our country and our race is involved. It is
expected that every unit will be brought into close contact with
the enemy and fight it out. I feel sure these words express
your own feeling and only send them to you in order to share your
burdens.

C. 4. (Telegrams)   Copies to:-

                              S. of S.
                              C.I.G.S.
                              Col. Jacob (10 copies)

                              The King.

Plate 3.8 Pride and Prejudice: A telegram from Churchill to Wavell demanding
fight to the death in Singapore to preserve imperial honour, 10 February 1942.

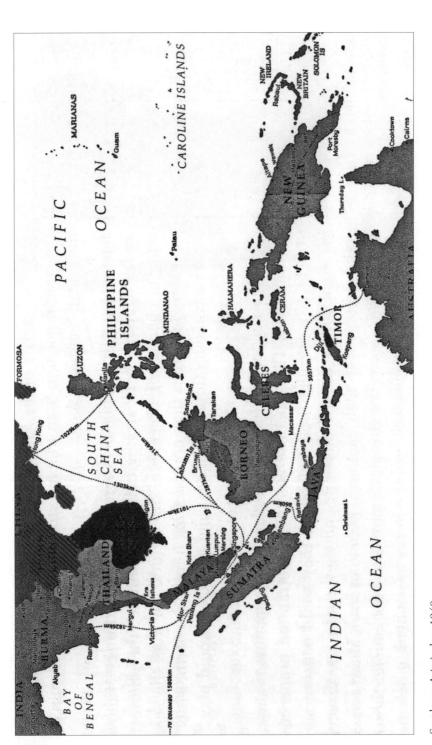

Southeast Asia in late 1940.

The British Empire is shaded dark brown; Netherlands East Indies: tan; French colonial territory: purple; Portuguese colonial territory: blue; USA: green; Japanese occupied territory: hatched red.

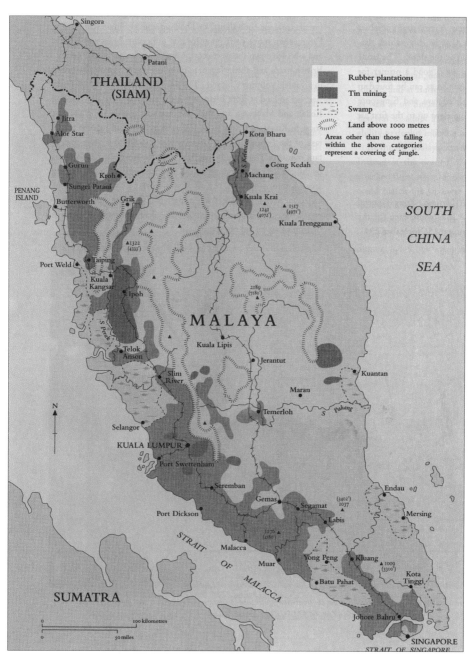

Malaya: Topography and land use, 1941.

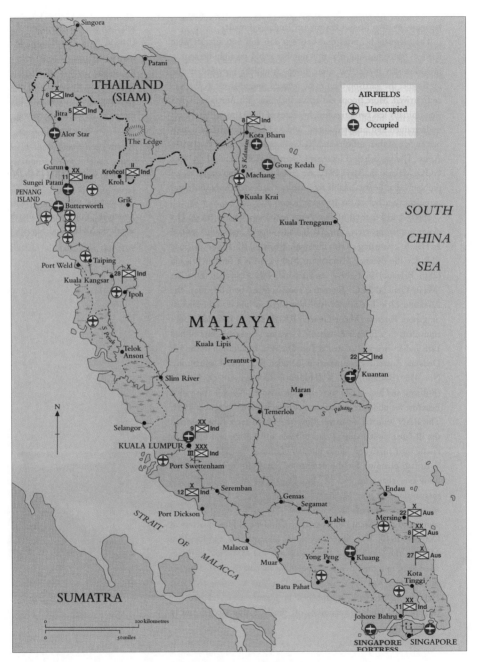

Malaya: Location of British Empire forces, 8 December 1941.

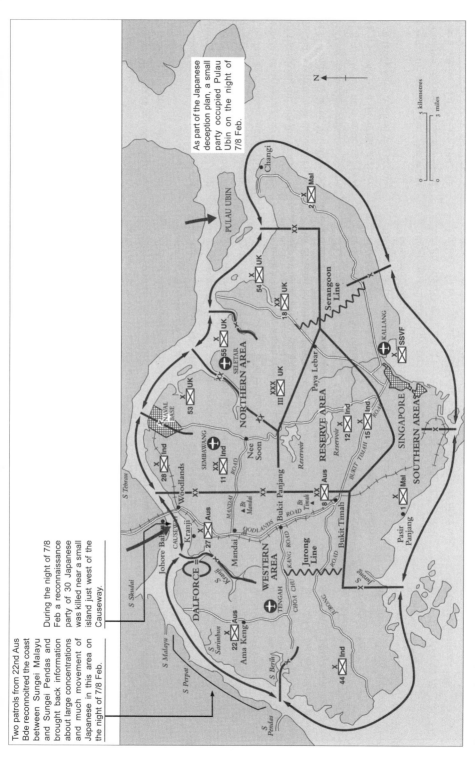

Two patrols from 22nd Aus Bde reconnoitred the coast between Sungei Malayu and Sungei Pendas and brought back information about large concentrations and much movement of Japanese in this area on the night of 7/8 Feb.

During the night of 7/8 Feb a reconnaissance party of 30 Japanese was killed near a small island just west of the Causeway.

As part of the Japanese deception plan, a small party occupied Pulau Ubin on the night of 7/8 Feb.

Singapore Island: British Empire defences.

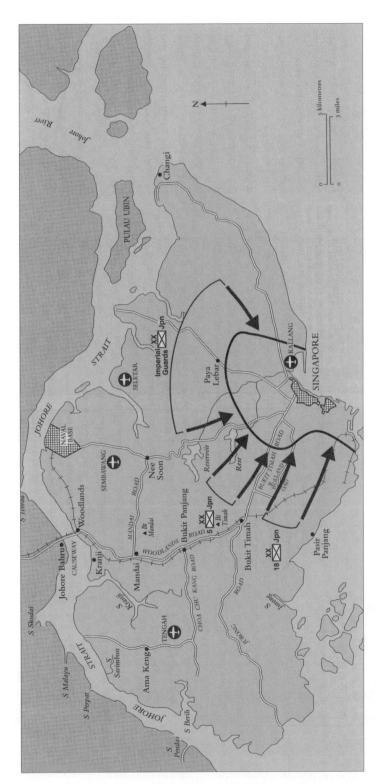

Singapore Island: Situation at time of capitulation, 15 February 1942.

CHAPTER 4

Churchill, Strategy and the Fall of Singapore

Geoffrey Till

"A complete amateur of strategy, he swamps himself in detail he should never look at and as a result fails ever to see a strategic problem in its true perspective". So wrote General Sir Alan Brooke of Winston Churchill, after a particularly difficult session of the COS Committee, meeting in July 1944. The aim of this chapter is to assess the validity of this view in regard to the fall of Singapore, and to British plans for its recovery.

At this point, some definitions are clearly necessary. According to Liddell Hart, strategy is simply "the art of distributing and applying military means to fulfil the ends of policy".[1] But as the great master, Clausewitz, reminds us, central to success in this endeavour is the fact that "the first, the grandest, the most decisive act of judgement which the Statesman and general exercises is rightly to understand [the nature of] the War in which he engages, not to take it for something, or wish to make of it something which it is not and which is impossible for it to be".[2] This raises the key issue of what the so-called "Singapore Strategy" was actually about. Churchill had four interconnected but distinct sets of objectives in his strategy for the defence of Malaya and Singapore.

The first was to deter, and if that failed, delay a Japanese attack. In the early days, this seemed to Churchill to be quite easy. In December 1939, while still First Lord of the Admiralty, he told the Australians that any such attack would be "a mad enterprise". He said, "Singapore is a fortress armed with 15-inch guns, and garrisoned by nearly 20,000 men. It could only be taken after a siege by an army of at least 50,000 men ... (a siege which) should last at least four or five months". Singapore was as far from Japan as Southampton was from New York; moving such an invasion force so far and keeping it supplied would be a forlorn endeavour. As soon as a British main fleet arrived, the besieging army would become prisoners of war. "It is not considered possible that the Japanese, who are a prudent people and reserve their strength for the command of the Yellow Sea and China, in which they are fully occupied, would embark upon such a mad enterprise".[3]

Of course, conditions could change, but even then, the prospects of attack seemed remote. In this "phoney war" period, Churchill was asked for an opinion of the consequences of Japanese "encroachments" upon the Dutch East Indies, in the event of a German invasion of the Netherlands. In this case, the Japanese would be deterred from any such encroachment by the knowledge that the United States would not tolerate the Japanese establishing bases west and southwest of the Philippines. "The contingency must, therefore, be regarded as highly improbable unless, of course Great Britain and France are getting the worst of it, when many evils will descend upon us all".[4]

This memorandum was an early expression of what became an enduring theme in Churchill's thinking on Singapore: that its security depended less on what the British did in theatre than on two closely intertwined developments elsewhere — the course of the war in Europe on the one hand and the support of the United States on the other. If Britain were clearly winning the European war, and if the United States were ranged steadfastly alongside it, Singapore, Malaya and the rest of the British Empire should be comparatively safe from Japanese attack. But, accordingly as the European situation deteriorated, through the Summer of 1940, then so did the danger in the Far East increase. After the fall of France, the Japanese "encroached" into French Indo-China through 1941, thereby increasingly undermining Churchill's geopolitical assumptions of November 1939.

In theory, the British were of course well aware of the possible implications of this. Early intelligence reports in the Autumn of 1940 however suggested that these moves were more directed at building up another avenue of attack on China than at threatening Singapore.[5] In the Summer of 1941, when the "encroachments" were all too obvious, the Americans sent "a stiff note" to the Japanese, Churchill reassured the anxious Prime Ministers of New Zealand and Australia in August 1941. The Japanese would need to know the outcome of the German invasion of Russia; the Siberian army which had completely outclassed the Japanese in 1939 was still intact and the Russian airforce "is capable of much dreaded bombing of Japan". Should the Japanese persist in their aggressive behaviour,

They would have about three-quarters of the human race against them, and I do not wonder they are plunged in deep anxiety and hesitation. I cannot believe the Japanese will face the combination now developing around them. We may therefore regard the situation not only as more favourable but less tense.[6]

There were two problems with Churchill's overall approach of defending Singapore through strategic deterrence. The first was that his hand never proved as strong as he had hoped, both in relation to the strength of the US commitment and to the unfolding of events in Europe. The second was much more serious, and that was a collective Japanese mindset and decision-making system that was simply impervious to such rational calculations. The Japanese were already involved in the mire of the China War, but in 1941, moved "to a position whereby it would initiate a general war in the Pacific and Southeast Asia against the world's greatest industrial power and the world's greatest empire while still committed to an unwinnable war against the most populous nation on the globe". If one adds that there seemed every prospect of war with Russia, the world's biggest country as well, it seems hardly surprising that Churchill and others regarded the imminence of the Japanese threat with some scepticism, but were caught out by the sheer irrationality or desperation of their adversary.[7]

Arguably, the Australians and New Zealanders had got closer to the heart of things in thinking that while it would not make sense for the Japanese to launch such a war, they might well do it anyway. Against this background, their acute concerns about the safety of Australia and New Zealand in the event of the fall of Malaya and the Dutch East Indies seem entirely understandable, even if the more detached Churchill thought such fears exaggerated. Shortly after he became Prime Minister, Churchill suggested that in the event of Japanese pressure on the Dutch East Indies in the wake of the disastrous European summer of 1940, that Japan be told this would lead to war with Britain. Not to do so would mean "allowing ourselves to be cut off from Australia and New Zealand, and they would regard our acquiescence as desertion". This did not, however, mean he would be prepared to undermine the British position in the Mediterranean by making excessive forces available to deal with lesser threats such as "a few attacks by cruisers".[8]

When strategic deterrence of this sort fails, the only recourse is an operational and tactical version of deterrence where the main focus is on being seen as able to *deny* the adversary operational and tactical success. This meant building up substantial forces in theatre capable of defeating any Japanese campaign which the Japanese themselves would recognise as such. But here too there were two main problems.

The first was that the competing demands of other theatres — success in which was believed to provide the main deterrent to Japanese attack — made it too difficult to build those local resources up, as shall be seen. The second was even more serious — and that was the overestimate of Singapore's strength and the related underestimate of Japanese fighting efficiency, and of the level of defensive resource needed to contain and defeat it. This major error derived partly from a persistent tendency to overrate the intrinsic strength of Singapore itself, indeed to regard it as a "fortress". With some justice, Churchill blamed his advisors for not making it clear to him that Singapore was no such thing. Indeed, his advisors seemed equally blind to the realities of the situation. Thus, even Major-General William Dobbie, who was well aware of the vulnerabilities of the British position, commonly referred to Singapore as a "fortress" when it was palpably no such thing.[9]

When to this was added a persistent tendency to underrate their prospective opponents' military capacities, the result was a clear failure to appreciate, on the part of both Churchill and his local representatives, what it was that they had to deter — and therefore the quality and quantity of the forces that deterrence, through the evident capacity to defend, would actually require. Worse still in many ways was the fact that the Japanese *knew* the British thought their forces in theatre were barely adequate, through their access to the War Cabinet Minutes of August 1940 captured on the SS *Automedon*.[10] Moreover, they failed to detect the *imminence* of the threat they needed to deter. While conceding that conflict at some stage was a real possibility, given the character of the Japanese regime, the British were always playing for time,[11] expecting that from 1942, the general correlation of forces between Britain and its possible adversaries would then start to show significant improvement. The Japanese were well aware that the opposite was true for them, the implications of which should, arguably, have been obvious to the British. Local commanders, moreover, assumed quite wrongly that once the dangerous Summer of 1940 was over, the onset of the Monsoon would rule out a large scale enterprise until early 1942. The extent to which local British commanders overestimated the deterrent effects of the Monsoon, despite ample evidence to the contrary, remains one of the major mysteries of this campaign.[12]

Churchill and Robert Menzies, for a time his opposite number in Australia, were quite clear about the second of Churchill's distinct objectives: the need for American assistance in the European war, and the deterrent effect of absolute American support in the Far East. "We do not want war, with Japan," Churchill told Stalin, "and I am sure the way to stop it is to confront those people who are divided and far from sure of themselves with the prospect of the heaviest combination".[13] The United States was the main element in that "heavy combination" and "[t]he stronger the action of the US towards Japan, the greater the chance of preserving peace".[14] Securing that, when it came, was arguably Churchill's ultimate triumph.[15]

The problem here was the constraints on Roosevelt's freedom of choice posed by hesitations in US political opinion about getting involved in Britain's wars.[16] Before the outbreak of the Second World War, the deterrent policies of both the United States and of Britain were weakened by the doubts they had about each other's steadfastness, and by the fear that their seeming to gang up on Japan might encourage war rather than deter it.[17] Such doubts and the realities of the US Constitution limited Roosevelt's capacity to do what he wanted. As Menzies reported in August 1941, "I do not think that there is any doubt that a firm and unequivocal attitude by the United States is the one thing that will deter Japan from continuing on a course leading to war ... I found Roosevelt extremely sympathetic but reluctant to be too precise. And yet precision and firmness are the real antidote to Japan".[18]

Churchill's task was then to cajole Roosevelt into the public firmness of support the Empire's security demanded. From time to time, this seemed a difficult task. A fortnight later, in temporary despair, he telegrammed Hopkins: "I ought to tell you that there has been a wave of depression through cabinet and other informed circles here about President's many assurances about no commitments and no closer to war etc. ... If 1942 opens with Russia knocked out and Britain left alone again, all kinds of dangers may arise".[19]

The cajolery required three things. First, Britain would have to pay a price for American support, sometimes in terms of future power, sometimes in terms of compromise in objectives, sometimes quite literally in terms of gold.[20] Second, it was necessary to show that the British Empire was not a lost cause for the Americans, that it was and would remain a strong and militarily effective partner in any coalition, and that the burden of helping it would be bearable for the United States. Hence his assurance to Roosevelt that in the event of Japan attacking the United States, a British declaration of war would follow "within the hour", even if Britain was apparently unaffected.[21]

This had military strategic consequences. Churchill had to show that Britain was fighting offensively and hard, not sitting on the shore and waiting for an American breeze. One of the most important reasons for

Churchill to send *Prince of Wales* and *Repulse* to Singapore was to impress the Americans and to provide a mechanism, and an incentive, by which cooperation between the two navies could be assured and developed. As well as hopefully helping to deter the Japanese, Force Z was a British sprat to catch an American mackerel. In essence, Churchill agreed with Menzies that the United States would not desert the British "if we show we are prepared to fight".[22] Hence also, Churchill's telegrams to Wavell in the closing days of the Malayan campaign that "no question of surrender be entertained until after protracted fighting amongst the ruins of Singapore City".[23] After the fall of Singapore, the need to rescue Britain's battered military reputation played a large part in Churchill's urging the decidedly premature Arakan I campaign, and his delighted support for, and political exploitation of, the quixotic Chindit operations.[24]

The third problem was to deal with the innate anti-colonialism of the American political establishment, a characteristic to which Roosevelt himself was by no means immune. As Roosevelt told his son on 19th November 1942, nearly a year after the Pacific war had begun, "Don't think for a minute that Americans would be dying in the Pacific tonight if it hadn't been for the short-sighted greed of the French and the British and the Dutch".[25] It was important, then, to show the Americans that the Australians, New Zealanders, Indians and all the rest were not the downtrodden victims of the British Raj but allies in a common cause, inspired by the same ideals as the American republic thought it was. "Alone among the nations of the world," he told the House of Commons in 1940 (and Roosevelt too) "we have found the means to combine Empire and liberty".[26] Hence also, the emphasis on the Atlantic Charter of January 1942.

The priority Churchill attached to the overriding strategic aim of securing American support was evident in his reply to the King over the loss of the *Prince of Wales* and *Repulse*:

> Quite apart from personal sorrow it is a very heavy blow, and our combinations formed in the Far East with so much difficulty from limited resources are disrupted ... [but] ... taking it together, I am enormously relieved at the extraordinary changes of the last few days.[27]

Despite the loss of two fine ships and the disaster at Pearl Harbor, the Americans were now in the war and ultimate victory was assured. After this, less crucial priorities could be sought. But for the rest of the war, managing that alliance whilst securing as much as he could of British interests was Churchill's immediate principal concern.[28]

Churchill was perfectly clear that sending reinforcements to Malaya before the Japanese attack began was, as far as he was concerned, a very low priority.[29] His third distinct objective was to make sure the defence of Singapore did not undo other campaigns he regarded as more important. In many ways, his attitude was an echo of his views of naval priorities before the First World War. So long as sufficient force was concentrated in European waters in order to defeat the main enemy, "we can put everything straight afterwards"; if that campaign was lost, though, "there will not be any afterwards".[30] It is hard to dispute the logic of this approach, although there is room for questioning the manner in which it was pursued.

"I deemed the Middle East," Churchill told Australian Prime Minister John Curtin in January 1941:

> a more urgent theatre than the now christened ABDA area ... It must be remembered that only three months ago, we faced in the Middle East ... the threat of a double attack by Rommel from the west and the overrunning of the Caucasus, Persia and Iraq from the north. In such a plight, all the teachings of the war have shown that everything should be concentrated on destroying one of the attacking forces. I thought it best to make a job of Rommel while forming with the rest of our resources the best Levant-Caspian front possible.[31]

Accordingly, the Middle East always commanded a much higher proportion of the air, land and sea forces available, although Churchill also sought to make it clear that if things in the Far East seriously deteriorated, these priorities would be changed. As he told Curtin's predecessor, Menzies, in December 1940, "We must try to bear our eastern anxieties patiently until this result is achieved, it always being understood that if Australia is seriously threatened by invasion we should not hesitate to compromise or sacrifice the Mediterranean position for the sake of our kith and kin".[32] This repeated the point Churchill had made a year earlier when still First Lord of the Admiralty:

> But we wish to make it plain that we regard the defence of Australia, and of Singapore as a stepping stone to Australia, as ranking next to the mastering of the principal fleet to which we are opposed, and that if the choice were presented of defending Australia against a serious attack, or sacrificing British interests in the Mediterranean, our duty to Australia would take precedence. It seems very unlikely, however, that this bleak choice will arise during the next year or two, which is what we have to consider at the present time.[33]

When the Middle East was secured, then more forces could be moved eastwards, although by definition, according to Churchill's impressions of Japanese strategic thinking, the need for this would in fact be less as this success would deter Tokyo from serious action against British interests in any case. The difficulty, of course, was that despite a very promising start by the end of 1940, the Greek adventure, the arrival of Rommel, and in late 1941, the threat of another German demarche past the reeling Soviet Army down into the area through the Caucasus, all meant the Middle East was far from secure. The radical improvements in the strategic position in the Mediterranean came about a year later than Churchill was anticipating, by which time it was far too late for the British position in the Far East to be rescued.

This can be seen by looking, in particular, at aspects of the naval, air and land deficiencies in the defence of Malaya. By the time the war started, the prospects of defending Singapore and Malaya by naval means had effectively been abandoned because of the deteriorating situation in Europe. The fall of France, the loss of its fleet, and the entry of the Italians into the war had exacerbated a naval strategic situation created in the Far East by the thorough modernisation of the Japanese battle fleet and carrier construction programme of the mid- to late 1930s. The British rearmament effort would only begin to improve the naval balance from 1942. Until these new battleships and carriers appeared, Churchill reported in December 1939, "we are now at the lowest point of our strength, compared to Germany or Japan" and could not afford any sizeable proportion of the fleet standing idle anywhere.[34]

Resolute action against both the French and Italian fleets in 1940 improved the situation, Churchill thought, and would have had the required deterrent effect on Japan, but "It is quite impossible for our Fleet to leave the Mediterranean at the present juncture without throwing away irretrievably all that has been gained there and all the prospects for the future ... Should the Italian fleet be knocked out as a factor ... we could send strong naval forces to Singapore without suffering any serious disadvantage".[35] But it was not to be. The Italians were not "knocked out as a factor" and the arrival of the Germans, their U-boats and *Fliegerkorps X* in the Mediterranean made the situation there even worse. Even so, the underlying situation was in fact improving sufficiently to allow the Admiralty to consider the:

> best disposition to make ... But I should like you to know that as they become available we contemplate placing a force of capital ships including first class units in the triangle Aden-Singapore-Simonstown

before the end of the year. All this will be without prejudice to our control to the eastern Mediterranean. I can assure you we are giving constant attention to all this, and you may be sure we shall never let you down if real danger comes. [36]

The arguments between Churchill on the one hand, and the First Sea Lord and his colleagues on the other, are now well known, about both what could be sent out and what any such force should do. The First Sea Lord, Admiral Sir Dudley Pound, wanted the steady build-up of a modest fleet based on the four old R class battleships and one carrier sent to the Indian Ocean in the Spring of 1942. The Admiralty was adamantly opposed to the despatch of *Prince of Wales* and *Repulse* to Far East, preferring a slower safer build up in the Indian Ocean at a pace even less likely to have a deterrent effect on the Japanese, or a reassuring one on the Australians, New Zealanders and Americans.[37] Instead, Churchill, impatient for a faster reaction to a suddenly deteriorating strategic situation, revived an earlier Admiralty idea of a "Flying Squadron"[38] of two capital ships and one aircraft carrier, swiftly to go out in the Autumn of 1941 and to act as an ambiguous fleet in being, rather like the *Tirpitz* in northern Norway waters, and hopefully deter or delay a Japanese attack and complicate their planning.[39]

The discussion as to whether this was a reasonable strategy and a worthwhile risk to take in the circumstances was heated at the time, and has hardly slackened since. But, in the event, the strategy failed in its effect. The Japanese decided on war the very day *Prince of Wales* arrived in Singapore. Much less often remarked upon was the recall in 1940 to the Mediterranean of the elite British 4th Submarine flotilla, which had practised wolf-pack attacks on incoming invasion forces in the South China Sea, whose presence in December 1941 might have had a significant deterrent effect on the Japanese.[40]

The result of all these privations was the despatch of the ill-fated *Prince of Wales* and *Repulse*, all that could be immediately spared after two years of war which had seen the sinking of two capital ships (*Royal Oak* and *Hood*), two fleet carriers (*Courageous* and *Glorious*), two heavy and nine light cruisers, 60 destroyers and 35 submarines. In addition, malign circumstance meant that in the period immediately before and after the Japanese attack, there were other serious naval losses amongst forces that otherwise could have been sent East; they included the grounding of the carrier *Indomitable* originally intended to join Force Z at Singapore, the sinking of *Ark Royal* (13 November 1941), *Barham* (25 November 1941), and the temporary immobilisation of *Queen Elizabeth* and *Valiant* by Italian frogmen (19 December 1941).

The naval situation in the Autumn of 1941 was thus in fact even worse than the Admiralty had foreseen in the Autumn of 1939, and amply justified the realistic view of 1940 that the primary response for the defence of Malaya and Singapore should shift from the Royal Navy to the RAF. But here there were also major problems. From the start of the European War, the Commander-in-Chief Far East, Air Chief Marshal Sir Robert Brooke-Popham, his colleagues and predecessors had been pressing for air reinforcements of all sorts, especially when they realised that "...aircraft reserves in the United Kingdom were now greater than any previous period in the History of Aviation".[41] Indeed, the very efficient British aircraft industry by then was out-producing its German equivalent. "We have made almost exactly two thousand aircraft in September," Churchill, who kept a close eye on such things, told Roosevelt jubilantly in October 1941, "and I think our first line strength tonight is slightly ahead of the Germans".[42] And of course, thousands of aircraft had been supplied by the United States under the agreement of 1940.

Brooke-Popham showed he was well aware of London's immediate priorities: "I realise that our main enemy is Germany and that any man or weapon which we have in the Far East surplus to our requirement is one less available for our main object of killing Germans".[43] All the same, he urged that more fighters, bombers and reconnaissance aircraft be sent, now that naval deficiencies meant that primary responsibility for the defence of Malaya would fall on the RAF. Reconnaissance aircraft were particularly important, since a long-range reconnaissance capability that could spot the Japanese invasion fleet as it sailed south from Hainan through the South China Sea would provide an opportunity for the British to prepare the appropriate diplomatic and military responses. Brooke-Popham had indeed specifically asked for these crucial resources but had been told by the Chiefs that "suggested air reconnaissance over the South China Sea appears too ambitious".[44] In itself, this and the consequent failure to detecting incoming Japanese forces early and well enough cast the whole strategy of the air defence of Malaya into jeopardy, even before the fighting stated.

The problem was that long-range reconnaissance aircraft were of particular use in the all-important campaign against the U-boats:

> It must not be forgotten that defeat of the U-boats carries with it the sovereignty of all the oceans of the world for the allied fleets, and the possibility of powerful neutrals coming to our aid, as well as the drawing of resources from every part of the French and British empires, and the maintenance of trade gathering with it the necessary wealth to continue the war.[45]

Accordingly, the Catalinas that Brooke-Popham wanted for long-range reconnaissance were denied him. "We certainly could not spare the flying boats to lie about idle there on the remote chance of a Japanese attack, when they ought to be playing their part in the deadly struggle on the North-Western approaches".[46]

It was the same story when it came to fighters and tanks. The aim in the Mediterranean in 1941 was to build up to 26 fighter squadrons, 17 medium and heavy bomber squadrons, two squadrons of Beaufort torpedo bombers, six army cooperation squadrons, five general reconnaissance squadrons and four transport squadrons, together with "substantial" reserves and the Royal Navy's Fleet Air Arm.[47] Furthermore, during the same period, Churchill undertook to send 200 fighters to Russia a month. Concerned at the implications of a Russian defeat, not least for Britain's position in the Mediterranean, aware of the staggering losses the Russians had suffered since June 1941, and no doubt responding to overwhelming public pressure, the British and Americans had agreed on a policy of major support to Russia through Persia and the Arctic convoys. By the end of October 1941, the British had themselves despatched 493 fighters to Russia (in the main Hurricanes and Tomahawks), and 315 tanks had arrived or been despatched, with the promise of more to come in successive months.[48]

In light of this, and in hindsight, it is hard to resist the conclusion rapidly arrived at by some of Churchill's critics in the House of Commons, that both the Mediterranean theatre and supporting Russia had become too absolute a priority. Even a few of those hundreds of fighters and tanks, if despatched early enough to Malaya to allow their acclimatisation, might have made all the difference to the British campaign to defend Singapore.[49] This impression is reinforced by the fact that it *was* indeed found possible to despatch substantial air reinforcements to the Far East, although these arrived too late and in too piecemeal a fashion to have a decisive regenerative effect on the British campaign.

Moreover, the recipient of much of Churchill's largesse, who had himself, perhaps not surprisingly, exaggerated the need for them given the approach of winter, was muted in his appreciation of the strategic effect of Britain's sacrifice. These aircraft, Stalin said, "will not be in a position to bring about any substantial change at the eastern front".[50] By the end of the year, an improvement in the strategic situation sufficient for an easing of the restrictions on reinforcement for the Far East was clearly evident, and despite the acute shortages of shipping that still hobbled the strategic mobility of British forces, such reinforcement was underway — but by then, of course, it was far too late.

The fall of Singapore changed the situation back to what it had been before. The fact that the Far East continued to be a secondary theatre as far as Churchill was concerned is best exemplified by the continuous appeals for more resources by Wavell's successors fighting the Burma campaign. Only when the European war was plainly coming to an end was it possible to think of a large-scale British return to the Far East.

There was never any ambiguity about Churchill's fourth and final distinct objective. "Without victory," Churchill told the House of Commons shortly after becoming Prime Minister, "there is no survival. Let that be realised; no survival for the British Empire, no survival for all that the British Empire has stood for".[51] Maintaining that Empire and recovering its lost prestige and geographic possessions were important to him, especially after the fall of Singapore. He had not, after all, "become the King's First Minister in order to preside over the liquidation of the British Empire".[52]

Part of this strategy meant assiduously cultivating the full cooperation, and thereby accessing the full resources, of the Empire, whether this was the rubber and tin of Malaya or the fighting resources of India, Australia, New Zealand, Canada, and so on. Part of the imperial bargain was to accede as much as was militarily sensible to the particular concerns of the Empire's main constituents. Here, maintaining the cooperation of Australia and New Zealand was the biggest challenge, since they tended to see, as Prime Minister Curtin claimed, "… the trend of the Pacific situation more clearly than was realised in London".[53]

Acutely aware of their vulnerability to attack through the islands of the Dutch East Indies, the southern Dominions pressed though the interwar period for the construction of strong defences in Singapore and Malaya as a protection against this. On that basis, they agreed that the bulk of Australian and New Zealand land forces were despatched to the Middle East. Even so, the Dominions insisted on their divisions having their own lines of command, which significantly complicated the running of the Desert War.[54] The discovery from the earliest days of the Malayan campaign that the British position in Malaya was not as strong as they had been led to believe, led to a major crisis in imperial relations and a fracturing of the sense of shared "Britishness" that actually held the Empire together.

All this was exemplified, even as the British campaign in Malaya unravelled, by the exchange of angry telegrams between Churchill, Curtin and Peter Fraser, Prime Minister of New Zealand, in January and February 1942, as Churchill was forced to explain how it was that he had so underrated both the imminence and the scale of the Japanese threat. "I sense your having been misled," Churchill also told Fraser, "by a too complacent expression of military opinion in the past on probable dangers in the Pacific area in general and to New Zealand in particular. But who could have foretold the serious opening setback which the United States fleet suffered on 7 December with what this, and the subsequent losses of our two fine ships entail? The events of the war have been consistently unpredictable, and not all to our disadvantage".[55] Fraser replied that "we have never been 'misled' by these appreciations which have, generally speaking, seemed to us to be more optimistic than the situation as we saw it warranted".[56]

Such recriminations over past priorities and expectations apart, Churchill was at one with the leaders of both countries in the new task at hand. Singapore should be reinforced and held if at all possible. "Our object", he said on 17 January, "... is to hold Singapore and to build up a fleet in the Pacific which will wrest naval control from the Japanese. All this is being worked out with the greatest despatch and in ceaseless communication with our American allies".[57] To do that, he warned against the local commanders frittering away scarce resources on defence in northern and central Malaya which Japanese control of local seas was likely to undermine anyway, and ordered the despatch of enough air and land forces, including the British 18th Division, to make the counter-stroke he hoped for possible in later February or early March.[58]

As late as 3 February, Wavell told Churchill that despite having to base British fighters back in Sumatra "there is every intention of holding Singapore".[59] Churchill was also undoubtedly encouraged in this vain hope by the persistence of Curtin and Fraser in saying that a toehold in the area must be held. On hearing that the Defence Committee back in London in January had considered abandoning the area, the Australian government notoriously pointed out that

> after all assurances we have been given, the evacuation of Singapore would be regarded in Australia and elsewhere as an inexcusable betrayal. Singapore is a central fortress in the system of the Empire and local defence ... we understood that it was to be made impregnable and in any event it was to be capable of holding out for a prolonged period until the arrival of the main fleet.[60]

But it turned out that Singapore was not a fortress after all, and that a fight to the finish in its shattered streets would achieve little of strictly military substance. Such a sacrifice might do something for British honour, although probably at unbearable cost in civilian lives, but it could not gain time for the construction of further defences to the south since the second wave of the Japanese assault on the area, the attack on Sumatra and the more or less defenceless islands beyond, was already underway. Accordingly, Singapore, grudgingly, was allowed to surrender. It was, Churchill told Roosevelt, "the greatest disaster in our history".[61]

The immediate issue was where now to try to hold the line? Australia and New Zealand argued strongly for the Dutch East Indies, or failing that, the direct defence of the two Dominions themselves. But in the immediate aftermath of the fall of Singapore, it was clear to both Roosevelt and Churchill that ABDA and the Dutch East Indies were probably a lost cause. They decided instead to focus on the maintenance in this area of a two front war. To the west, the Australia/New Zealand/Fiji/New Caledonia area would be easiest for the United States to reinforce and to the east, Burma/China/India would remain a British responsibility.[62] This chimed perfectly with what Wavell had told Churchill three days before. Java was indefensible against a scale of attack which included four Japanese divisions, 400–500 fighters and 300–400 bombers. The 7th Australian Division currently returning from Europe should, he recommended, go to Burma which is "only theatre in which offensive land operations against Japan possible in near future. It should be possible for American Troops to provide reinforcement of Australia if required".[63]

This difference of view prompted a furious spat between Churchill, who urged that the 7th Australians should be diverted to Burma, and Curtin, who insisted they and the following two divisions should come home. Churchill put a great deal of pressure on Curtin, pressure which included enlisting the support of Roosevelt and even ordering the diversion of the convoy in question, in order to give Curtin more time to think about things. Curtin had his way in the end — illustrating thereby the new political realities of the British Empire. He did however in early March offer the sop of peeling off two Brigade groups from the 6th Division, last of the two returning Australian Divisions, to offer temporary support for Ceylon.[64]

Churchill's thinking on all this was clear. As he told the Governor of Burma the day after the fall of Singapore, "I regard Burma and contact with China as the most important feature in the whole theatre of war".[65] He regretted continuing to reinforce a losing campaign in Singapore with the British 18th Division and wished that he had diverted them instead to Burma, because "they could almost certainly have saved Rangoon". Not being able to make use of the Australian 7th as it passed through the theatre was therefore deeply frustrating. As a result, Rangoon, and in the end the whole of Burma, fell as well. The disaster for the British Empire was complete.

The question was, what to do next, in this new and desperate situation? Whatever his private doubts, Churchill never wavered from the view that the Empire *would* fight back and that in the end, it would be successful. As evidence of this, London soon set up a unit whose task was to prepare for the British re-occupation and rehabilitation of a Singapore assumed to be devastated by the ravages of war.[66] This buoyant optimism about the future stood in some contrast to the pessimism (or realism!) of some of those around him.

The daunting scale of the task of restoring the Empire militarily in the early months of 1942 was revealed by an entry in Brooke's diary just before Singapore's final fall:

> I have during the last 10 years had an unpleasant feeling that the British Empire was decaying and that we were on a slippery decline!! I wonder if I was right? I certainly never expected that we should fall to pieces as fast as we are and to see Hong Kong and Singapore go in less than three months plus failure in the western Desert is far from re-assuring! We have had a wonderful power of recuperation in the past. I wonder whether we shall again bring off a comeback? ... We are paying very heavily now for failing to face the insurance premiums essential for security of an Empire! This has usually been the main cause for the loss of Empires in the past.[67]

In this situation, Churchill's determination to restore what he valued above all else seems wholly admirable, something of a necessary corrective to the doom and gloom all around him. But paradoxically, his assumptions and presumptions were in danger of being self-defeating since he failed to appreciate the extent to which survival depended on change, with the Empire in effect needing to be transformed into the Commonwealth.

Even after the fall of Singapore and Burma, Churchill was insufficiently aware of the need to woo the leaders and peoples of the British Empire with concessions that would win their continuing support by giving them the prospect of greater consultation in the immediate future and more autonomy, even independence, in the longer term future. He seemed to have missed the opportunity, for example, to regain lost ground with Curtin, who for all the arguments of 1942, remained loyal to the concept of close association with Britain, especially when the limits of American sympathy and support for Australia became clear.[68] Australia and New Zealand, both of necessity and with the agreement of Churchill, turned to the United States for urgent reinforcement and protection; but they also wanted a reappraisal of the extent to which their strategic interests and perspectives were represented in London's decision-making processes. Churchill, though, remained as unsympathetic to the idea of allowing Dominion leaders a larger share in deciding Imperial strategy as he had been before the First World War. He seemed to think that power, whether it was the power of strategic decision or the power represented by naval forces, should be concentrated for maximum effect in London, not dissipated around the Empire.[69] The result, arguably, was a degree of strain between Britain and its Antipodean Dominions that could have been avoided.

Churchill's strategy towards India seems in retrospect equally un-yielding. It put considerable strain on his relations with Roosevelt.[70] Churchill thereby missed the chance for an accommodation with the emerging rulers of India that might have avoided the distractions and uncertainties of the political threats of the Indian National Army and the "Quit India Movement". When urged by Field Marshal Smuts to reward Indian efforts in the forthcoming campaign to drive Japan from Southeast Asia, with the promise of Dominion status after the war, Churchill re-plied this was an issue which "does not lend itself to simple solutions".[71] Churchill was right of course, and India performed its Imperial duty all the same, doing so to a much greater extent in the recovery of Burma than he was grateful for, or even aware of.[72] Fortunately, most of his local commanders were much more enlightened and realistic.

Such long-term considerations apart, the first and most immediate requirement was to reinforce British naval strength in the Indian Ocean, by concentrating a fleet centred on the four old R class battleships, *Warspite* and hopefully some modern carriers too, to be based at Trincomalee and to "deter sea-borne attack on India".[73] Although under no illusions about the weakness of this force, Churchill hoped "to regain our sea power in the Indian Ocean in the next two or three months, and this should enable minor offensive action to be taken by us against the Japanese conquered islands".[74] He made the point that the Japanese were now spread very thinly around their new conquests, with large distractions in China and the prospect of war with Russia, and so must be vulnerable to counter-attack. Nonetheless, the immediate dangers of a further Japanese naval demarche into the Indian Ocean were clear, and to Roosevelt, he expressed "hope that your forces in the Pacific will prevent the Japanese bringing over the bulk of their fleet to the Indian Ocean".[75] What would happen if this proved not the case was made crystal clear by the success of the Japanese raid on Ceylon and the Indian Ocean in April 1942.

In the longer term, it was a question of rebuilding naval strength until the desired counter-offensive could take place, subject of course to the more pressing priorities in the European theatre, which in effect delayed that counter-offensive for the next two years. After the final surrender of the Italian fleet, September 1943 became the turning point for real planning for a British counter-offensive in Southeast Asia.[76]

The need to do so was dramatically demonstrated when leading elements of the Japanese fleet turned up at Singapore in February 1944. Churchill, in an unconscious echo of the original justification for the Singapore base, pointed out that naval forces there were "equally well placed for operations in the Pacific or in the Bay of Bengal. Singapore had the best docking and maintenance facilities outside Japan and is remote from air attack ... The presence of the Japanese battlefleet in Singapore may be induced by reports that we are contemplating amphibious operations based on India". He assured the Dominions that forces would be built up to cope. Moreover, he told Roosevelt, "From your point of view, it should open up fine opportunities in the Pacific ... to the American fleet".[77]

Churchill had a variety of options in his determined campaign to recover lost ground, battered prestige and strategic advantage. They were complex and interwoven. Further, all Far East options were constrained by the continuing priority given to Europe. It was never likely to be a case of either this campaign or that one. Even with a shortage of resources, the real issue was the balance to be struck in the priorities attached to a mix of operational possibilities in the Far East, where the British would try to back as many horses in the race as they could.

At heart, the issue was about whether Britain should participate in the final campaign against Japan in the Pacific, or whether it would be sensible for it to pick off the "ripe fruit" as Dill (now in Washington) put it to Churchill on 14 March 1944, and instead focus on the campaign to recover Burma, Malaya and, especially, Singapore. None of these were easy options however.[78]

Both alternatives had their attractions and their disadvantages. Getting together the British Pacific Fleet and participating in the final maritime campaign against Japan, and even in the invasion of Japan's home islands, was an ambitious, almost Homeric enterprise at that stage of the war, when voices back home were warning of the need to prepare for a demanding peace.[79] Moreover, Admiral Ernest J. King and others in the US Navy were unenthusiastic about the British unnecessarily participating in the Pacific campaign, their historic revenge for Pearl Harbor. King insisted that the British bring everything they would need with them, and this demand further reduced prospects in Southeast Asia.

On the other hand, anxious that the sinking of *Prince of Wales* and *Repulse* should be properly avenged, Admiral A.B. Cunningham, for his part, was absolutely determined that the Royal Navy enter the final stages of the Pacific War in the best way it could. The Australians, the New Zealanders and even the Canadians felt the same; the desire to be "in at the kill" would be emotionally and strategically satisfying for all concerned. The COS thought it a more realistic option because, initially, it was less demanding in manpower terms. Finally, it seemed a good way of staying alongside the Americans into an uncertain future. The COS, clearly intruding into the political domain, admitted that their desire to stay alongside the Americans in the final assault on Japan had "as much a political as a strategical objective".[80]

But focussing on the recapture of Burma and, even more, launching a large-scale amphibious operation to recapture Malaya and Singapore would more immediately restore the prestige of the Empire, and do something to wipe out the stain of the defeat of 1941–1942. As Mountbatten observed, failure to do so would "irretrievably impair our prestige in the Far East".[81] Accordingly, Churchill, with the backing of Mountbatten, enthusiastically advocated Operation *Culverin*, an amphibious assault on Sumatra, and, somewhat less so, Operation *Buccaneer* (an adulterated version aimed at the Andamans), outflanking the Japanese in the jungles of Burma and facilitating a satisfyingly direct assault on occupied Singapore. Such a plan would also avoid the difficulties of what Churchill anticipated would be a long, gruelling and difficult campaign in central and southern Burma.[82] He ordered that "All preparations will be made for amphibious action across the Bay of Bengal against the Malay peninsula and the various island outposts by which it is defended, the ultimate objective being the re-conquest of Singapore".[83] The minutes of a later meeting made the point even more explicitly: "In his [Churchill's] opinion, the shame of our disaster at Singapore could only be wiped out by our recapture of that fortress".[84] This again was more an emotional/political than a military need; the COS, bearing much less personal responsibility for the original disaster, were decidedly cool about the whole idea.

Another problem was that direct and radical progress back to Singapore was however dependent on a particular type of reinforcement — landing craft, which were absurdly short. "How it is that that the plans of two great empires like Britain and the United States should be so much ham-strung and limited by a hundred or two of these particular vessels will never be understood by history," Churchill complained. He urged Roosevelt to step up their production, saying in March 1944, "It is my earnest wish to operate against the Japanese as soon as our amphibious resources are released from the European Theatre and I very much hope you will find it possible to meet this request".[85] As far as the COS were concerned, this proposal had all the imaginative, flowing big-hand-small-map characteristics of much of Churchill's approach to strategy, and it caused a dispute between Churchill and his COS that became so rancorous at times they thought about resigning en masse, and occasioned Brooke's comment about Churchill's strategic deficiencies with which this chapter began. Certainly, the British suffered serious shortages in manpower and materiel but Brooke was unconvinced by the whole idea, anyway. The project he said should be "tested by one essential question — what would it contribute to the shortening of the war against Japan?" By this criterion, it failed.[86] For the COS, winning the war in the East meant defeating Japan; for Churchill, it also meant winning the peace afterwards, in which he included the requirement to recover the Empire.

Reluctantly, the COS were however prepared to accede to an overland approach in Southeast Asia. A steady state campaign in northern Burma would have the advantage of re-opening the Burma Road to China, thereby keeping the Americans happy. For this reason, the Americans would be prepared to provide the air assets and, to some extent, the landing craft, that such a strategy required. It is clear that neither Churchill nor the COS appreciated the extent of Slim's victory at Kohima-Imphal in the Summer of 1944, nor the strategic possibilities that it opened up for central and south Burma, Rangoon and beyond if properly supported.[87] The outstanding successes of the 14th Army caught London by surprise and were the most "Imperial" enterprise imaginable. Even after the war, Churchill, in his memoirs, was slow to recognise the achievements of this extraordinary campaign, which would surely have ended with the re-occupation of Singapore had time not run out.[88] Torn all ways, Churchill and the COS argued heatedly about the balance to be struck between these competing alternatives in "... waffling that there has been for nearly nine months over the basic question of our strategy in the Far East", which Pownall believed "will be one of the black spots in the record of British higher direction of War",[89] and which ended in the compromise of pursuing all three options — to some extent.

The British contribution to the Pacific campaign was the British Pacific Fleet, which indeed earned the eventual respect even of Admiral King. Air forces and land forces were on the way too, until the dropping of the atom bombs on Hiroshima and Nagasaki ended the war unexpectedly early. Churchill got his amphibious operations in the end, *Dracula*, to retake a Rangoon abandoned by the fast-retreating Japanese shortly before, and *Zipper*, the campaign to retake Malaya and Singapore, which was indeed mounted but only after the Japanese had surrendered.

The fleet carriers necessary for a faster and more ambitious amphibious strategy in Southeast Asia had long since been despatched to the Pacific. At the same time, British forces, crucially supported by American airpower, inflicted the biggest defeat on the Japanese Army it had ever suffered at Imphal-Kohima, with the Japanese losing 53,000 of the 84,000 troops they committed. Moreover, despite the climate and the appalling difficulties of the campaign, the 14th Army went on to retake the whole of Burma with the Japanese in full retreat. All of this had been achieved by a truly Imperial army of Indians of every persuasion (still largely British-officered), East and West Africans, Burmese irregulars, South Africans and UK British, the latter making barely a third of the total of forces in theatre.[90] An Empire, in the process of transformation, had indeed finally struck back with decisive strategic effect.

Churchill clearly knew what he was about in the Far East in a way in which the Japanese certainly did not. He showed an acute awareness of the need, if he was to secure his four major objectives, of accommodating military strategy to political realities, and to be prepared as much as possible for the peace that would follow. That despite the manifest weaknesses of the British, Churchill managed to achieve three of his four grand objectives, speaks for itself. He won, after all. In Clausewitz's terms, and quite unlike the Japanese, Churchill understood the war he was in and what had to be done to secure what he thought the country needed.

Brooke's adverse comment on Churchill as a strategist, with which this paper began, proceeded from one of the many tussles the COS had with the Prime Minister, over the future direction of affairs in Southeast Asia. It reflected the classic problem of where the line should be struck between the statesman and the military professional in the construction of strategy, and was exemplified by quarrels and disagreements over both the objectives of strategy (ideally the statesman's prerogative) and the method (ideally the military man's). In practice, both need to intrude into the other's province, of course.

With the major exception of the despatch of Force Z, the COS had no quarrel with Churchill's strategic priorities before the fall of Singapore, but they most certainly did in his desire two years later to retake it, as we have seen. They paid less attention to the recovery of imperial prestige than he did and more to the political attractions of fighting alongside the Americans, in the final campaign against Japan in the Pacific. They underestimated the difficulties of this campaign and overestimated the time which they had to solve them.

The COS' real venom, though, was reserved for Churchill's major incursions into "their" sphere of deciding the *means* by which the objectives were to be secured. After the contested despatch of Force Z to Singapore in 1941, the worst example of this was their exasperation over his, to them, wilful refusal to accept the infeasibility of large-scale amphibious operations across the Bay of Bengal until late 1945. Two things may be said in defence of Churchill's habitual optimism. The first is that he was in fact acutely conscious of British weaknesses and saw in both the radical reform of what would now be called the defence acquisition process, and in the American connection, the major means for dealing with them. Second, Churchill's approach was continually more optimistic about current and future prospects than professional opinion could accede to, and this was the cause of countless clashes with his military advisors, whose function, it was increasingly clear, was to inject a sense of reality where it was lacking.

For his part, Churchill listened, and usually bowed, to what he once called "the difficulties so industriously assembled" and the "general attitude of negation". On one occasion, Churchill remarked: "Why, you may take the most gallant sailor, the most intrepid airman, or the most audacious soldier, put them at a table together — what do you get? The sum total of their fears!" He saw his task as constantly to goad and ginger up his "Safety First" Admirals, Generals and Air Marshals into the kind of aggression that characterised their Japanese adversaries. The result of such painful and often frustrating encounters was a compromise that in the end delivered what was necessary.[91] In 1944 his secretary, John Colville, noted that with Churchill's imagination and resolution:

> Whatever may be the PM's shortcomings, there is no doubt that he does provide guidance and purpose for the Chiefs of Staff and the Foreign Office on matters which, without him, would often be lost in the maze of inter-departmentalism, or frittered away by caution and compromise.[92]

And in the final analysis, even after such disasters as the fall of Singapore, it is hard to disagree with this. Indeed, much of the obloquy directed at Churchill's role in the fall of Singapore, his biggest failure in the Far East, seems due more to the total irrationality of the Japanese than to his intrinsic failings as a strategist.

Notes

1.   B.H. Liddell Hart, *Strategy: The Indirect Approach* (London: Faber and Faber Limited, 1967), p. 335; Alex Danchev and Daniel Todman, eds., *War Diaries 1939–1945: Field Marshal Lord Alanbrooke* (London: Weidenfeld & Nicolson, 2001), p. 568.

2. Carl von Clausewitz, *On War*, Book I, "On the Nature of War" (London: N. Trübner, 1873).

3. CAC, Churchill Papers, CHAR 20/15, First Lord of the Admiralty Memorandum, Australian Naval Defence Winter 1939, 17 December 1939.

4. Ibid.

5. CAC, Churchill Papers, CHAR 20/16, Weekly Intelligence Commentary No. 55, 5 September 1940.

6. CAC, Churchill Papers, CHAR 20/42A/39, Churchill to Prime Ministers of Australia and New Zealand, 30 August 1941. In fact, the Soviet air forces had never prepared for strategic bombing in the way that the British and the Americans had, and were soon wholly absorbed by the desperate campaign to defend Moscow, Stalingrad and Leningrad against the advancing Germans.

7. Haruo Tohmatsu and H.P. Willmott, *A Gathering Darkness: The Coming of War to the Far East and the Pacific, 1921–42* (Lanham, MD: SR Books, 2004), pp. 93–4. The industrial, economic and military deficiencies of Japan at this time are explored on pp. 59–60, 84–7. The Japanese argument for initiating the war now seemed to reflect a view that the correlation of military forces would only get worse from the Japanese point of view.

8. Quoted in Martin Gilbert, *Winston S. Churchill*, Vol. VI, *Finest Hour 1939–41* (London: Heineman, 1983), pp. 678–86; Martin Gilbert, *Churchill: A Life* (London: Pimlico, 2000), p. 695. In some circumstances, Churchill and Admiral Pound seemed willing to think about *not* intervening should Japan attack the East Indies. See Gilbert, *Finest Hour*, p. 1047.

9. Churchill has been heavily criticised for imagining Singapore to be a fortress. But it is hardly surprising that he thought so since his advisors both on the spot and in London frequently used that term. Thus, General Dobbie, 17 March 1936 and May 1938; Karl Hack and Kevin Blackburn, *Did Singapore Have to Fall? Churchill and the Impregnable Fortress* (London: Routledge, 2004), p. 40; and even in a note of 21 January 1942 on minute from Prime Minister to General Ismay, dated 19 January 1942, NA, WO 106/2528; Churchill, *The Second World War*, Vol. IV (London: Cassell, 1951), pp. 43–4. See also Percival lecture of January 1937 reproduced in Louis Allen, *Singapore 1941–42* (London: Davis-Poynter Ltd, 1977), p. 272.

10. Peter Elphick, *Far Eastern File: The Intelligence War in the Far East 1930–1945* (London: Hodder & Stoughton, 1998), pp. 255–67.

11. Gilbert, *Finest Hour*, p. 686.

12. See Percival's comments on this cited in Allen, p. 46.

13. CAC, Churchill Papers, CHAR 20/42A/29, Churchill to Stalin, 28 August 1941.

14. CAC, Churchill Papers, CHAR20/20, Churchill to Roosevelt, 20 October 1941.

15. Gilbert, *Finest Hour*, pp. 743, 783.

16. Ibid., p. 1161.

17. Greg Kennedy, "Symbol of Imperial Defense: The Role of Singapore in British and American Far Eastern Strategic Relations", in *Sixty Years On: The Fall of Singapore Revisited*, eds. Brian P. Farrell and Sandy Hunter (Singapore: Eastern Universities Press, 2002).

18. CAC, Churchill Papers, CHAR 20/41/95, Menzies to Churchill, 8 August 1941. Churchill absolutely agreed with this: Gilbert, *Finest Hour*, p. 825.

19. CAC, Churchill Papers, CHAR 20/42A/35, Churchill to Hopkins, 28 August 1941.

20. Gilbert, *Finest Hour*, pp. 968–77.

21. CAC, Churchill Papers, CHAR 20/20, Churchill to Roosevelt, 20 October 1941.

22. CAC, Churchill Papers, CHAR 20/41/105-06, Menzies to Churchill, 11 August 1941.

23. CAC, Churchill Papers, CHAR 20/68B/124, Churchill to Wavell, 21 January and 10 February 1942. See also Brian P. Farrell, *The Defence and Fall of Singapore* (Stroud: Tempus, 2005), pp. 355–6. Brooke participated in the drafting of these final orders, for which Churchill is often criticised. See Danchev and Todman, eds., *Brooke Diaries*, entries for 9 February and 14 February 1942, p. 228.

24. Raymond A. Callahan, *Churchill and his Generals* (Lawrence, KS: University Press of Kansas, 2007), pp. 196–201.

25. Cited in William Roger Louis, *Imperialism at Bay: The United States and the Decolonisation of the British Empire* (New York: Oxford University Press, 1978), p. 180. Roosevelt's personal anti-colonialism endeared him and the US even such nationalists as Ho Chi Minh: Marilyn B Young, *The Vietnam Wars 1945–1990* (New York: HarperCollins, 1991), pp. 2–10. British-American differences over the shape of the post-war world were at their most acute over the future of India and Southeast Asia. Christopher Thorne, *Allies of a Kind: The United States, Britain, and the War Against Japan 1941–45* (London: Hamish Hamilton, 1978), p. 702.

26. Gilbert, *Finest Hour*, p. 836.

27. CAC, Churchill Papers, CHAR 20/20, Churchill to King George VI, 12 December 1941.

28. Nor was this easy. Thorne, *Allies of a Kind*, pp. 699–729.

29. Hack and Blackburn, pp. 44–6; Kirby, pp. 64–5.

30. Churchill to Haldane, 6 May 1912, cited in Randolph S. Churchill, ed., *Winston S. Churchill*, Vol. II, Companion 3 (London: Heinemann, 1969), p. 1549.

31. CAC, Churchill Papers, CHAR 20/68B, Churchill telegram to Curtin, 19 January 1942. Because Russian resistance proved greater than expected, Churchill's fears for a German lunge through the Caucasus against Britain's strategic interests in the Middle East never materialised. For that reason, the prospect has rarely commanded the attention it did at the time: Gilbert, *Finest Hour*, p. 889.

32.   CAC, Churchill Papers, CHAR 20/14, Churchill to Menzies, 23 December 1940.

33.   CAC, Churchill Papers, CHAR 20/15, First Lord of the Admiralty Memorandum, Australian Naval Defence Winter 1939, 17 December 1939.

34.   Ibid.

35.   CAC, Churchill Papers, CHAR 20/14, Churchill to Menzies, 23 December 1940.

36.   CAC, Churchill Papers, CHAR 20/42A/39, Churchill to Prime Ministers of Australia and New Zealand, 30 August 1941.

37.   The Admiralty, however, thought that the four R class battleships (*Royal Sovereign, Revenge, Resolution* and *Ramillies*), if joined by the newer *Rodney, Renown* and *Nelson*, and aided by shore-based airpower, should be able to hold their own against Japanese forces likely to be sent into the Indian Ocean. Gilbert, *Finest Hour*, p. 1257.

38.   Christopher M. Bell, *The Royal Navy, Seapower and Strategy Between the Wars* (London: Macmillan, 2000), pp. 86–8 and Malcolm H. Murfett, "Admiral Sir Roger Roland Charles Backhouse" in *The First Sea Lords* (Westport, CT: Praeger, 1995), pp. 173–84.

39.   This was one of the choices advocated in the immediate aftermath of the Japanese landings. The other was for the ships to join the battered US Pacific Fleet at Hawaii. Gilbert, *Finest Hour*, p. 1271.

40.   Alastair Mars, *British Submarines at War* (London: William Kimber, 1971), pp. 21, 24, 47–52.

41.   LHCMA, Brooke-Popham Papers, 6/1/11, Brooke-Popham to Air Ministry, 24 March 1941.

42.   CAC, Churchill Papers, CHAR 20/43/75, Churchill to Roosevelt, 4 October 1941. The strength of the British aircraft industry is a major theme of David Edgerton, *England and the Aeroplane: An Essay on a Militant and Technological Nation* (London: Macmillan, 1991).

43.   LHCMA, Brooke-Popham Papers, BPP 6/1/11, Brooke-Popham to Air Ministry, 20 August 1941.

44.   LHCMA, Brooke-Popham Papers, BPP 6/1/6, COS to Brooke-Popham, telegram 39, 10 January 1941.

45.   CAC, Churchill Papers , CHAR 20/15, First Lord Statement to the French Admiralty, 3 November 1939.

46.   CAC, Churchill Papers, CHAR 20/14, Churchill to Curtin, 23 December 1940. Catalina flying boats, like the one ruthlessly shot down by the Japanese before the invasion, were in particularly short supply and were an urgent requirement from the United States. Gilbert, *Finest Hour*, pp. 738, 772.

47.   CAC, Churchill Papers, CHAR 20/42B, Churchill to Menzies, 12 September 1941. Paradoxically, this was written in order to reassure the Australians that their forces in Tobruk and elsewhere would still be provided with sufficient air support.

48. CAC, Churchill Papers, CHAR 20/43/83, Churchill to Stalin, 6 October 1941. The total plan over nine months was for Britain to dispatch 1,800 Hurricanes and Spitfires, 900 American fighters and another 900 American bombers. Gilbert, *Finest Hour*, p. 1210.

49. Louis Allen quotes Sir Archibald Southby to this effect, Hansard 378 HC Debates 61, in *Singapore 1941–42*, p. 17.

50. CAC, Churchill Papers, CHAR 20/42A/64, Stalin to Churchill (undated but late August/early September 1941).

51. Quoted in Martin Gilbert, *Churchill: A Life*, p. 646.

52. Speech of 10 November 1942, House of Commons, quoted in ibid., p. 734.

53. CAC, Churchill Papers, CHAR/20/68B, Curtin to Churchill, 22 January 1942.

54. Niall Barr, *The Pendulum of War: The Three Battles of El Alamein* (London: Pimlico, 2005), pp. 44, 408.

55. CAC, Churchill Papers, CHAR 20/68B/107-08, Churchill to Fraser, 17 January 1942. The unpredictable but "good" things that had happened, he thought, included German errors during the Battle of Britain and the Battle of the Atlantic, and the unexpected success of Russian resistance to the German invasion.

56. CAC, Churchill Papers, CHAR 20/68B/107-08, Fraser to Churchill, 20 January 1942.

57. CAC, Churchill Papers, CHAR 20/68B/107-08, Churchill to Fraser, 17 January 1942.

58. For this, see Hack and Blackburn, pp. 138–9; CAC, Churchill Papers, CHAR 20/68B/77-79, Churchill to Curtin, 14 January 1941.

59. CAC, Churchill Papers, CHAR 69B/109, Wavell to Churchill, 3 February 1942.

60. CAC, Churchill Papers, CHAR 20/69A/6, Curtin to Churchill, 24 January 1942.

61. CAC, Churchill Papers, CHAR 20/71A/44, Churchill to Roosevelt, 5 March 1942.

62. CAC, Churchill Papers, CHAR 20/70/74, Roosevelt to Churchill, 19 February 1942.

63. CAC, Churchill Papers, CHAR 20/70/59, CINCSWPAC to WO, 16 February 1942.

64. CAC, Churchill Papers, CHAR 20/70/93-94, Churchill to Curtin, 20 February 1942; CHAR 20/70/101, Curtin to Churchill, 22 February 1942; CHAR 20/70/115, Curtin to Churchill, 23 February 1942; CHAR 20/71A/21, 3 March 1942.

65. CAC, Churchill Papers, CHAR 20/70/59, Churchill to Dorman-Smith, 16 February 1942.

66. O.W. Gilmour, *With Freedom in Singapore* (London: Ernest Bonn, 1950), p. 24. The planners also worked to the assumption that the liberation of Singapore might well happen sooner than it did.

67. Diary entries for 11 and 12 February 1942, in *Brooke Diaries*, eds. Danchev and Todman, pp. 228–9.

68. See Peter Edwards, "Churchill, Singapore and Australia's Strategic Policy", Chapter 6 in this volume.

69. For a useful summary of Churchill's views on the advantages of concentration before the First World War, see Christopher Bell, "Winston Churchill and Dominion navies, 1911–1914", in *The Canadian Navy and the Commonwealth Experience*, ed. Richard Gimblett (forthcoming). As Churchill told Sir William Graham Greene on 14 October 1913: "It is high time that the Dominions had the true strategic conception on which the Empire is conducted impressed upon them": NA, ADM1/8375/108.

70. Arthur Herman, *Gandhi and Churchill* (London: Arrow Books, 2009), p. 509.

71. CAC, Churchill Papers, CHAR 20/68B/130, Smuts to Churchill, 20 January 1942. For Churchill's views on the internal complexities of the India problem, see his memo of 3 March 1942, CHAR 20/71A/27 and Herman, pp. 92, 185, 517–39, 567.

72. Callahan, pp. 227–34.

73. CAC, Churchill Papers, CHAR 20/71A/44, Churchill to Roosevelt, 5 March 1942.

74. CAC, Churchill Papers, CHAR 20/71B, Churchill to Fraser, 15 March 1942.

75. CAC, Churchill Papers, CHAR 20/71A/44, Churchill to Roosevelt, 5 March 1942.

76. H.P. Willmott, *Grave of a Dozen Schemes: British Naval Planning and the War Against Japan, 1943–1945* (Annapolis, MD: Naval Institute Press, 1996), p. 6. This book provides the most detailed account of the tortuous process that followed.

77. CAC, Churchill Papers, CHAR 20/158, Churchill to Prime Ministers of Australia and New Zealand, 3 March 1944; CHAR 20/157, Churchill to Roosevelt, 25 February 1944.

78. NA, PREM, 3/164/6.

79. The strategic preference of the COS, this option depended on the gathering together of carrier forces, supply ships and a logistical infrastructure in Australia of daunting size and complexity, which its advocates tended rather to underestimate: Willmott, pp. 11–3. Moreover, getting British air and ground forces into the Pacific theatre proved to be a long, slow and difficult process; the unexpectedly sudden end to the war invalidated the whole scheme.

80. Notes on COS meeting, 4 May 1944, quoted in Nicholas Evan Sarantakes, *Allies Against the Rising Sun: The United States, the British Nations and the Defeat of Imperial Japan* (Lawrence, KS: University Press of Kansas, 2009), p. 79. For further discussion, see Jon Robb-Webb, "The British in the Pacific", in *The Triumph of Neptune? Seapower and the Asia-Pacific: Adjusting to New Realities*, eds. Patrick Bratton and Geoffrey Till (forthcoming).

81. Philip Ziegler, *Mountbatten: The Official Biography* (London: Collins, 1985), p. 282.

82. Ibid., p. 161.

83. Sarantakes, p. 49.

84. Ibid., p. 99. For a summary of the COS position, see Danchev and Todman, eds., *Brooke Diaries*, p. 526.

85. CAC, Churchill Papers, CHAR 20/16/14, Churchill to Dill for Marshall, 16 April 1944, and to Roosevelt, 4 April 1944.

86. Ziegler, p. 266. See also Sarantakes, p. 50. This immediate focus on the defeat of the main adversaries rather than the peace that followed was also occasionally characteristic of the Americans too. Gilbert, *Finest Hour*, p. 986. Even after Kohima, Brooke toyed with the idea of closing the Burma campaign down, not expecting Slim to be able to reconquer the country so speedily.

87. Field Marshal Viscount Slim, *Defeat Into Victory: Battling Japan in Burma and India, 1942–1945* (New York: Cooper Square Press, 2000), p. 374.

88. Callahan, p. 210.

89. Quoted in Ziegler, p. 277.

90. Slim, pp. 508–34.

91. Quoted in Gilbert, *Churchill: A Life*, p. 708; quoted in Gilbert, *Finest Hour*, p. 876; and Gilbert *Churchill: A Life*, p. 758.

92. Quoted in Gilbert, *Churchill: A Life*, p. 773.

CHAPTER 5

An Imperial Defeat?
The Presentation and Reception
of the Fall of Singapore[1]

Richard Toye

In his memoirs, Churchill described the loss of Singapore as "the worst disaster and largest capitulation in British history".[2] The future Prime Minister of Singapore, Lee Kuan Yew, apparently discerned at the time that the battle foretold "the end of the British Empire".[3] The defeat resonated around the world, giving a field day to German propagandists such as William Joyce ("Lord Haw-Haw"), who spoke of "Winston Churchill, the undertaker of the British Empire".[4] According to Churchill's doctor, Lord Moran, "The fall of Singapore on 15 February [1942] stupefied the Prime Minister". Churchill was both incredulous to learn of the inadequate state of the island's defences and self-reproachful for having failed to find out the true position himself earlier. According to Moran's account:

> There was another more crucial question, to which the Prime Minister could find no answer. How came 100,000 men (half of them of our own race) to hold up their hands to an inferior number of Japanese? Though his mind had been gradually prepared for its fall, the surrender of the fortress stunned him. It left a scar on his mind. One evening, months later, when he was sitting in his bathroom enveloped in a towel, he stopped drying himself and gloomily surveyed the floor: 'I cannot get over Singapore,' he said sadly.[5]

Churchill's involvement in, and the degree of his responsibility for, the catastrophe (and associated military errors) has received much discussion from historians, as has the way he dealt with the issue when he came to write *The Second World War*.[6] The purpose of this chapter, by contrast, is to consider the symbolism of the loss of Singapore. Its focus is less on high policy and military strategy than on the imperial language of Churchill and others, and its reception in Britain and elsewhere.

Ronald Hyam has suggested that Churchill "was not all that interested in the empire, apart from its rhetorical potentialities, and as distinct from what he regarded as the larger and more portentous issues of international relations".[7] Yet if we want to understand fully how he and his contemporaries attempted to promote their views in Britain and abroad, then the "rhetorical potentialities" of Empire are exactly what we need to consider. Historians of empire discuss the language of imperialism a great deal, although they do not tend to distinguish between (written) "discourse" and (spoken) "rhetoric".[8] Meanwhile — in contrast to the thriving state of rhetorical studies in the United States[9] — scholars of modern Britain have paid comparatively little explicit attention to political rhetoric. There are signs that this may be changing, with some recent work considering the imperial and post-imperial dimensions of British political rhetoric.[10] Churchill is one of the few British figures whose rhetoric has been examined at length, although the focus has generally been on his great wartime and Cold War speeches; the imperial dimension has not received sustained analysis.[11] If it is to be fruitful, such an analysis must do more than examine the particular rhetorical effects that Churchill sought; his language must be put in the context not only of his own career and ideology, but also of the norms and ideological expectations of the society that surrounded him. That is to say, without an understanding of "the context of refutation" — that is, the arguments a speaker is attacking and seeking to rebut — a narrow focus on a series of "great speeches" will not take us very far.[12] We must also remember that Churchill was not just a political actor in the story of Empire and its decline, but also a symbol of it. His reputation was subject to manipulation and contestation in the rhetoric of others — and it was also, of course, a resource upon which he could draw himself.

In recent years, there has been much historical debate about the degree to which the British people were informed about, or cared about, their Empire. Bernard Porter has argued, controversially, that they were largely indifferent to it; and though he takes the story only up to the interwar years, he suggests that "the lack of imperial commitment that characterised the majority of the British people from the 1940s onwards was simply a continuation of what had gone before".[13] For this period, there is a considerable amount of survey evidence that can help us judge if Porter is correct. The material generated by the sociological organisation Mass-Observation (MO) is well-known; less familiar are some of the reports of the BBC's Listener Research Department, which used similar techniques, deploying 2,000 volunteer "Local Correspondents" to report back on opinion in their own circles.[14] Coverage of Empire themes is patchy in these reports, but what there is lends some support to Porter's viewpoint. A BBC report on the state of public opinion regarding India, carried out a few months before the fall of Singapore, found that the general point of view was one of benign indifference. Relatively few people considered themselves either "proud" or "ashamed" of Britain's Indian record. (Working-class people were more likely than middle-class ones to be ashamed.) A pharmacist in Blackpool reported that "Only about 10% of my contacts showed any interest in the Indian problem. On the whole, India is looked on as a foreign country — some parts of the British colonies in Africa are also similarly regarded — as distinct from Canada, Australia, New Zealand, etc., which are looked on as definitely English". Overall, the report found that the predominant opinion could be summarised in the following propositions:

(a) I suppose I ought to be interested in India, but it's all so complicated.

(b) We can safely leave Indian questions to be settled by the British Government.

(c) Britain genuinely intends to give India self-government as soon as she is ready for it.

(d) There is no inconsistency between our policy in India and our fight for freedom in Europe, because conditions are so different.

(e) We are bound to postpone any increase in self-government in India till after the war.[15]

Churchill could probably have taken a fair degree of comfort from this report. Although the mainstream public was seemingly far less emotionally involved with the Indian issue than he was, and perhaps keener on self-government for India, he would certainly have assented to propositions (b), (d) and (e) and might even have been prepared to pay grudging lip service to (c). Although he faced major battles within his own government over India, public opinion was quiescent. This would seem to prove Porter's point that there was no intense interest in imperial matters, but on the other hand, there seems to have been a general belief in Britain's good intentions and capacity to carry them out, albeit it was accepted that self-government was the likely outcome in the long term.

What kinds of information were available to the British people about Singapore itself? In his memoirs, Churchill described his shock at learning that the island was not an impregnable fortress, but it is worth noting that the image which had gained such a hold on him was in fact something of a novelty. During the controversy surrounding the 1924 Labour government's decision — later reversed — to abandon construction of the base, Lord Sydenham wrote to *The Times*. In his letter, he argued that "unlike Singapore, Pearl Harbor can easily be made impregnable".[16] The former General Sir Ian Hamilton (who was a friend of Churchill) replied, pouring scorn on the idea that any port could be made invulnerable to attack: "Port Arthur was 'impregnable' — until it was taken".[17] In a 1929 speech — in which he sought to play down the idea that the base posed any threat to Japan — Churchill himself dwelt not on any supposed "impregnability" of Singapore but on the part it could play in connecting Australia and New Zealand with the motherland.[18] In the late 1930s, however, with the naval base nearing completion, the British public was increasingly given the mistaken impression — which Churchill too absorbed — that the island was a "fortress".[19] In 1937, for example, the *London Illustrated News* ran an article headlined "Combined Manoeuvres Which Proved Singapore 'Invulnerable'".[20] In April 1941, a *Times* journalist writing on Japan's ambitions pointed out that although "Impregnable by sea, Singapore is exposed to land attack by the Malay peninsula and to air attack, if bases can be established within effective range".[21] However, the message of "impregnability" — reiterated by the Australian politician Sir Earl Page just days before Japan's attack on Pearl Harbor — was the dominant one.[22] This sense of complacency continued, even as the Japanese swept into Malaya. On January 1942, a Pathé newsreel package featured film of soldiers digging trenches, over which the announcer intoned: "North of Singapore in the Malay peninsula Australian troops help to make every inch of the way to the fortress island a death-trap for the yellow plague infecting the Straits Settlement".[23]

With this prior context in mind, let us consider the extent to which the loss of Singapore was understood in an imperial context. The events were, of course, mediated not only through press and radio reporting but also through Churchill's own public comments on the defeat: members of the public looked to him to interpret and explain things to them. On 15 February 1942, the BBC six o'clock news announced both that Churchill would speak that evening at nine and that the Japanese had announced the unconditional surrender of the garrison at Singapore.[24] Churchill presented his speech as a general review of the war. He stressed that, with the USA as a new ally, and with the USSR fighting more successfully than had seemed possible a few months earlier, Britain was in a better strategic position than it had been at the time of his previous broadcast, made in August 1941. His discussion of the fall of Singapore was brief, but he did acknowledge it to be a very serious "British and imperial defeat". He was silent on its causes; an omission perhaps prompted in part by security concerns, yet perhaps also by the difficulty of providing an explanation that was both reassuring and credible. He concluded by presenting the crisis as an opportunity which, as in 1940, would allow "the British race and nation" to demonstrate "its quality and its genius".[25] There was no suggestion in the speech that Singapore and Malaya in and of themselves had any particular imperial meaning or symbolic significance, and this was perfectly consistent with the relatively low priority that Churchill gave to the Pacific theatre. We may, however, surmise that his use of the term "imperial defeat" was not just a reference to the fact that Australian and Indian troops had been present in Singapore. Leo Amery, the Secretary of State for India, noted the next day that in Cabinet, Churchill was "eloquent [...] on the general loss of the white man's prestige. That indeed is pretty serious".[26]

Some, Amery included, found Churchill's speech impressive.[27] The overall response, however, was lukewarm. Harold Nicolson MP felt that his call for national unity and not criticism was reminiscent of Neville Chamberlain, and wrote in his diary that the broadcast "was not liked. The country is too nervous and irritable to be fobbed off with fine phrases".[28] With the exception of the *Daily Express*, those papers that offered comment tended to be critical. "We must endure anything, certainly", observed the *Daily Mail*, "but to go on offering us tears, sweat and blood in monotonous gloom of stoical resignation is now to confess ... that something is seriously wrong with the conduct of the war as a whole".[29] Cecil King, who directed the editorial policies of the *Sunday Pictorial* and *Daily Mirror*, wrote in his diary:

> He [Churchill] offered no suggestion of new men or new methods, but said that in the Russians' darkest hour they had supported Stalin, and we should support our leaders in the same way. Of course there is no parallel at all between Churchill, his record of failure and his Government of odds and ends, and Stalin, who has led Russia with much success for twenty years [...] The speech has had a reception in the newspapers this morning varying from hostile to chilly.[30]

Some concrete evidence of the reaction of the population as a whole can be gained from a BBC Listener Survey Report on the speech. This document, reproduced here as an appendix, is valuable, not least as equivalent surveys were not conducted for Churchill's other wartime speeches. Even so, it was prepared on the relatively narrow basis of 46 Local Correspondent reports. 65.4% of the adult population heard the broadcast and it achieved a "Popularity Index" of 62, which the report considered to be "undeniably a low figure".[31] It was indeed 30 points less than that achieved by Sir Stafford Cripps — former ambassador to Russia and now a leadership rival to Churchill — for his broadcast in the "Postscript" series the previous week.[32] Although some positive comments from listeners were reported — "Told us how things really are, straight from the shoulder" — the general feeling was that Churchill had failed to allay people's fears. The survey concluded:

> The reports reveal that a number of elements clearly played a part in determining the public reaction to the Prime Minister's broadcast. First there was grave concern at recent bad news. Secondly, long standing trust in Mr. Churchill as leader. Thirdly, considerable misgivings about some of the P.M.'s colleagues. Over against these came the broadcast which some felt was 'making the best of a bad job', while others felt it to be 'beating about the bush'. It is impossible not to detect a note of disappointment, both from those who hoped for better news in the broadcast, from those who hoped for new light on the recent perplexing set-backs, and from those who looked to the P.M. to provide new inspiration in dark times.[33]

It is notable that the report contains no explicit mention of the Empire: although Churchill had described the debacle as an "imperial defeat", it appears that the respondents saw it more as a military and leadership issue. This can also be seen, for example, in the comments of MO diarist Pam Ashford, who was a secretary in Glasgow: "Singapore! That is news indeed! There are recriminations galore! People say Mr. Churchill has taken on too much, he is a dictator etc., but when asked if they want Mr. Churchill to go, they hastily reply, 'No, but they want to see about half the cabinet go.'"[34]

There is, however, some evidence of the surrender having an impact on popular attitudes to Empire. A March 1942 MO survey on the latter topic found that "There is a very considerable body of guilt-feeling about the way the Empire has been acquired, and the way the colonies have been administered. This feeling, in some cases, seems to mitigate any apprehension or regret people may feel at the present precarious position of parts of the Empire". The report also concluded that few people seemed to be surprised to learn about "the 'bad' aspects of the Empire"; if anything, they were surprised at suggestions of its "good" aspects. The report concluded: "It would thus seem that events in Singapore, Malaya etc. fall into the preconceived pattern of a considerable number of people,

Plate 5.1 Cartoon by David Low: "Inquest on Malayan Reverses"

and a half-pleased half-despairing note of 'told you so' finds expression". This, though, was probably a less widespread viewpoint than the report suggested, as the sample included a heavily disproportionate number of "non-party socialists", who were likely to have had stronger anti-imperial feelings than the rest of the population.[35] A BBC survey the following year — at which point, of course, feelings induced by the loss of Singapore may have dissipated — found that only small minorities felt either unmixed pride or shame about Britain's colonial record. The vast majority believed the record was mixed, but over 70 per cent felt that the good outweighed the bad.[36]

It is also worth noting that left-wing attitudes to Empire were more complex than the MO report seemed to imply. Guilt and condemnation were not always uppermost. Nearly a month before the surrender, cartoonist David Low, a New Zealander, drew a cartoon captioned "Inquest on Malayan Reverses" (Plate 5.1).

Its message was that the public were paying too much attention to the "Out of date colonial system" as a cause of defeat when the real problem was "Not enough tools" (i.e., weapons).[37] Although critical of "Blimpish" attitudes to Indian and colonial freedom, Low was not hostile to the Empire per se, which he seems to have conceived of in terms of a relationship of equality between self-governing Dominions. As he recalled in his memoirs, "even before the shooting war with Japan began and especially after the miscalculations and errors of judgement of the Malayan campaign had arrived at the fall of Singapore, I had run a string of newspaper cartoons advocating closer consultation with the Pacific Dominions about their defence".[38] In this case, the impact of Singapore was double-edged. On the one hand, it provided an argument for greater imperial cohesion. On the other, it stimulated propaganda for the "Commonwealth ideal" based on mutual interdependence rather than diktat from London, thus potentially weakening imperial ties.

Elite figures seem to have been more likely than the majority of the population to view the Singapore defeat in imperial terms. Two days before the surrender, the Tory MP "Chips" Channon noted that "The country is more upset about the escape of the German battleships [through the English channel] than over Singapore".[39] Harold Nicolson, whose own diary confirms this point, took the opportunity for self-laceration: "We intellectuals must feel that in all these years we have derided the principles of force upon which our Empire is built".[40] Alan Brooke, the Chief of the Imperial General Staff, wrote in his diary: "If the army cannot fight better than it is doing at present we shall deserve to lose our Empire!"[41] The catastrophe does appear to have prompted some rethinking within government and the media of Britain's imperial role. In March, Africa expert Margery Perham published articles in *The Times* calling for a re-evaluation of the system of colonial administration in light of what had happened.[42] Taking its cue from this, *The Times* itself editorialised about the "lessons of Malaya", arguing that "The defect of the British Colonial system [...] is that it has been too long and too deeply rooted in the traditions of a bygone age, and that it has retained too much of that 'stratified' spirit of inequality and discrimination, whose last strongholds are now being attacked and eliminated in our contemporary [British] society".[43] Historian Wendy Webster has argued that in the aftermath of Singapore, British imperial propaganda increasingly emphasised "partnership and welfare".[44] These high ideals were of course frequently not lived up to in practice, but the shift in language was itself significant. This is not to say that racist attitudes were absent from the reaction to the defeat. *Daily Mail* cartoonist Leslie Illingworth depicted Japanese Prime Minister Hideki Tojo as a monkey, preening himself in colonial garb, including a plumed hat marked "Singapore", with the caption "Fun while its lasts"

Plate 5.2   Cartoon by Leslie Gilbert Illingworth: "Fun While it Lasts"

(Plate 5.2).[45] The Japanese, therefore, were presented as an inferior race unsuited to wear the white man's imperial clothes.

The Singapore surrender was a key factor in forcing Churchill to reconstruct his government. In particular, he was obliged to accept Cripps into the War Cabinet; and soon afterwards, he was forced to consent to a mission to India, headed by Cripps, carrying a plan to offer the country self-government after the war. On 11 March, after Churchill announced this in the Commons, "Chips" Channon recorded: "The House appreciated the solemnity of the moment, and that our great Empire of India was perhaps to be bartered away".[46] (The mission turned out to be a failure, but the very offer of self-government set a precedent from which it would be difficult to row back.) Churchill also had to manage discontent in Parliament. In Secret Session on 23 April, he rejected calls for an official inquiry into what had gone wrong, although he admitted that the army had underperformed. "Australian accounts reflect upon the Indian troops," he noted. "Other credible witnesses disparage the Australians". To probe too deeply, in other words, would open a wide field for intra-imperial recrimination and thus damage the prosecution of the war. (Churchill had been persuaded to tone down the original draft of this passage, but when the speech was published in 1946, it nonetheless created a furore in Australia.) After his disquisition on Singapore, he remarked: "I now leave the lesser war — for such I must regard this fearful struggle against the Japanese — and come to the major war against Germany and Italy".[47] Raymond Callahan hints that this reflected Churchill's sense of strategic priorities, which is undoubtedly true.[48] But it should also be noted that Churchill was making an astute rhetorical manoeuvre. By suggesting that too much investigation would damage the Empire and the war effort, and that the Far Eastern theatre was at any rate a second order problem, he successfully deflected some of the heat from his own government, whilst simultaneously disclaiming any intention to safeguard his administration. The Tory MP Cuthbert Headlam wrote: "Today's effort [i.e., Churchill's speech] was, I thought, a very fine one — and none of his critics made any reply to it — not even complaining at his refusal to hold an enquiry on Singapore — they prefer to speak in public so that they can advertise themselves".[49]

The loss of Singapore, of course, was not just a military fact or a domestic political problem; it was a global media event. Enemy propagandists, therefore, rushed to exploit it, heaping scorn on Churchill's speech in the process.[50] Some of the German propaganda aimed at Britain was cack-handed. "Well workers, Churchill has been spouting again, and we're just about sick and tired about it," ran one broadcast. "The trouble about Churchill is that he's a skunk, and that nothing can de-skunk him".[51] William Joyce, by contrast, was comparatively subtle, making play with Churchill's implicit admission that Britain was now reliant on the power of the USA:

> It was [...] natural to wonder what Churchill would say to assure his people that some barrier would be created to arrest, if only for the time, the flood of defeat which is now pouring over the British Empire. Read the speech twenty times and you will find no such assurance [...] In the past the British used to say: 'We may lose every battle but the last. The last battle, however, we win.' But now that hope is gone, for apparently Churchill is expecting the United States to win the last battle for him.[52]

It is doubtful that these arguments had much effect in Britain. In Germany of course — although some ran the risk involved in listening to the BBC — the population was almost wholly dependent on Nazi sources for their information. Even there, however, the reaction to the surrender and to Churchill's speech was surprisingly ambivalent. This is clear from an SS report on public opinion. Although there was pleasure at the triumph of Germany's Japanese ally, there was also a sense that not only the British but white people in general had suffered a defeat. There was much talk of the "yellow peril" (*Gelben Gefahr*). The extracts from Churchill's speech and commentaries on it that the German media provided attracted much attention. Many people noted that Churchill did not hesitate to report bad news and to outline the severity of Britain's situation. They concluded from this that in spite of their heavy defeats, the British people were holding their nerve and remained steadfast.[53]

Axis broadcasts aimed at India and the Arab world were potentially more dangerous to the Allied cause than those received in Britain. The "Voice of Free Arabs" station noted that Churchill's speech had made no effort to turn the surrender into a "heroic defeat" on the lines of Dunkirk:

> We thought that Churchill, as usual, would speak of so-called glorious British victories, converting defeats into outstanding victories, but we were surprised when this criminal butcher told the truth [...] The fall of Singapore means the defeat of the British Empire [...] We, the Arabs, are well aware of the fact that the British Empire [,] which has been built up on tyranny and savagery, will not survive this war.[54]

Similar messages, adjusted for the different audiences, were broadcast in Afrikaans to South Africa and in Hindustani to India. According to the BBC monitoring report, one broadcaster "addressed himself to Churchill personally, saying that 'your treacherous bastard nation has kept India in slavery'".[55] A report to the British Cabinet in March 1942 noted that "The fall of Singapore and the further advances made by the Japanese inevitably increased anxieties in India, particularly in the cities and towns of the Eastern seaboard. The spread of anti-war and defeatist rumours throughout the month [of February], encouraged by Axis broadcasts and by stories circulated by-evacuees from the overrun territories, caused serious concern".[56] The image of Churchill with his cigar proved to be a poor tool for the British in their own Indian propaganda. As an intelligence report observed in July, "the Indians' conception of a leader involves the spiritual and the symbolic, not the prosaic and ordinary".[57]

Predictably enough, the reception of the fall of Singapore in different parts of the Empire varied according to the nearness or otherwise of the

Japanese threat. In Canada, secure by virtue of its proximity to the United States, press comment "was marked by an attitude of dejection", according to a report to the British Cabinet:

> The fall of Singapore was regarded as almost inevitable, so that no particular surprise was evinced, at the news of its capture [...] The escape of the German battleships from Brest overshadowed, however, even the bad news from Singapore. Many Canadian newspapers quoted angry United Kingdom press comment on the incident, but, in general, themselves maintained a reasonable and balanced view.[58]

Meanwhile, Canadian Prime Minister W.L. Mackenzie King noted the fall of Singapore in his diary but appears to have seen this "momentous" event primarily as a problem for Britain, rather than for Canada or for the wider Empire. He praised Churchill's broadcast as "a manly endeavour to brace the country against the most desperate situation with which it has been faced since the fall of France", but he also commented on Churchill's "terrible omission which was no reference to Canada". Whilst claiming to understand this, Mackenzie King grumbled about it at some length, complaining that Churchill consistently paid him and Canada less attention than Roosevelt did. "Is it to be wondered at that some peoples [sic] some times think that Canada counts for little in the eyes of Britain except where she can be used to some purpose", he wrote.[59]

In the Southern Dominions, the anxiety was more intense and the reaction complex. Even before the surrender, British-Australian relations had become fractious, with politicians in Canberra increasingly concerned that the British were giving insufficient priority to their defence.[60] In a famous New Year message to his people, Labour Prime Minister John Curtin declared that Australia refused to "accept the dictum that the Pacific struggle must be treated as a subordinate segment of the general conflict" and that the country now looked "to America, free of any pangs as to our traditional links or kinship with the United Kingdom".[61] Arguably, the significance of this as an imperial rupture has been exaggerated; Curtin himself remained attached to the British and Empire connections, which he viewed in terms of "race patriotism".[62] In the short term, relations between Curtin and Churchill deteriorated. British officials tended to contrast the "narrow, selfish" Australians with the (more distant and safer) New Zealanders, who were seen as "a tower of strength".[63] Australian fears were heightened a few days after the Singapore surrender when the Japanese launched a major air attack on Darwin. However, the consequences for imperial cohesion were not all negative: "Although anxiety for the safety of Australia increased rapidly, the attitude of the general public in regard to United Kingdom leadership steadied, and criticism of this country practically disappeared now that war is at the very gates of Australia". Moreover, although the week of the fall of Singapore and the escape of the German battleships "was regarded in Australia as one of the grimmest of the war [...] the general reaction to these events was to maintain the belief in Mr. Churchill's leadership". Churchill's Cabinet changes were also well received; and the inclusion of the Secretary of State for the Dominions Affairs in the War Cabinet, in the person of Clement Attlee, helped kill off previous pressure for direct Dominion representation in it. The New Zealanders, for their part, did not quite live up to their caricatured reputation for pluck and loyalty: "The fall of Singapore, when it came, quickened apprehension in New Zealand over the country's relative impotence, and an undercurrent of defeatist talk was noticed, arising probably from the insidious influence of Tokyo broadcasts, which have had a large audience". The Cabinet was also told that the fall of Singapore had "done much to destroy the South African attitude of detachment towards the war", with even the Afrikaner nationalist opposition press acknowledging the possibility of a direct attack on South Africa. Nevertheless, these newspapers lost "no opportunity of indulging in carping criticism of the Government [of J.C. Smuts] for having continued in the war".[64] Interestingly, in 1924, Smuts' earlier administration had been the only Dominion government to support Ramsay MacDonald's plan to abandon the construction of the Singapore base.[65]

The United States' reactions were also of vital significance. A report from the British Embassy in Washington noted on 19 February, "The events of the past week have led to greatly increased criticism of Great Britain in this country".[66] From Churchill's perspective, the chief danger was that perceptions of British military-colonial incompetence would contribute to an upsurge in US anti-imperialism, with consequences for the shape of the post-war world. Churchill's own differences of opinion with Americans over the question of Empire pre-dated the Boer War.[67] Now, the celebrated and widely-syndicated columnist Walter Lippmann wrote:

> As Mr. Churchill explained in his speech on Sunday, the main burden of the Eastern war rests upon the United States. With this responsibility must go authority in the political conduct of the war. Now it is evident that for the American people the objective of the Eastern war is not and cannot be the recapture and restoration of the white man's empire [...] And now that Singapore and what it represents and symbolizes have fallen, we are bound to wage the war on the principle that the freedom and security of the peoples of Asia is the best guarantee of our own future in the Pacific.[68]

Later in the year, Wendell Willkie, the Republican candidate defeated by Roosevelt in 1940, called for the "orderly but scheduled abolition of the colonial system".[69] Such views, in combination with the growing demand that in future, colonies should be subjected to some form of international control or "trusteeship", form the essential context for understanding Churchill's famous speech at London's Mansion House in November 1942.[70] On that occasion, which took place shortly after the victory at El Alamein and the turning of the war's tide in favour of the Allies, the Prime Minister declared: "We mean to hold our own. I have not become the King's First Minister in order to preside over the liquidation of the British Empire".[71] As Mackenzie King observed to Roosevelt, the "liquidation" remark "was an answer to Willkie", who in turn criticised Churchill's defence of "the old imperialistic order".[72] Moreover, the assumption, articulated by Lippmann, that American military power on the ground should translate into responsibility for determining the political future of the Far East, was a danger to Britain's interests as viewed by Churchill. This meant that Britain had to secure its own stake by playing as big a role in the Pacific theatre as it could, irrespective of immediate necessity; the British had to be seen to re-conquer their lost Asian Empire themselves, in order to safeguard their future role in the region. Hence, when the Allied South-East Asia Command (SEAC) — which was eventually to reconquer Burma — was created under Lord Louis Mountbatten in 1943, the Americans nicknamed it "Save England's Asiatic Colonies".[73]

In conclusion, examining the domestic, imperial and international reception of the loss of Singapore and of Churchill's rhetoric about it points to a number of lessons. First, Churchill proved unable to convert the surrender into a "heroic defeat" as had been done with Dunkirk; in fact, he did not even try to do so. Arguably, no amount of linguistic skill could explain away or compensate for the abject military failure at Singapore, a failure which some, like Lippmann, portrayed as symbolic of the failure of the British colonial system as a whole. Although Churchill's broadcast was not received too badly under the circumstances, his acknowledgment of US military strength — intended to comfort British listeners in the face of their own country's military weakness — could be used against him by enemy propagandists and American critics of Empire alike. The evidence suggests, however, that Churchill's defiant speech was more successful in achieving its intended effect in Germany than it was at home.

Second, the debacle did little to damage the British people's confidence in Churchill's personal leadership, even though it cast doubt on the competence of the conduct of the war in general. Moreover, the fall of

Singapore was not understood by the British people primarily in imperial terms, nor even as important militarily as the escape of the German warships, an episode which, after all, took place considerably closer to home. As the MO diarist Henry Novy put it, "The Far East is bad enough but when you hear the English Channel is a clear passage to three German battleships … well!"[74] In the Dominions, by contrast, the defeat did cause some questioning of the imperial relationship, but there was also an element of drawing together in the face of adversity. Although opinion in the "non-white" parts of the Empire is difficult to assess, it seems that the fall of Singapore was much more likely to be seen there as heralding "the end of the British Empire". This, of course, was a common theme of enemy propaganda, but such propaganda could only be successful insofar as it played on genuine pre-existing grievances, which were manifold.

Together, these points may help explain why there is little if any memorialisation of the battle of Singapore in Britain — unlike in Australia, or in Singapore itself. From around 1938, and particularly during 1941, the British had been subject to fairly heavy propaganda depicting the island as an impregnable fortress, and they undoubtedly disliked losing it, especially to a "yellow" race.[75] As Cuthbert Headlam MP wrote on 8 February 1942, "clearly the defence of Singapore is not going to last much longer", adding, "to be beaten and humiliated in this way by Asiatics is almost more than a Victorian Englishman can bear!"[76] Yet it is notable that he was more upset by the damage to his racial pride then by the loss of Singapore per se. Military catastrophe made Singapore look like the symbol of everything that was wrong with the British Empire, but not at the expense of any particularly strong or positive popular image. Churchill may not have been able to get over the loss of Singapore; but, with the notable exception of those POWs who lost their lives or their health in Japanese camps, most of the rest of the British people seem to have succeeded in getting over it very well.

LR/713

A Listener Research Report
Confidential

THE PRIME MINISTER'S BROADCAST

before the 9.00 p.m. News on Sunday, 15th February, 1942

1. Normally one section of the panel of Local Correspondents report on each Sunday night Postscript. On Sunday, 15th February, however, there was no Postscript. Instead, the News was preceded by a long broadcast by the Prime Minister. Most Local Correspondents, therefore, made no report, but as 46 did so, and as their reports like all those of Local Correspondents, reflect the reactions of the circles in which they move, this report upon them has been prepared.

2. As always when he broadcasts at a peak listening hour the Prime Minister has an enormous audience, 65.4% of the adult population listened to him (61.5% kept their sets on for the News afterwards).

3. The Popularity Index, calculated on the admittedly slender basis of 46 reports, was, however, only 62. This is undeniably a low figure and is 30 points less than the Popularity Index for Sir Stafford Cripps' Postscript the previous Sunday. The Index might have been higher had the sample been bigger, but it must be admitted that there is just as much likelihood that it erred on the high as on the low side.

4. The following comments illustrate the tenor of public opinion as revealed by these replies:

    > Told us how things really are, straight from the shoulder — no false optimism, but not despondent. If only we had more men like him.
    >
    > (NCD 2753) Shearer, Sheffield

Dismaying and serious as the situation was he compelled one to see things in a truer perspective.

(NCD 2808) House Duties, Harrogate

Whilst still courageous, brave and pugnacious, the speech did nothing to allay the fears of further failures and feelings of frustration. There was no new attitude to the war, to strategy or production. We are tired of soothing syrups and are neither children nor fools.

(NX 1657) Housewife, Barnoldswick

The fall of Singapore, plus the scramble from Brest left people anxious. Harking back to 1940 was not good psychology, the address was too long; in substance it should have been — we can take defeats but will not take final defeat — we must fight! fight! and win!

(MX 1094) Estate Office Clerk, Walsall

What he said was good, but what he did not say was more significant.

(NCD 902) Housewife, Bacup

To many devoted admirers of the P.M. this was his first Postscript (sic) that failed to convince and inspire.

(NX 973) Social Welfare Worker, Leeds

5. The reports reveal that a number of elements clearly played a part in determining the public reaction to the Prime Minister's broadcast. First there was grave concern at recent bad news. Secondly, long standing trust in Mr. Churchill as leader. Thirdly, considerable misgivings about some of the P.M.'s colleagues. Over against these came the broadcast which some felt was "making the best of a bad job", while others felt it to be "beating about the bush". It is impossible not to detect a note of disappointment, both from those who hoped for better news in the broadcast, from those who hoped for new light on the recent perplexing set-backs, and from those who looked to the P.M. to provide new inspiration in dark times.

Listener Research Department
3rd March 1942

Notes

1. I am grateful to Richard Overy and Kristine Vaaler for assistance and suggestions. Any errors are of course my own responsibility.
2. Winston S. Churchill, *The Second World War, Vol. IV: The Hinge of Fate* (London: Cassell, 1951), p. 81.
3. Christopher Bayly and Tim Harper, *Forgotten Armies: Britain's Asian Empire and the War with Japan* (London: Allen Lane, 2004), p. 130.
4. Talk by William Joyce, in English for England and North America, 16 February 1942, quoted in Daily Digest of Foreign Broadcasts, 16–17 February 1942, BBC Written Archives, Caversham.
5. Lord Moran, *Winston Churchill: The Struggle for Survival, 1940–1965* (London: Constable, 1968 [1966]), p. 43.
6. See, in particular, Raymond A. Callahan, "Churchill and Singapore", in *Sixty Years On: The Fall of Singapore Revisited*, eds. Brian Farrell and Sandy Hunter (Singapore: Eastern Universities Press, 2002), pp. 156–72; Christopher Bell, "The 'Singapore Strategy' and the Deterrence of Japan: Winston Churchill, the Admiralty, and the Dispatch of Force Z", in *English Historical Review* 116 (2001): 604–34; ibid., "Winston Churchill, Pacific Security, and the Limits of British Power, 1921–41", in *Churchill and Strategic Dilemmas before the World Wars*, ed. John H. Maurer (London: Frank Cass, 2003), pp. 51–87; and David Reynolds, *In Command of History: Churchill Fighting and Writing the Second World War* (London: Allen Lane, 2004), pp. 294–8.
7. Ronald Hyam, *Britain's Declining Empire* (Cambridge: Cambridge University Press, 2006), p. 172.
8. For example, Richard Koebner and Helmut Dan Schmidt, *Imperialism: The Story and Significance of a Political Word, 1840–1960* (Cambridge: Cambridge University Press, 1964), and David Spurr, *The Rhetoric of Empire: Colonial Intercourse in Journalism, Travel Writing, and Imperial Administration* (Durham, NC: Duke University Press, 1993).
9. A key text is Jeffrey K. Tulis, *The Rhetorical Presidency* (Princeton, NJ: Princeton University Press, 1987).
10. H.C.G. Matthew, "Rhetoric and Politics in Britain, 1860–1950", in *Politics and Social Change in Modern Britain*, ed. P.J. Waller (Brighton: Harvester, 1987), pp. 34–58; Jonathan Charteris-Black, *Politicians and Rhetoric: The Persuasive Power of Metaphor* (Basingstoke: Palgrave Macmillan, 2005); Alan Finlayson and James Martin, "'It Ain't What You Say …': British Political Studies and the Analysis of Speech and Rhetoric", *British Politics* 3 (2008): 445–64; and Ben Jackson, "The Rhetoric of Redistribution", in *In Search of Social Democracy: Responses to Crisis and Modernisation*, eds. John Callaghan *et al.* (Manchester: Manchester University Press, 2009), pp. 233–51. For the Empire/Commonwealth dimension, see Philip Williamson, *Stanley Baldwin: Conservative Leadership and National Values* (Cambridge: Cambridge University Press, 1999); Frank Myers, "Harold Macmillan's 'Winds of Change'

Speech: A Case Study in the Rhetoric of Policy Change", *Rhetoric & Public Affairs* 3 (2000): 555–75; and Andrew S. Thompson, "The Language of Imperialism and the Meanings of Empire: Imperial Discourse in British Politics, 1895–1914", *Journal of British Studies* 36 (1997): 147–77.

11. For discussion of Churchill's rhetoric, see, for example, Manfred Weidhorn, "Churchill the Phrase Forger", *Quarterly Journal of Speech* 58 (1972): 161–74; Henry B. Ryan, "A New Look at Churchill's 'Iron Curtain' Speech", *The Historical Journal* 22 (1979): 895–920; David Cannadine, *In Churchill's Shadow: Confronting the Past in Modern Britain* (London: Allen Lane, 2002), Chapter 4; and John Lukacs, *Blood, Toil, Tears & Sweat: The Dire Warning* (New York: Basic Books, 2008).

12. Stefan Collini, *Liberalism and Sociology: L. T. Hobhouse and Political Argument in England 1880–1914* (Cambridge: Cambridge University Press, 1979), p. 9.

13. Bernard Porter, *The Absent-Minded Imperialists: Empire, Society and Culture in Britain* (Oxford: Oxford University Press, 2004), p. 282. See also ibid., "Further Thoughts on Imperial Absent-Mindedness", *Journal of Imperial and Commonwealth History* 36 (2008): 101–17, and John M. MacKenzie, "'Comfort' and Conviction: A Response to Bernard Porter", *Journal of Imperial and Commonwealth History* 36 (2008): 659–68.

14. The listener research reports for 1937–1950 are now available online, via subscription, at <www.britishonlinearchives.co.uk>, with a valuable introduction by Siân Nicholas: "The Good Servant: The Origins and Development of BBC Listener Research 1936–1950".

15. BBC Listener Research Department, "A Listener Research Report: 'India': The State of British Public Opinion on India in the Autumn [of] 1941", LR/382, 20 October 1941.

16. Lord Sydenham to the editor of *The Times*, 24 March 1924.

17. Ian Hamilton to the editor of *The Times*, 25 March 1924.

18. Speech of 16 August 1929, in David Dilks, *'The Great Dominion': Winston Churchill in Canada, 1900–1954* (Toronto: Thomas Allen, 2005), pp. 73–4.

19. "The Manoeuvres at Singapore", *The Times*, 5 February 1937; Reynolds, *In Command of History*, p, 115.

20. *London Illustrated News*, 27 February 1937.

21. "Greater East Asia", *The Times*, 1 April 1941.

22. "Pacific Defences Impregnable", *The Times*, 26 November 1941.

23. The segment, entitled "News From Singapore", was released on 15 January 1942. It is available at <www.britishpathe.com>.

24. Helen D. Millgate, ed., *Mr. Brown's War: A Diary of the Second World War*, Stroud, 2003 (1998), p. 149 (entry for 15 February 1942).

25. "Mr. Churchill's Call For New Resolution", *The Times*, 16 February 1942.

26. John Barnes and David Nicholson, eds., *The Empire at Bay: The Leo Amery Diaries, 1929–1945* (London, 1988), p. 774 (entry for 16 February 1942).

27. Ibid., p. 773 (entry for 15 February 1942). See also Millgate, *Mr. Brown's War*, p. 149 (entry for 15 February 1942).

28. Nigel Nicolson, ed., *Harold Nicolson: Diaries and Letters 1939–1945* (London: Collins, 1967), pp. 211–2 (entries for 15 and 16 February 1942).

29. Quoted in "Churchill Assures British Allies are Capable of Squaring All Accounts", *Evening Independent* (St Petersburg, Florida), 16 February 1942.

30. Cecil King, *With Malice Toward None: A War Diary* (London: Sidgwick and Jackson, 1970), pp. 158–9 (entry for 16 February 1942).

31. BBC Listener Survey Department, "A Listener Report: The Prime Minister's Broadcast before the 9.00 p.m. News on Sunday, 15th February, 1942", LR/713, 3 March 1942.

32. Churchill disliked Cripps' Postscript and Cripps was highly critical of Churchill's broadcast. Mark Pottle, ed., *Champion Redoubtable: The Diaries and Letters of Violet Bonham Carter, 1914–1945* (London: Weidenfeld & Nicholson, 1998), pp. 235, 239 (entries for 11 and 19 Febuary 1942).

33. BBC Listener Survey Department, "A Listener Report: The Prime Minister's Broadcast before the 9.00 p.m. News on Sunday, 15th February, 1942", LR/713, 3 March 1942.

34. Pam Ashford diary, 16 February 1942, in *Private Battles: How The War Almost Defeated Us*, ed. Simon Garfield (London: Ebury Press, 2007 [2006]), p. 214.

35. "Feelings About the British Empire", Mass-Observation File Report 1158, March 1942, Mass-Observation Archive, University of Sussex. Moreover, MO was a self-consciously "progressive" organisation, and some observers may have been inclined to interpret what they heard so as to fit in with their own point of view.

36. BBC Listener Research Department, "The British Empire: Some Aspects of Public Opinion on the British Empire, and in Particular, the Colonial Empire (January 1943)", LR/1558, 22 February 1943.

37. *Evening Standard*, 16 January 1942.

38. David Low, *Low's Autobiography* (London: Michael Joseph, 1956), p. 345.

39. Robert Rhodes James, ed., *'Chips': The Diaries of Sir Henry Channon* (London: Weidenfeld and Nicolson, 1993 [1967]), p. 321 (entry for 13 February 1942). Similarly, see George Orwell, "The British Crisis: London Letter to *Partisan Review*", 8 May 1942, in *The Collected Essays, Journalism and Letters of George Orwell, Vol. 2: My Country Right or Left, 1940–1943*, eds. Sonia Orwell and Ian Angus (London: Penguin, 1970 [1968]), pp. 246–7: "It is hard to assess how much the man in the street cared about the Singapore disaster. Working-class people seemed to me to be more impressed by the escape of the German warships from Brest".

40. Nicolson, *Harold Nicolson Diaries*, p. 214 (entry for 27 February 1942).

41. Alex Danchev and Daniel Todman, eds., *War Diaries, 1939–1945: Field Marshal Lord Alanbrooke* (London: Weidenfeld and Nicolson, 2001), p. 231 (entry for 17 February 1942).

42. Margery Perham, "The Colonial Empire", I and II, *The Times*, 13 and 14 March 1942.

43. "The Colonial Future", *The Times*, 14 March 1942.

44. Wendy Webster, *Englishness and Empire 1939–1965* (Oxford: Oxford University Press, 2005), pp. 26, 28–9.

45. *Daily Mail*, 18 February 1942.

46. Rhodes James, *'Chips'*, p. 324 (entry for 11 March 1942).

47. Charles Eade, ed., *Secret Session Speeches By the Right Hon. Winston S. Churchill O.M., C.H., M.P.* (London: Cassell and Co, 1946), pp. 55, 65. For the modifications to the speech, see Allen Packwood's Chapter 3 in this volume. For the post-war controversy, see "Singapore Inquiry Needed 'To Clear the Air'", *Sydney Morning Herald*, 28 January 1946; "Defence of Singapore's Vanquished", *The Straits Times*, 31 July 1947; and the correspondence in the UK National Archives, Kew, London, PREM8/316.

48. Callahan, "Churchill and Singapore", p. 160.

49. Stuart Ball, ed., *Parliament and Politics in the Age of Churchill and Attlee: The Headlam Diaries, 1935–1951* (Cambridge: Cambridge University Press for the Royal Historical Society, 1999), pp. 308–9 (entry for 23 April 1942).

50. Interestingly, Reich Propaganda Minister Joseph Goebbels, who spent much of 1941 predicting the collapse of the British Empire, published an article in November of that year suggesting that this was unlikely to take place imminently. Goebbels considered Churchill to be a formidable opponent. Ernest K. Bramsted, *Goebbels and National Socialist Propaganda 1925–1945* (N.P.: The Cresset Press, 1965), pp. 423–4, 428–35.

51. "Workers' Challenge", in English for England, 16 February 1942, quoted in Daily Digest of Foreign Broadcasts, 16–17 February 1942, BBC Written Archives.

52. Talk by William Joyce, 16 February 1942, quoted in Daily Digest of Foreign Broadcasts, 16–17 February 1942, BBC Written Archives.

53. Report of 19 February 1942, in *Meldungen Aus Dem Reich 1938–1945: Die geheimen Lageberichte des Sicherheitsdienste der SS*, Vol. 9, ed. Heinz Boberach (Berlin: Pawlak Verlag Herrsching, 1984), pp. 3338–9.

54. Voice of Free Arabs, 16 February 1942, quoted in Daily Digest of Foreign Broadcasts, 16–17 February 1942, BBC Written Archives.

55. "In Afrikaans for South Africa", 16 February 1942, and "In Hindustani for India", 16 February 1942, both quoted in Daily Digest of Foreign Broadcasts, 16–17 February 1942, BBC Written Archives.

56. NA, CAB68/9/17, "Report for the Month of February 1942 for the Dominions, India, Burma and the Colonies, and Mandated Territories", WP(R) (42)17, 25 March 1942.

57. "Monthly Intelligence Summary no. 7", 6 July 1942, quoted in Philip Woods, "From Shaw to Shantaram: The Film Advisory Board and the making of British propaganda films in India, 1940–1943", *Historical Journal of Film, Radio and Television* 21 (2001): 293–308, at 299.

58. NA, CAB68/9/17, "Report for the Month of February 1942 for the Dominions, India, Burma and the colonies, and mandated territories", WP(R) (42)17, 25 March 1942.

59. W.L. Mackenzie King diary, 15 February 1942, at <www.collectionscanada. gc.ca>.

60. For the Anglo-Australian dimension of the Second World War, see David Day, *The Politics of War* (Sydney: Harper Collins, 2003), and also Graham Freudenberg, *Churchill and Australia* (Sydney: Macmillan, 2008), Chapters 13–31.

61. "Battle for the Pacific Comes First", *Canberra Times*, 29 December 1941.

62. James Curran, "An Organic Part of the Whole Structure': John Curtin's Empire", *Journal of Imperial and Commonwealth History* 37 (2009): 51–75.

63. Ian Jacob diary (27 December 1941), in *The Churchill War Papers, Vol. III: The Ever Widening War: 1941*, ed. Martin Gilbert (New York: W.W. Norton & Co., 2000), p. 1698.

64. NA, CAB68/9/17, "Report for the Month of February 1942 for the Dominions, India, Burma and the Colonies, and Mandated Territories", WP(R) (42)17, 25 March 1942.

65. The Irish Free State and Canada were non-committal, whereas Newfoundland, New Zealand and Australia protested at the decision, which, of course, was later reversed by Stanley Baldwin's Conservative government. "Dominion Premiers Differ Regarding Singapore Project", *Montreal Gazette*, 26 March 1924.

66. H.G. Nicholas, ed., *Washington Despatches 1941–1945: Weekly Reports from the British Embassy* (Chicago: University of Chicago Press, 1981), p. 19.

67. Richard Toye, *Churchill's Empire: The World That Made Him and the World He Made* (London: Macmillan, 2010), p. 23.

68. Walter Lippmann, "The Post-Singapore War in the East", *Montreal Gazette*, 21 February 1942.

69. "Commonwealth of the World", *The Times*, 28 October 1942.

70. William Roger Louis, *Imperialism at Bay: The United States and the Decolonization of the British Empire, 1941–1945* (Oxford: Oxford University Press, 1977), p. 8.

71. Speech of 10 November 1942, in *Churchill Speaks 1897–1963: Collected Speeches in Peace and War*, ed. Robert Rhodes James (Leicester: Windward, 1981), p. 810.

72. Mackenzie King diary, 5 December 1942; "Old Imperialistic Order", *The Times*, 18 November 1942.

73. Philip Ziegler, "Mountbatten, Louis Francis Albert Victor Nicholas, first Earl Mountbatten of Burma (1900–1979)", in *Oxford Dictionary of National Biography* (Oxford: Oxford University Press, 2004); online edition, January 2008.

74. Henry Novy, diary entry for 15 February 1942, in *Our Longest Days: A People's History of the Second World War*, ed. Sandra Koa Wing (London: Profile Books, 2008 [2007]), p. 115.

75. Henry Novy, diary entry for 15 December 1941, in ibid, p. 107.

76. Ball, *Parliament and Politics*, p. 294 (entry for 8 February 1942).

CHAPTER 6

Churchill, Singapore and Australia's Strategic Policy

Peter Edwards

Australians have long been ambivalent towards Winston Churchill. His courage and leadership during Britain's, and his, finest hour have been fully recognised; his reputation as perhaps the greatest statesman of the 20th century seldom challenged. Australians were among the most generous donors to the Churchill Trust that established the Churchill Fellowships.[1] But alongside these positive attitudes have been currents of reservation, at times open hostility, which have left their mark even into this century. If one had to distil the reasons for those negative attitudes into two words, they would be Gallipoli and Singapore. To many Australians, April 1915 and February 1942 represent the sacrifice of Australian men because of bad strategic planning, some would say bad faith, on the part of the British politico-military establishment in general and of Churchill in particular.

In Australian popular history, a frequently heard myth links Churchill, Australia and the fall of Singapore. Most commonly voiced by Australian Labor Party sympathisers, but by no means confined to them, it goes like this. The Labor Prime Minister John Curtin, who stood up for Australian interests unlike his predecessor, the arch-imperialist Robert Menzies, exchanged a series of terse and bitter cables with Winston Churchill in late 1941 and early 1942. In these, Curtin demanded, and finally succeeded in gaining, the return of Australian troops from the Middle East to defend Australia against the Japanese threat. He also denounced the incompetence and bad faith surrounding the defence of Malaya and Singapore, at one point telling Churchill that one proposed action would constitute an "inexcusable betrayal" of Australia. Churchill was, of course, infuriated but Curtin's stand, according to the popular account, was not only brave, but right. Curtin became so disillusioned with Britain that he made his famous statement that "Australia looks to America, free of any pangs as to its traditional links and kinship with the United Kingdom". He established a close relationship with General Douglas MacArthur, Commander of allied forces in the South West Pacific Area. This, according to the longstanding myth, was the origin of the Australian-American alliance, which has been the foundation of Australia's foreign and defence policies ever since.

Historians have challenged this simplistic interpretation from a number of different directions for nearly 40 years, but it retains a strong hold on the Australian public mind and variations on this theme are still common. This chapter will approach it from a different direction, re-assessing the place of the fall of Singapore in February 1942, and the association of Winston Churchill with that catastrophe, in the long-term development of Australian strategic policy, between the 1920s and 1930s, and the 1950s and 1960s.

For most of the last 200 years, Australians' approach to their national security has generally been based on the tension between two fundamental concepts, each of which has a strong hold on the public mind. One asserts that Australia is a large but sparsely populated continent, set in an alien and potentially hostile environment, far distant from the sources of its culture and values, and incapable of defending itself without close relationships with the countries that its longest-serving Prime Minister, Robert Menzies, famously called "our great and powerful friends", meaning Britain and more recently the United States. The other perspective asserts that to rely on these powerful but distant allies is highly problematic; that they may lack the desire and/or the capacity to help Australia in its hour of need; that close association with these powerful but distant allies leads to Australian involvement in "other people's wars"; and that Australia must therefore make its own way in the Asia Pacific region, asserting its independence and assuring its security by making its own friends and alliances in the region. The tug between these two views has often been portrayed as the struggle between imperial alliance and national independence, or between our history and our geography. It might better be seen as the debate between a global and a regional perspective. Participants in the never-ending debate between these two positions draw their evidence from conflicts ranging from Sudan in the 1880s to Afghanistan today, but they most frequently turn to the early years of the Second World War. That is why Australian books, movies, documentaries and websites turn again and again to discussions of Churchill and Menzies, Churchill and Curtin, Curtin and MacArthur, and the like.

Australian Prime Ministers have often been accused — and not only from within Australia — of leaning too far towards either the global or the regional view. In fact, in peacetime, they have usually tried to develop policies that would satisfy the Australian electorate that both these concepts were being addressed, and that any tensions between them were being resolved to the greatest extent possible in the geopolitical circumstances of the day. Towards this end, they have generally taken three steps. First, Australian governments have long sought the best possible access to the highest politico-military councils of their allies, if necessary by creating new structures to create that access. Second, while accepting that Australian forces will usually be deployed as part of a British-led or American-led coalition, Australian leaders have placed great emphasis on the right to state how and where their forces would be deployed within that coalition. And third, and importantly but often overlooked, Australian governments, whatever their party, have sought in peacetime to establish a strategic formula that responded to both the global and the regional imperatives in the public mind, to satisfy the electorate that the government knows that the public wants Australia to maintain strong alliances, but to do so in a way that is consistent with our national pride and our regional relationships. In effect, when critics have said that Australia has been too willing to fight "other people's wars", the political and military leaders have responded that they were getting powerful friends to fight, or preferably to prevent, our wars. All this has been true of every significant Prime Minister, from Alfred Deakin to Kevin Rudd.

Let us now place Churchill and the fall of Singapore into this longer-term perspective of Australian strategy. The famous cables exchanged by Curtin and Churchill in late 1941 and early 1942, so important in Australian mythology, did not come out of a clear blue sky of Anglo-Australian cooperation and reciprocal trust. For nearly half a century, it seemed to Australian governments that (in present-day jargon) Churchill simply did not get it — that is, he could not accept the validity of the national and regional element in Australian strategic thinking; nor could he countenance any view of the British Empire other than one in which London took all the major strategic and operational decisions, with at most token gestures towards consulting the overseas Dominions. Perhaps it reflected the fact that he never set foot in Australia — or New Zealand, or indeed Singapore — so that he never saw the world through Antipodean eyes. Whether in government or in opposition, whether he was a Liberal or a Conservative or part of a national coalition, he always opposed Australian leaders, from across the political spectrum, who were asserting the need for consultation, access or influence on the conduct of the Empire's political and military affairs, or who were asserting the need to balance the global and the regional imperatives in Australian policy.

Conflict over such matters began in 1907 when, as Parliamentary Under-Secretary for the Colonies in a Liberal government, Churchill opposed the efforts of Alfred Deakin to gain a greater voice for the Dominions in imperial councils. Between 1911 and 1915, as First Lord of the Admiralty, Churchill insisted on concentrating the Empire's naval forces in home waters, despite the obvious anxieties of the Antipodeans. But even then, Churchill showed that he understood one element of the Australian worldview. In early 1914, discussing Australian and New Zealand fears of an aggressive Japan, Churchill said:

> There are no means by which ... Australia and New Zealand can expect to maintain themselves single-handed. If the power of Great Britain were shattered on the sea, the only course of the five million of white men in the Pacific would be to seek the protection of the United States.[2]

Half a century and two world wars later, that is precisely what did happen: and the question we must ask is the extent to which Churchill in the 1940s helped to bring about precisely the result that he had feared.

In the 1920s and 1930s, the formula that was supposed to resolve the tension between Australia's imperial loyalty and its regional concerns was the Singapore Strategy. The majority of Australians remained deeply loyal to the Empire and its unity in world affairs, perhaps even more than they had been before 1914; but they also retained the conviction, which had dominated official and public thinking since 1905, that their greatest potential threat came from Japanese expansionism in the Pacific. Their longstanding concern was that Britain might not be able to take effective action against a Japanese threat, if Britain were preoccupied by challenges from major European powers. The Singapore Strategy was intended to reassure Australia that the creation of the naval base and the promised despatch of a fleet at the appropriate time would deter, or if necessary defeat, any such threat.

Throughout the 1920s and 1930s, successive Australian leaders wondered whether they could trust the repeated assurances from British leaders that the Singapore Strategy would work, despite the expenditure cuts imposed by successive Chancellors of the Exchequer — not least, of course, Churchill himself in the 1920s. Their uncertainty was all the greater when the assurances came from Churchill, as First Lord of

Admiralty (again) in 1939–1940 and then as Prime Minister after May 1940. By this time, Australians could look back on more than 30 years of frustrating differences with Churchill over diplomatic consultations, military deployments and strategic policies. Those frustrations were bipartisan — indeed tri-partisan, for they were felt and expressed by all three Australian Prime Ministers between 1939 and mid-1945, Robert Menzies, Arthur Fadden and John Curtin, who led three different parties in the Australian Parliament. It was, as David Reynolds has shown, quite misleading for Churchill to have implied, in his *magnum opus* on the history of the war, that all his problems were with Australian Labor Prime Ministers.[3] The Menzies-Fadden Government fought a general election in September 1940 on the slogan "Back The Government That's Backing Churchill", and the frontispiece to Menzies' post-retirement memoirs showed him in a cordial conclave with Churchill, but behind the scenes from the outbreak of war to late 1941, there were acrimonious disputes over consultation (over Dakar), over the deployment of troops (most notably to Greece and Tobruk), and not least over the viability of the Singapore Strategy, and the British assurances on which that strategy depended.

So, at one level, Singapore could be seen as the latest in a long line of international crises during the previous 30 years and more, on which Australian leaders had clashed with Churchill. But the fall of Singapore was far more than just another military setback that could be laid, fairly or otherwise, at Churchill's door. The fall of Singapore meant the failure of the fundamental strategic concept that had governed Australia's approach to national security for a generation. The term "inexcusable betrayal", which understandably offended Churchill, was probably coined by that most undiplomatic of foreign ministers, Dr H.V. Evatt, rather than by the milder-mannered Curtin, and it referred to a proposed evacuation of troops, which now looks to have been an eminently sensible idea. But Menzies, who had far more sympathy with Churchill's strategic approach, had also long expressed his doubts about Churchill's judgement, and his understanding of Australia's legitimate concerns.

This is not the place to go over the longstanding arguments over the extent to which the blame for the fall of Singapore should be sheeted home to Churchill personally. What we can say is that he was at least cavalier, if not downright disingenuous, in giving repeated assurances to the Australian government that the Singapore Strategy was sound and the British promises of support would be upheld. Given the pressures that Churchill was under in 1940–1941 and the resources that were at his disposal, it is easy now to have some sympathy with his attitude to troublesome Dominion Prime Ministers. His strategic concept of concentrating forces for the decisive battle in the decisive theatre was sound. And of course he did send a fleet. It was not his fault that one of its principal components, an aircraft carrier, ran aground in the West Indies en route to Singapore, nor that, for this and other reasons, the *Prince of Wales* and the *Repulse* were denied the air cover that might perhaps have saved them. But such niceties had no place in Australian thinking. To the political elite and the general public alike, the fall of Singapore meant that Australia had been at least badly let down, if not downright betrayed, by Winston Churchill, and by no means for the first time.

What is often overlooked, in the repeated accounts of British-Australian relations during the war, is Churchill's relationship with Curtin and the Australian government during the later years of the war, after the crisis of late 1941 and early 1942. To this day, many people regard Curtin's celebrated statement of December 1941, that "Australia looks to America, free of any pangs as to our traditional links and kinship with the United Kingdom", as the definitive turning point in Australian strategy, the founding point of the Australian-American alliance. While that statement, or at least that one sentence, is repeatedly quoted, far less attention has been given to the meeting between Curtin and General MacArthur on 1 June 1942. The date is significant: it was the morning after Japanese midget submarines entered Sydney Harbour, and Australian anxiety about the support from major allies was at its most intense. In that atmosphere, General MacArthur bluntly told Curtin that Australia should not turn to the United States for support; that American forces had come to Australia not out of friendship but simply because it was the most convenient forward base for the counterattack against Japan; that the United States had no interest in, or desire for, a continuing strategic relationship with Australia; and that Australia's best hope for such a rela-tionship lay with the United Kingdom, precisely because of those tradi-tional links and kinship that Curtin's statement appeared to have scorned.[4]

For the rest of his life — Curtin died on 5 July 1945, the same day as the general election in which Churchill was humiliatingly defeated — Curtin did exactly as MacArthur had proposed. No Prime Minister, not even Menzies who famously proclaimed himself "British to the bootstraps", was a more passionate advocate of close relations with the Mother Country. Curtin spoke with great warmth of the traditions of what he sometimes rather quaintly called "the British-speaking race". To the puzzle-ment, if not downright embarrassment of some of his colleagues, espe-cially those of Irish nationalist heritage, Curtin "wrapped himself in the Union Jack" during the campaign for the 1943 election, where he was returned with a comfortable majority. Moreover, it was not the great empire loyalist Menzies, but the Labor leader Curtin who became the only Prime Minister to nominate a member of the royal family — Prince Henry, Duke of Gloucester, the King's brother — to become Governor-General of Australia. To his internal party critics, he defended this decision on strategic grounds. This, he said, would help to persuade Britain to retain substantial forces in the Far East after the European threat had been countered.[5]

Moreover, in 1944, when Curtin came to London for a meeting of the Empire-Commonwealth's Prime Ministers, he presented a proposal for a secretariat that would coordinate the foreign policies of the constituent nations, once again outflanking the most imperialist of the conservatives. Curtin's proposal echoed many of the ideas that Alfred Deakin had brought to the Colonial Conference of 1907; but if Curtin's attitudes had radically changed in a couple of years, it seemed that Churchill's had not changed over nearly four decades. He did not even attend the conference session at which Curtin's proposal was aired, and the idea disappeared.

Again, it is easy to understand that Churchill's priorities at this time lay in far weightier matters, including negotiations with Franklin Roosevelt and Joseph Stalin about ensuring victory and shaping the post-war world. Nevertheless, it is possible to note with regret that Churchill missed a potential opportunity to bring Australia, and the other Dominions, into a new system that would help to coordinate strategic policies across the Empire-Commonwealth, in war and peace. While less London-centric than Churchill's preferred *modus operandi*, it might well have added to, rather than subtracted from, Britain's diplomatic weight.

It was by failing to understand what Curtin was doing in 1943 and 1944, almost as much as by his actions in 1941–1942, that Churchill helped to bring about precisely what he had feared in early 1914, the transfer of Australia's principal strategic relationship from Britain to the United States. In the late 1940s and early 1950s, Australian governments once again sought a new strategic formula to resolve that basic tension between the global-imperial and the national-regional imperatives. By this time, two new elements dominated. One was the emphasis on Asia, especially Southeast Asia, as the focus of Australia's security concerns. The other was the negotiation of the ANZUS Security Treaty, signed in September 1951, the month before Churchill was returned to office as peacetime Prime Minister. First as Leader of the Opposition, then as Prime Minister, Churchill vehemently opposed the idea that Australia and New Zealand should sign a treaty with the United States to which the United Kingdom was not a party. He regarded this as a major blow to the standing of the British Empire in the Pacific, and an indication that henceforth

Canberra and Wellington would look to Washington, rather than to London, for their security concerns.[6]

The strength and persistence of Churchill's objections to the ANZUS treaty puzzled the ministers of the Menzies Government who had secured this diplomatic prize. At the time, they certainly did not envisage a complete transfer of loyalty from Britain to the United States. As they saw it, they had gained a second string to their strategic bow. They wanted to have the support of both Britain and the United States, but felt obliged to accept America's insistence that Britain be excluded from the ANZUS treaty. At this time, many countries would have done almost anything to gain a strategic guarantee from what was far and away the world's most powerful nation.

So, for the next two decades, the formula governing Australia's strategic policy was known as "forward defence". It prescribed that Australian forces would be shaped and directed towards fighting in Southeast Asia — and not, for example, the Mediterranean or the Middle East — but those forces would only fight alongside Britain or the United States, or preferably both. For some years, Australian defence planning placed more emphasis on the South East Asia Treaty Organization (SEATO), of which both Britain and the United States were members, than on ANZUS. In the 1950s and 1960s, Australia's military commitments in Korea, Malaya and Borneo were in Commonwealth formations, and in the latter two cases, the United States was not involved. Not until 1965, when Australia made its major commitment to the Vietnam War, did Australia enter a conflict to which the United States was heavily committed, but in which the UK had no combat forces.

And yet, for all that, it is true that Churchill was to a degree prescient. To use a metaphor of which he was fond, he could distinguish between the great tides of global affairs and the smaller eddies. Australia's turn towards the United States was one of the great tides. It happened long after Churchill's speech of 1914; it took two world wars and several smaller conflicts to come about; it came a decade and a half after Churchill's vehement opposition to British exclusion from ANZUS; but since the late 1960s, the United States, and not the UK, has been central to Australia's defence and security policies. Ironically, it was some of Churchill's actions, and some of his omissions, that helped to bring about precisely the result that he had long feared. And in the Australian public mind, hovering over that transition and over all the debates on Australia's strategic policy has been the shadow of the fall of Singapore, and its association with the man whom Australians still regard with some ambivalence: the greatest statesman of the 20th century, the lion of Britain's finest hour, and yet someone who could not really grasp that the world looked different when seen from the Antipodes, rather than from the Admiralty or No. 10 Downing Street.

Notes

1. On Churchill's post-1945 reputation in Australia, see John Ramsden, *Man of the Century: Winston Churchill and His Legend since 1945* (New York: Columbia University Press, 2003), Chapters 10 and 11.
2. Quoted in Graham Freudenberg, *Churchill and Australia* (Sydney: Macmillan, 2008), p. 47.
3. David Reynolds, *In Command of History: Churchill Fighting and Writing the Second World War* (London: Allen Lane, 2004), especially pp. 257–9.
4. See Peter Edwards, "From Curtin to Beazley: Labor Leaders and the American Alliance", John Curtin Day lecture at the John Curtin Prime Ministerial Library, 8 October 2001, available at <http://john.curtin.edu.au/events/speeches/edwardsp.html>.
5. Peter Edwards, "Labor's Vice-Regal Appointments: The Case of John Curtin and the Duke of Gloucester, 1943", *Labour History* 34 (May 1978): 68–73.
6. John Williams, "ANZUS: A Blow to Britain's Self-Esteem," *Review of International Studies* 13, 4 (October 1987): 423–63.

CHAPTER 7

"The Times they are a-Changin'": Britain's Military Commitment to Singapore, 1967–1971[1]

Malcolm H. Murfett

"A week is a long time in politics"[2]

Harold Wilson's experiences in and out of the corridors of power in Whitehall had led him to see politics as an intensely volatile environment in which even the most elaborate government plans could be undone — almost at a moment's notice — by some dramatic event occurring either at home or abroad. Long before the Lebanese market quant Naseem Nicolas Taleb had made his fortune by conjuring up the concept of the "Black Swan", Wilson had seen the descent into randomness first hand on numerous occasions.[3] Regardless of what David Lloyd George might have thought about it, promises — in Wilson's lexicon — were like pie crust, and as such, likely to be broken if the exigencies of the moment (that ghastly contractual term) demanded they should be. Wilson, whose reputation never really recovered from his astounding devaluation broadcast in November 1967, was inclined to promise now and change later.[4]

His political nemesis Edward Heath, whom he had remarkably little time for, was less cynically driven. Much misunderstood, Heath was a reflective man of probity, not given to self advertisement or the catchy sound byte that the telegenic M.P. for Liverpool Huyton could be relied upon to provide for the media.[5] On the contrary, Heath would have been temperamentally disinclined to offer hope where none existed. He seemed to mean what he said; but was his apparent sincerity a reflection of genuine reality or worrying naiveté? Would he respond deftly to sudden change or be compromised by it? Only time would tell. Surely he could not outdo Wilson when it came to chutzpah — or could he?[6]

This paper will investigate the evolution of the Conservative Party's foreign and defence policy as far as maintaining a British military presence in Southeast Asia was concerned, and how that commitment was shaped by remarkable and unforeseen events happening far from the island of Singapore.[7] Enraged by the Labour government's plans for a complete military withdrawal from East of Suez by the end of 1971, the Tories had immediately promised in January 1968 to reconsider this shameful scuttle if they were returned to power at the next General Election. It did not take them long to review their own policy. By the summer of 1968, the stark promises of only a few months before had become remarkably less strident. Within another year, their agenda had changed fundamentally as Charles de Gaulle shuffled off into retirement and Georges Pompidou re-emerged like a phoenix from the ashes to claim presidential power in France. By the time the Tories were swept into power in June 1970 — as President Nixon had confidently and gleefully predicted they would be — Heath and his Cabinet were looking to Europe, rather than the US and the Far East, for their future orientation.[8] Thereafter, the prospect of a belated entry into the European Economic Community (Common Market) became a distinct possibility for the UK. It was a policy orientation that suited Heath perfectly. He was the leading Europeanist in his party.[9]

But what would this new policy orientation mean for the repatriation of British troops from Southeast Asia? Lord Carrington, Secretary of State for Defence, might claim he was doing far more than his predecessor Denis Healey had planned to do, but essentially this was more a case of "smoke and mirrors" than anything else. When one removed the layer of political posturing, there was little to choose between the Tory government's post-1971 policy in Southeast Asia and the stalled one which Healey tried to devise. A key feature of both schemes was cooperation in security matters. Carrington sought to wind up Far East Command and replace the Anglo-Malaysian Defence Agreement with a consultative scheme — the Five Power Defence Arrangements between the UK and Australia, Malaysia, New Zealand, and Singapore. If the truth be known, this was an identical mechanism to that which Healey vainly sought to establish in order to replace the leading British defence role in the region. So what was all the fuss about in January 1968? Was it the usual stuff of everyday politics: here today and gone tomorrow? For an answer to this beguiling question, we need to look closer at what was going on in the corridors of British power back in the mid-1960s.

Far East Command, the headquarters of British military forces in the region, was situated at Phoenix Park in Singapore. Each of the three services — British Army, Royal Navy (RN) and Royal Air Force (RAF) — had extensive facilities which they owned and occupied on the island. In total, the British military establishment occupied 59 square kilometres, or roughly one-tenth, of the entire island. Apart from 1,857 warehouses, the Army owned 354 workshops, 680 administrative offices and a fuel depot. Ships of up to 100,000 Gross Registered Tons could berth at the impressive Sembawang naval base, which was also home to a Far East Fleet that consisted of 50 to 60 warships. Sembawang was equipped to repair and overhaul ships of all kinds. In addition, it also boasted a communications centre and a huge oil dump and weapons facility. Not to be outdone, the RAF had three air bases on the island: short haul transport aircraft and a contingent of helicopters were based at Seletar; fighters, Canberra bombers and visiting V-bombers with their nuclear payloads were based at Tengah; while Changi was the centre of Transport Command and the headquarters of the RAF in the Far East.[10]

At the end of *Konfrontasi* with Indonesia in 1966, Far East Command was home to 91,000 servicemen. To house the troops assigned to Singapore, the British built 10,175 dwellings of all types from luxurious black and white bungalows with extensive grounds for high ranking officers to much less salubrious quarters for the NCOs and enlisted men. In addition, there were 645 barracks for single enlisted men, or those troops serving without family dependents being stationed with them. 58 churches and mosques, 21 schools and 201 clubs catered to the varied needs of the troops and their families, while an extensive range of recreational possibilities including 19 cinemas, seven golf courses, 153 assorted indoor sports courts, 115 sports fields, 25 swimming pools, and 131 tennis courts were also on tap in what was basically "a city within a city" — a rather closed military community with its own police forces, electrical power generators and sources of water supply.[11]

None of this came cheap. In terms of foreign exchange, the cost of maintaining the Singapore base alone doubled from roughly £40M in 1961 to £80M in 1966. According to *The Financial Times*, the Singapore government estimated in 1966 that as many as 150,000 local Singaporeans were either directly or indirectly dependent upon the military base for their livelihood, and in an interview with *The Mirror*, on 16 May 1966, Singapore Prime Minister Lee Kuan Yew confirmed that the bases were responsible for generating 25% of the infant republic's income.[12]

While it was abundantly clear the bases were invaluable to the Singaporeans, what was the official view expressed by those at or near the top of the "greasy pole" in the UK? In a memorandum drawn up for Sir Alec Douglas-Home's government in September 1964, the Defence and Oversea Policy Committee (DOPC) found that 15% of the British defence budget was devoted to maintaining a military base in Singapore and keeping troops in Hong Kong at a time when Southeast Asia provided only 3% of British trade and under 6% of investment revenue — a figure smaller even than that generated by British involvement in Latin America![13] Douglas-Home's successor as Prime Minister, Harold Wilson, was known to favour a world role for the UK. It had enabled him to once visualise the British frontier as being drawn up along the borders of the Himalayas.[14] As such, he was temperamentally disinclined to see foreign and defence policy reduced to a crude table of profit and loss figures. His attitude was underlined by his statement in the House of Commons on 16 December 1964:

> I want to make it quite clear that whatever we may do in the field of cost effectiveness, value for money and a stringent review of expenditure, we cannot afford to relinquish our world role ... Our maritime tradition, our reputation, our mobility ... above all our Commonwealth history and connections, mean that Britain can provide for the Alliances and for the world peace-keeping role a contribution which no other country, not excluding America, can provide ... If we are to fulfil our overseas role ... we need most, if not all, of the bases we now hold...[15]

It rarely happened that Wilson's views would echo those of *The Daily Telegraph*, but they did intriguingly coincide on the value of the Singapore base.[16] Interestingly enough, however, editorials within the left-leaning *Guardian* newspaper disagreed fundamentally with the British Prime Minister's global perspective. At the end of *Konfrontasi* in the summer of 1966, it declared unambiguously: "Whatever our commitments to the people of Malaysia and Singapore this situation cannot continue. We are trying to defend them on a scale which is obviously beyond our means. A country which owes 997M pound sterling to overseas bankers cannot afford imperial gestures".[17]

Wilson's Labour Party struggled across the electoral line in October 1964, ending 13 years of Tory rule to be greeted by a balance of payments situation that almost defied belief. Expecting something along the lines of a £400M deficit, James Callaghan, the newly installed Chancellor of the Exchequer, was duly informed by his Treasury officials that the true picture was roughly double that amount![18] Grim news of this nature called for immediate action. Wilson, a former Economics don at New College, Oxford, knew the various policy options better than his Chancellor, but set his face against devaluation as much for political as economic reasons. In these days of fixed exchange rates, any devaluation was not seen as merely an exercise of adjusting internal prices to external realities. Instead, it was seen, quite simply, as a fundamental sign of financial failure on the part of the government. Remembering how Attlee's administration had been pilloried for devaluing in 1949, Wilson was determined that Labour must not be seen henceforth as the "party of devaluation".[19]

So devaluation was eschewed in favour of an alternative set of economic strategies. Unfortunately, the prices and incomes policy only worked for a time, and the much vaunted "white heat of technology" that was supposedly going to drive the industrial fortunes of the UK forward into the modern era was desperately short of a sustained supply of money for long term research and development.[20] Add a trade union movement restless and obstreperous, with leaders anxious to use their dislocative power over the economy to win better deals for their members; and international speculators, who could spot a financial crisis a mile off and homed in on the weakening pound and put it under increasingly sustained pressure; and all the elements were in place for chaos and catastrophe. Not surprisingly, therefore, sterling crises came and went on an annual basis. Wilson and his Cabinet might woo the IMF and the US and receive significant help in a bid to prop up the overvalued pound, but the bailout of sterling did not, alas, lead to the kind of improvement in British industrial competitiveness that was so eagerly sought.[21]

Something would have to give, but the question was *what*? Public expenditure needed to be reined in, but this was a Labour administration, and as such, it was not supposed to cut social welfare and education programmes — surely, that was the province of the Tories when they were in crisis mode? On the other hand, defence budgets were not sacred cows, but slaughtering some of the most costly of these beasts would have to be put on hold as long as *Konfrontasi* lasted. Even then, defence cuts in Southeast Asia would be bound to stir controversy with the Johnson administration, who expected nothing less than a further ten-year defence commitment East of Suez from the British as a quid pro quo for the US$1.4 billion of aid they received from the IMF in the early summer of 1965.[22] Could Wilson afford to retain his Olympian view of the UK's role on the world stage? A meeting with senior members of the Cabinet at Chequers, his weekend retreat in Buckinghamshire, in mid-June 1965 suggested that the "good old days" were finally gone, as agreement was reached on a 16% cut in defence expenditure (£400M) by 1969–1970. It was the start of a process which ended up unravelling the East of Suez policy later in the decade.[23]

Labour's calculations were aided, of course, by the Untong coup of 1 October 1965, which succeeded in transforming the political situation in Indonesia and the strategic picture on the island of Borneo. With Suharto firmly in the driving seat and Sukarno forlornly yesterday's man, *Konfrontasi* passed into history on 11 August 1966, having cost the UK anywhere between £1–2M a week while it lasted.[24] By then, however, the economic crisis at home had driven the Wilson government from pillar to post. A seaman's strike in May, and a further speculative attack on sterling in July, led Wilson, Callaghan and the rest of the Labour team to introduce stringent deflationary policies, and contemplate further cuts in defence expenditure.[25] As autumn wore on, so Healey at the Ministry of Defence came under sustained pressure to start cutting troop numbers and significantly reduce overseas expenditure. By December 1966, Healey and George Brown, the abrasive and hot-tempered Foreign Secretary, co-authored a paper that sought a 50% cut in Far East Command. Healey's apostasy over the East of Suez policy was confirmed by his admission to Wilson in March 1967 that there was no realistic alternative to halving all British forces in Malaysia and Singapore by 1970–1971, and withdrawing them completely by 1975–1976.[26]

Wilson's Cabinet, stung by their abysmal irrelevance to both Israel and the Arab states during the Six Day War in June 1967, finally conceded that if they could not affect matters in the Middle East, what real chance did they have of doing so even further afield?[27] This was a sobering fact of life for the ministers, and it consolidated support across the board for the irrevocable withdrawal from East of Suez that was confirmed by the publication of the Supplementary Statement on Defence Policy on 18 July 1967.[28]

Once again, the matter did not rest there. Indeed, the picture darkened considerably as a crippling dock strike and slumping trade figures brought the day of final reckoning ever closer. Eventually, Wilson and Callaghan were forced to admit that the thing they had avoided for three years at a cost of £1billion — devaluation of the pound — was finally upon them.[29] On 18 November 1967, Wilson announced the 14.3% devaluation ($2.80–$2.40 = £1) but contrived to say that somehow the pound in the pocket of the British citizen was not worth less than it had been before the devaluation. Even for a New College don, this was pretty rum.[30]

As Callaghan folded his tent and moved off to the Home Office, his successor as Chancellor, Roy Jenkins, a Europeanist rather than an East of Suez aficionado, wasted little time convincing a rather shell-shocked Wilson that the UK was no longer a superpower, and that it made no sense to go on trying to play a role beyond its economic strength. If Wilson needed any further proof of this lamentable fact, President Charles de Gaulle delivered it on 27 November with a crushing "*Non*" to the latest British application to join the EEC. Frustrated by this latest rebuff from Paris, Jenkins believed the British would have to get their house in order; overseas expenditure was far too high and would have to be slashed, and the sooner it was done, the better. He proposed that the first casualty of this policy should be the "East of Suez" commitment and sought the Prime Minister's support for bringing forward the date for the total withdrawal of British forces in Aden, Malaysia and Singapore, from 1975–1976 to March 1971.[31] Wilson became a zealous convert to the cause. George Thomson, Secretary of State for Commonwealth Affairs, was dispatched to inform authorities in Kuala Lumpur, Singapore, Canberra and Wellington of the momentous news. This visit was never going to be a junket and so it proved. When he reached the Singapore Istana, for instance, Thomson found Lee Kuan Yew almost apoplectic with rage.[32] Brown, charged with telling the Americans the same unpalatable information, failed to fare any better with Dean Rusk, US Secretary of State. In what the British Foreign Secretary described as "a bloody unpleasant meeting" in Washington on 11 January 1968, an exasperated Rusk denounced the decision to withdraw from Southeast Asia and angrily lectured his opposite number on the shortcomings of the UK as an international partner. A chastened Brown, with no room to manoeuvre, left the State Department with Rusk's condemnatory "for God's sake be Britain" ringing in his ears.[33] For his part, an indignant Lee Kuan Yew and his senior ministers took themselves off to London for an urgent meeting with Wilson, Jenkins and Healey. Out of this set of crisis meetings came a nine-month extension of the withdrawal date to 31 December 1971.[34] It was, as Churchill might have said, a time pregnant with possibilities.

After Wilson had duly informed a packed and highly partisan House of Commons on 16 January 1968 about the accelerated withdrawal from "East of Suez", the leading members of the Conservative Opposition took to the floor over the course of the next few days and flayed the government for its craven irresponsibility. Healey was repeatedly called upon to resign for his seemingly villainous and treacherous conduct. Heath considered the withdrawal detrimental to British interests in the region as a whole and accused the government of "indecisiveness and vacillation" and dishonourable behaviour; Reginald Maudling worried that a pull out of British forces from Southeast Asia might lead to an American retreat back into isolationism — a move which would seriously undermine Western unity; and Douglas-Home regarded the end of the "East of Suez" policy as a dereliction of government stewardship of an unprecedented degree.[35] Iain Macleod, never one to beat about the bush, described the decision as "perfidious" and indicated that a future Conservative government would review the accelerated withdrawal from the Far East. He promised members of the Commons that if the Tories found it "practicable and helpful to maintain a presence in the Far East, we shall do so". Asked by the inveterate Labour left-winger Emanuel Shinwell whether this constituted a pledge of future action, Macleod responded emphatically: "Yes and one we will keep".[36] As a former Secretary of State for the Colonies, Macleod took an imperious line accusing the government of leaving its Malaysian and Singaporean friends in the lurch and complaining about the UK abandoning its peacekeeping duties in Southeast Asia before it needed to do so. Linking the decision to quit the region to the negative effect it may have upon the ongoing Vietnam War, Macleod posed the question: "Is it not dangerous to leave a vacuum on the southern flank and might it not encourage continuance of a war which everyone wants to see ended?"[37] He did not need to add that it was bound to cause problems with the Americans, who did not need SEATO being denuded in this way — and the more so when the Tet Offensive was launched at the end of the month, catching them unprepared and more vulnerable than for a long time.[38]

Reinforcing his opposition to the withdrawal by homing in on the economic aspects of the matter, Heath robustly attacked Jenkins, the Chancellor of the Exchequer, by indicating that the much vaunted savings he hoped to make from this ill-conceived demarche would prove to be illusory:

> If one looks at the at the profit and loss account of investment and income from the Far East and the Near East one sees that what we stand to lose is so immense that cannot believe that the sacrifice he is prepared to make set against what he will gain from a saving in overseas expenditure is justifiable. This is not so on a profit and loss basis.[39]

Jenkins was, of course, unrepentant. He had already gone on record in the House on 17 January as indicating that the changes announced in British defence policy were "... no more than the recognition — some will say the belated recognition — of basic currents in the tide of history. We are no longer, and have not been for some time, a super Power. It does not make sense for us to go on trying to play a role beyond our economic strength".[40] Returning to this theme later in the debate, Jenkins intimated that while no withdrawal could be painless, it was far better to do it sooner rather than later. "This has been true from Ireland to India and the

Conservative Party or, half of it at any rate, has always been left clinging to an untenable concept".[41] He was firmly supported on this point by the Foreign Secretary who chose a reflective rather than combative approach for a change, declaring almost wistfully perhaps: "Today the special pleading has to stop. Britain has to become strong ..."[42] Brown soon resumed his more choleric approach, and his clash with Douglas-Home and Heath from the Tory front bench a few days later in the Commons was vivid.

Douglas-Home began the proceedings on 24 January by provocatively contending that it was just as well that Labour and its draconian spending plans had not been in government earlier in the decade, otherwise Malaysia and Singapore would have forfeited their independence and been absorbed by an Indonesia that had sold itself at least temporarily to the Chinese communists. Douglas-Home then went on to sketch out what role the UK should adopt in Southeast Asia. It was definitely not the old knee-jerk reaction so typical of the Kiplingesque Monday Club. Instead, it illustrated what modern Conservatism stood for in the late 1960s:

> Britain's purpose in South-East Asia should be something parallel, but on a smaller scale, to what the United States were doing in Thailand. This would mean training Singapore and Malaysia ultimately to take over their own defence ... Britain might consider becoming a member of an Anzam [sic] alliance devoted to keeping open the sea and air approaches to South-East Asia in the Indian Ocean and Indonesian seas ... I am not pressing for a roving commission in the traditional sense expected of a great power. I am asking the Foreign Secretary to deal particularly with those areas where we can establish that a British interest lies, and [has] assets, and where Britain can contribute to political stability, and where we should maintain a presence for limited but vital periods.[43]

Brown was profoundly unimpressed by this line of argument. Although admitting that British interests remained worldwide in nature, as could be expected of a great commercial nation, he asserted that the UK could no longer afford to assume the burden of maintaining a policing role around the globe, and that Labour recognised this and the Tories manifestly did not. This infuriated Heath, who struck back immediately by declaring that Brown distorted the Tory position which had already been unambiguously outlined by Douglas-Home. Heath continued: "We do not propose this country should have what the Foreign Secretary terms 'a world policing role.' What we do believe is that our interests, which have been clearly and specifically defined in the Gulf, Singapore and

Malaysia, should be maintained, and these are two clear and specific commitments on which the present government has ratted".[44]

Brown was now in his element. Rejecting the vulgar reference, he managed to ridicule Douglas-Home and impugn the honour of Heath in a few mischievous sentences, and refused to give way to those maligned on the Opposition benches. Uproar resulted. Possessing both presence and a booming voice, Brown held the floor and presented the government's case for drawing back from East of Suez and looking to NATO for its future strategic focus. Unperturbed by the hubbub going on around him, Brown proposed that the UK could exercise its influence in the world without having expensive military bases dotted around the globe. According to *The Times* correspondent, Brown then added a rather intriguing and surreal note to the proceedings by making the following suggestion: "There could be a British presence without a military presence. There could be British influence without British armies on the spot. The influence which many of our friends in Asia looked to us to provide could be more effective without military backing".[45] Quite what he meant by this impenetrable statement perhaps only he knew. One fancies he would have got short shrift from the Americans had he tried that tactic on them.

On the following day, the embattled Denis Healey rose to defend the government's controversial decision to quit "East of Suez". Healey was known not to suffer fools gladly and was not about to be lectured on defence policy by the Tories who, he claimed, had performed a continuous series of somersaults on defence policy while they were in office — their only consistency being in the way they changed the very defence ministers (nine in 13 years) who constructed these haphazard policies in the first place. Rejecting calls for his resignation, the longest serving Defence Minister since 1950 vigorously counterattacked those churlish enough to criticize him:

> What frightens me most about the Opposition proposal to keep forces in Singapore, even when no carriers and F111s are available, is that they are breaking this fundamental principle and putting the lives of our Servicemen in jeopardy. It was no good putting a handful of troops in the Gulf or Singapore if they were not backed by ships, aircraft and other reinforcements.[46]

Instead of harking back to the past and engaging in old fashioned wishful thinking, he described British foreign and defence policy as having a "new and necessary realism".[47]

Thrust and counterthrust continued in the debate, but essentially the crucial battlelines were drawn; the Conservatives regarded the withdrawal as a breach of faith as well as contract and regretted both. Labour rejected what they saw as the Tories steeped in a culture of living beyond their means and saw their own decision on withdrawal as an unavoidable realignment of British power and responsibility, at a time when they could not afford to do everything they might wish to do on the world's stage.

Over the next few months, the Labour government tried — rather unsuccessfully as far as Tunku Abdul Rahman, Prime Minister of Malaysia was concerned — to sweeten the bitter pill of military withdrawal by agreeing upon a fixed set of ex-gratia payments to its former equatorial colonies.[48] Further discussions took place in Kuala Lumpur in June 1968, with the Australians and New Zealanders joining their Malaysian hosts, a lively Singaporean delegation, and a British contingent led by Denis Healey and George Thomson. It was not a particularly convivial conference since each of the Commonwealth partners looked for different things from it.[49] While the British sought the most satisfactory terms for disengagement, the Australians and New Zealanders had yet to determine whether a military withdrawal was appropriate for them also. As for the two former colonies most directly affected by the "East of Suez" decision, the Singaporeans actively sought a sustainable and effective Integrated Air Defence System (IADS), while the Malaysians were anxious to preserve the Anglo-Malayan Defence Agreement (AMDA) and retain a solid British commitment to the area in the post-1971 period. Therefore, Healey had his work cut out for him to convince everyone present that the British were capable of not only presenting a good case to those in need but were also prepared to put their words into subsequent action, if need be. There was a discomforting ambiguity about Healey's statements — lots of well-meaning talk interspersed with largesse (the free transfer of fixed assets), offers to help run the Jungle Warfare School at Kota Tinggi and helm a major reinforcement exercise from the UK to Malaysia in 1970. Ultimately, the conference achieved perhaps the most that could have been expected, since at least it accepted conceptually some form of future defence cooperation between the five powers that could operate in and around Malaysia and Singapore in the post-1971 period.[50]

For their part, the Tories — with no imminent prospect of being returned to government — had the luxury of criticising Labour's foreign and defence policies without having to implement anything in return. Tory leaders still considered it fair game to attack the Wilson government's abandonment of its friends in the East, and Heath, on a world tour, chose the third anniversary of Singapore's independence from Malaysia (9 August 1968) to return to the idea of a future Tory administration reviewing the repatriation process if the party won the next General Election, which would have to take place before 31 March 1971. "If we are returned, the phasing-out programme will not have been completed and it will be possible for us to carry on Britain's defence role in the Far East".[51] What kind of role it was likely to be was not spelt out with any clarity by the Tory party leader. Here was an instance when he sought to create a "feel good" factor by avoiding making specific promises, settling instead for general observations that could mean different things to different people.

Heath showed this beguiling ambiguity at a press conference in Sydney later in the month to mark the end of his 13-day tour of Australia. Underlining what he saw as the fundamental difference between his party's stance on "East of Suez" and that of the existing Labour government, Heath claimed: "By pulling forces out of South-east Asia, the British Government would save very little in foreign exchange".[52] It was of course utter nonsense, but since he did not provide any figures that could be refuted, the statement managed to escape close scrutiny from a sympathetic Commonwealth press corps. According to *The Straits Times*, Heath resolutely defended the stationing of British forces "East of Suez". "The British Government says it has earmarked a brigade group in Europe for use (East of Suez) should the need arise. But if they're simply earmarked in Europe, they're no deterrent here".[53]

Although Heath was prepared to hold out the prospect of some kind of enhanced role for the British in Southeast Asia beyond 1971, there was much less of the "sound and fury" from the Tories that accompanied Wilson's announcement of the military withdrawal in January 1968. Instead he mentioned the need to forge a joint five-power lease of Singapore's giant naval base at Sembawang. Dismissing the prospect of the British playing the anchor role in such a naval enterprise, he spoke optimistically of the five Commonwealth powers — the UK, Singapore, Malaysia, Australia, and New Zealand — sharing the responsibility on an equal basis.[54] Less than a month later, he was quoted by *The Times* as confirming that the British defence role in Southeast Asia would be subject to change: "We shall do it on a new basis. We shall establish a new and equal partnership with our friends".[55] Quite what this meant for AMDA, let alone SEATO, was, naturally, a moot point.

Equally, Heath's remarks seemed to suggest there had been a distinct narrowing of the gulf between the Tories and Labour on the "East of Suez" policy. Had it now become little more than a semantic difference to them and if so why?[56] What might have brought about a level of bi-partisanship on this withdrawal that seemed unthinkable only a few months before? Had the rapid cooling of the European Cold War, following the ruthless imposition of the Brezhnev Doctrine and the cruel suppression of the "Prague Spring", changed the overall strategic picture for Heath and his

Shadow Cabinet? Was imminent change in the White House another lurking reason for Heath's decision to recast the Tory position on Far East Command? Whatever the trigger was — and perhaps it was a mix of both these factors — the Tories now seemed to be in favour of devising a far more equal and consensual approach to future regional security issues with the Malaysians and Singaporeans as well as the Australians and New Zealanders.[57]

Over the course of the next few months, as the attention of the British politicians shifted much closer to home and the Australians became more introspective on Southeast Asian defence issues, the Joint Planning Staff at Far East Command began devising a detailed plan for the running down of its military forces in Singapore. It proposed that some 16% of its Headquarters staff and 20% of its logistic support staff would be withdrawn by the end of the 1969–1970 financial year; while another 39% would leave HQ and 45% of its support staff would be phased out in 1970–1971. This would leave 45% of the HQ detail and 35% of its support staff to go between April and December 1971.[58] Once these permanent forces were withdrawn, of course, it would be very difficult to reinstall them whichever government was in power at the time.

A few days before the powers met at the Commonwealth Prime Ministers Conference in London in January 1969, John Gorton, the abrasive Australian Prime Minister, added his own distinct touch to the proceedings by finally announcing that both the Australian and New Zealand forces that formed a basic constituent of the 28th Commonwealth Brigade would leave their base at Terendak and withdraw to Singapore, once the British troops began withdrawing from the same camp in Malacca.[59] Needless to say, Gorton's announcement won him few friends in Kuala Lumpur — the more so when it became clear the New Zealanders would have preferred to remain at Terendak but could hardly do so alone. Gorton's tetchy relations with the Tunku and his Deputy Tun Abdul Razak were not improved by his failure to provide any kind of reassurance on the Sabah problem, but the craggy Australian leader did do something to repair his tarnished image in the region by making a joint declaration with Keith Holyoake, the New Zealand Premier, on 25 February 1969 to the effect that Australian and New Zealand forces would remain in Malaysia and Singapore beyond the end of 1971.[60]

Benefiting from the fact that the Malaysians appeared to reserve their deepest suspicious for Gorton and the Australians, Healey went to the next five power conference, held in Canberra from 19–20 June 1969, offering help with future training and arms sales, but steadfastly refusing to renegotiate the 1971 withdrawal, and rejecting any idea that he could make any binding military promises — diplomatically couched as "obligatory commitments" — to come to the aid of Malaysia and Singapore after the withdrawal finally took place. Healey obviously hoped the conference might provide for a useful exchange of views rather than an endless series of recriminations, but, not surprisingly, in the rather unstable political environment of the time, he got a bit of both.[61] Malaysia-Singapore relations, never entirely easy and always open to misunderstanding after the August 1965 denouement between them, were further strained by communal violence that broke out in Kuala Lumpur on 13 May. Lee Kuan Yew had not expected much from the conference and still less from the Malaysians, but he still managed to be infuriated by Gorton's boorish mistreatment of Tun Razak and vitriolic about Australians in general, whom he described as "a pretty miserable lot".[62] Describing Holyoake as "a pompous old ninny" and the New Zealanders in general as "backward but civilized", Lee had not set the bar very high for much in the way of positive results from the five-power gathering.[63]

In fact the conference proved to be far more productive than was anticipated, since it approved a slew of agreements that dealt with defence issues: arrangements were approved for both Exercise *Bersatu Padu* (Complete Unity) to be staged in 1970 and the establishment of a Commonwealth Jungle Warfare Centre at Ulu Tiram, near Kota Tinggi in the southern Malaysian state of Johor; Malaysia and Singapore agreed on a range of naval matters; and the British decision to sell Bloodhound missiles to Singapore and contribute to training its air force was also approved.[64] While political control over IADS remained a thorny issue, the constituent parts of the system itself had largely been settled.[65] On the whole, therefore, the delegates could feel reasonably satisfied with their efforts. Five Power consultation was proving to be more sustainable than perhaps the most optimistic advocate would have imagined hitherto.[66]

Sensing that this new willingness to share defence responsibility in Southeast Asia played into his own hands, Edward Heath sought to remind the public where his party stood on this aspect of foreign and defence policy. On 6 October *The Mirror* in Singapore quoted him as saying: "Our policy is to retain a presence in Singapore and Malaysia as part of a joint five-power presence".[67] Again the Tory leader left out any specifics as to how many troops and service units this might involve, but these vital ingredients could be waved away on the grounds that a defence review could be made if (or once) his party had won power at a future General Election. Such a victory could no longer be dismissed as being highly unlikely. Wilson's star was waning considerably; his equivocal support of

Barbara Castle's *In Place of Strife* plans for bringing the trade unions into line was backfiring upon him, and the "Troubles" in Northern Ireland that broke out in late 1968 added immeasurably to his government's unpopularity.[68] Much to Heath's satisfaction, the European political environment had also undergone another series of momentous upheavals. De Gaulle had permanently left the Élysée for his village in the Haut-Marne (Colombey-les-Deux-Églises) and was replaced as French President by Georges Pompidou, whom he had outrageously sacked after the Paris troubles of May 1968, while Willy Brandt came to the fore as the first socialist Chancellor of West Germany. Heath glimpsed a new alluring Europe beckoning from across the Channel. This was a concept he believed in; could the UK finally make it into the EEC at the third time of asking? [69]

By the time the Tory leader visited Southeast Asia again in January 1970, he found the rundown of British forces going on apace. 43,000 servicemen would remain under Far East Command in May 1970 and this figure was scheduled to decline to about 32,000 by April 1971.[70] Moreover, the 28th Commonwealth Brigade had been withdrawn from Terendak Camp in Malacca and transferred to Singapore in late 1969.[71] While Australian and New Zealand forces were set to remain in the region beyond 1971, just how much longer they could be expected to stay on for was debatable. As such, the Commonwealth Strategic Reserve's continuing commitment to SEATO was looking increasingly frail.

Faced with something of a *fait accompli*, Heath spoke warmly of the UK contributing to a balanced five-power military force operating in the area around Malaysia and Singapore, and endorsed Lee Kuan Yew's shrewd observation of the psychological benefits to be gained from actually being in the area. Whether the British would benefit from this arrangement quite as much as Lee's own citizens would was left unanswered. Moreover, and as usual, Heath's support for a shared military role in Southeast Asia beyond the next election came without any quantifiable commitment, but he referred to it as "a modest insurance premium for continuing stability and prosperity".[72] Dr. Goh Keng Swee put his finger on the issue when referring to Heath's visit and that of Roy Mason, the President of the Board of Trade in Wilson's government: "Both are agreed upon the important stakes Britain has in this part of the world and the great opportunities awaiting British trade and investment here".[73]

When back on his own turf once again, Heath wrote an article in the sympathetic *Daily Mail* on 30 January reiterating the position he had adopted in Singapore. Writing of the need for some British forces to

remain in Singapore and Malaysia, Heath conceded: "The British contribution would not be, as in the old days, the preponderant one. This is to
be an entirely new concept of joint cooperation and joint responsibility
with the object of fulfilling a common purpose: the maintenance of
stability in Singapore and Malaysia against threat from outside".[74]
Eschewing what he termed "a big unwieldy imperial juggernaut with all the
paraphernalia of expensive bases", Heath sought "a joint five-Power force
based on the co-operation of local government". Interviewed on the BBC
TV programme *Panorama*, which aired on 2 February, he admitted that
the emphasis should be on providing the type of naval and air defence that
the two Southeast Asian states found most difficult to provide themselves.
Without mentioning any numbers, Heath spoke of a cost of approximately
£100m per annum. Without any numbers to crunch, who could say
whether this figure was realistic or not? What it did do, however, was to
pinpoint the likelihood that ground forces were unlikely to feature in any
meaningful way.[75]

When Douglas-Home, now Shadow Foreign Secretary, came through
Singapore in early March 1970, he was a little more forthcoming about
the defence of Southeast Asia than his leader had been earlier in the year.
Speaking privately and off the cuff, he mentioned a Commonwealth
Brigade and talked of two British battalions being in Singapore and
Malaysia. In an interview he gave to the local press, however, Douglas-
Home focussed on the long term objective of the People's Republic of
China (PRC) which, he claimed, was to make regional governments sub-
servient to Beijing:

> In this connection he commented that neither SEATO, ANZAM or
> ANZUS was a suitable nucleus for an effective South East Asian security
> grouping and implied that a five-power Commonwealth arrangement,
> with a permanent British component, was essential if the defence of
> Malaysia and Singapore were to be adequately assured against external
> 'interference'.[76]

Douglas-Home met Lee Kuan Yew and leading members of his Cabinet
at the Istana and found the Singaporean leader refreshingly candid about
the future:

> … Lee had stressed to him that he did not want a large British presence
> in Singapore. Lee appears to be thinking of one battalion in Malaysia
> and one in Singapore but probably attaches more importance to having
> an air force and naval presence here … It is clear that Lee wants us to
> stay here not in any great strength but on a scale which would provide a
> visible token of commitment and be the core round which a Five-power
> arrangement in which he would have confidence could be built up.[77]

Across the border in Malaysia, the leaders were not quite so sanguine. They knew Healey's White Paper of February 1970 confirmed that all British defence signs were pointing to NATO rather than AMDA.[78] Douglas-Home's visit, therefore, was welcome since it offered hope that something might be saved from the ruins of the "East of Suez" policy. Everyone in authority knew, of course, that the leading members of H.M. Opposition could talk up a good case, but they had no executive power and were in no position to effect change until they possessed it.

Despite the launching of the elaborately expensive Exercise *Bersatu Padu* in April, the problems thrown up by the military manoeuvres and the political sensitivities that had been exposed as a result meant that the prospect of mounting a large scale reinforcement programme from over-seas — should such be needed in the future — looked exceedingly problematic.[79] Evidently, the loss of Far East Command would be keenly felt in Southeast Asia. Healey's pious hope that AMDA might be replaced with a five-power consultative agreement also won him few friends or much influence among the leaders in the region and beyond. Those intimately involved in his plan chose to mark time since a defeat for the Labour government at the forthcoming British General Election would change the dynamic, ushering in a Conservative government that might offer a better alternative than the one on hand.[80] In mid-June 1970, the hopes of the regional powers in Southeast Asia for a change of government in London were rewarded in the most dramatic way.

Victory in the General Election of 18 June 1970 propelled the underestimated Heath into Downing Street, much to the bemusement of Mr. Wilson and his Cabinet colleagues who were forced to surrender their seals of office far earlier than they expected. Heath's surprising victory at the polls was greeted with official pleasure by the governments in KL and Singapore, and by a mixture of relief and optimism from the civilian employees of the British forces in Southeast Asia who hoped that the entire withdrawal might now be set aside.

Lee Kuan Yew did not share their views and in a meeting with the unionised representatives of the workers on the British bases, he was at pains to point out that the Tory victory did not mean a reprieve. Talking of his recent meetings with Heath and Douglas-Home, Lee made the following observations:

> I learned that it was not their intention to keep any of the ordnance depots or any of the paraphenalia [sic] in a base complex that adds so much to annual recurring costs ... The British units that will be here after 1971 will be those operating sophisticated aircraft and naval vessels

and some ground forces. Unless the British Prime Minister and his colleagues change their minds, there will be some quote teeth unquote units, without expensive quote tail unquote outfits to inflate costs.[81]

Heath's choice of Lord Carrington as his Defence Minister was a remarkably astute one. Carrington, both genial and able, was no workaholic like Healey and saw no earthly reason for becoming a pale imitation of the intellectual bruiser from the Leeds East constituency. On the contrary, Carrington, carrying a touch of "Old School" gentility about him, admitted that he much preferred reading executive summaries — prepared by his staff — than wading through a vast amount of detailed memoranda on his own. He also wryly observed that while he respected logic, he had a certain regard for hunches too.[82] This combination of brain and gut sensitivity — he would have preferred calling it intuition — was to stand him in good stead on some issues but not, alas, on all during his career.[83]

Carrington knew the Tory diehards would expect him to beef up British defence policy around the globe, but he equally realised that the financial situation would not enable him to do so to the extent his party activists would like: "There was no question of completely putting the clock back; we accepted much of the situation as we found it, although we had been, in Opposition, very sceptical of it".[84] As the sentiments of Bob Dylan's classic folk hit of 1964 had long since indicated, the times were a-changing, and the Defence Secretary's tricky problem was to change traditional Conservative policy with them. His task — no mean feat to accomplish — was to devise a defence policy that would safeguard British economic interests in Southeast Asia, not disappoint their Commonwealth allies, and yet not cost the earth. He did not need reminding that it would not be easy to arrive at an acceptable solution for all concerned. Meanwhile, the rundown of British forces under Far East Command, already 40% down on the April 1968 figures, would proceed as planned.[85]

Before Carrington took himself off to Southeast Asia and Australasia to discuss these issues with the regional powers-that-be, he needed to brief his Cabinet colleagues on the available policy options. While these detailed memoranda were being prepared, his Prime Minister added to the general level of anticipation by informing the House of Commons on 2 July that a five-power agreement on Southeast Asian security needed to be made to help the 200 million people living in the region.[86]

As a result of the ministerial briefings he received, Carrington distributed a series of memoranda to his Cabinet colleagues later in the month outlining what he proposed to say to the political leaders he would meet on his travels to the equator and southern hemisphere during the parliamentary recess, in late July and early August. He noted that Douglas-Home, now Foreign Secretary, had recommended that the UK retain no political commitments beyond those which Australia and New Zealand were prepared to undertake themselves. Douglas-Home was firmly of the opinion that AMDA had outlived its usefulness and would have to be replaced with a looser consultative agreement that would involve discussions between the signatory powers about measures to be taken in the event of an armed attack, or threat thereof, against Malaysia and Singapore. While this new scheme would be markedly less rigid than the existing AMDA structure, it was still thought that a continuing military presence in these states would contribute to stability within the region, and act as a deterrent against those powers who might otherwise pose a threat to both Malaysia and its southern neighbour.[87]

Carrington's professional background and extensive overseas experience had accustomed him to appreciate the underlying priorities in both British foreign and defence policy, and the dangers of compromising them by being pulled hither and thither.[88] Referring to the British commitment to NATO, he observed:

> We shall need to settle the composition of our military presence in South East Asia in a way which will minimise the risk of the adverse repercussions which would be certain to follow from any suspicion that our commitment to NATO and European defence was being reduced.[89]

For all of these reasons, Carrington spelt out what he thought the UK military contribution to the proposed joint defence arrangements should be. In his view, British forces should be small in number and backed by a minimum of facilities; they should only be retained as long as they were welcome to their Commonwealth allies. He was adamant that they should neither be predominant nor more sophisticated than necessary for creating a sense of stability within the region. What did this mean in practice? Carrington felt that this role could be accomplished by a battalion group with an air defence platoon, an artillery battery, a flight of six Whirlwind helicopters, up to four Nimrod long-range maritime reconnaissance aircraft and five frigates or destroyers, one of which might be a guided missile destroyer, plus possibly an "O" class submarine that would roam the seas East of Suez and take in Hong Kong as well.[90] In manpower terms, the new garrison force would be roughly 3,000 servicemen with 4,000 dependents and the approximate cost of deploying them in Singapore might be at least £5m annually for the first three years.[91]

Replacing AMDA with a new five power defence agreement would not come cheap. Modest though Carrington's proposals were for the new British defence contribution in Southeast Asia and limited in the first instance to a trial five-year period, they would still prove to be far costlier than the sums envisaged by the Wilson government — a point that Maurice Macmillan, Chief Secretary to the Treasury, raised adroitly in a DOPC meeting on 22 July. Nonetheless, the Committee gave the green light to the recommendations of both Douglas-Home and Carrington, as did the Cabinet at its meeting on the following day.[92]

Carrington was under no illusions that the easier obstacles had been overcome and that he was likely to face a far sterner test of his credentials when he met his equatorial and Antipodean hosts in the days to come. Carrington's poise and unfailing charm carried him through the jetlag and the blustering of Lee and Gorton.[93] In truth, Heath and Douglas-Home, as well as the British diplomatic staff resident in the capitals he visited, had laid much of the groundwork for the urbane old Etonian. His hosts knew, or at the very least suspected, what gifts he would be bringing with him. They may still have been too little for Malaysia, who bemoaned the loss of AMDA and doubted the intrinsic value of multilateralism, but even in Kuala Lumpur, Tun Razak went on record as expressing satisfaction with the two days of talks his side had with the affable peer of the realm and his British delegation. Only time would tell, of course, whether the five powers could establish an operationally sound defence policy that would bring stability to the area, reassure the Malaysians and their southern neighbours, while posing an effective deterrent to all potential enemies of the two states lying within a degree or two of the equator.[94]

Meanwhile, Douglas-Home had few doubts about the success of Carrington's visit and described his tour of the four capitals as "a cracking success" that "laid a firm foundation for what we want to do...."[95] Carrington was inclined to agree with his former Premier since he had encountered less trouble than he anticipated. Far from being pushed to do more, he found general acceptance by the other four powers of the proposed British military contingent that would replace Far East Command after it was wound up at the end of 1971.[96] Carrington brought his proposals, now costing somewhere between £5m–£10m, to the DOPC on 5 October and had them endorsed as the basis for the Draft White Paper on Defence that he would unveil in the House of Lords at the end of the month.[97]

Interestingly enough, the "euphoria" that greeted Carrington on his visit in late July and early August began to erode in the weeks after he left the region. Replacing AMDA and the loss of the anchor role performed in it by the UK — never popular in the region — had become far more contentious with the other four powers the closer it came to terminating the old standard arrangement. In the absence of any formal document from the British on their future plans, dissatisfaction grew and the Malaysians, in particular — now with Razak as Prime Minister — responded to this lack of official information from London by becoming far more assertive and notably less sanguine about defence matters.[98] Although Working Parties had been weighing up the specific service issues in the interim period, Heath's government looked to be dragging its feet on this issue at some cost to itself.[99] At long last, the Foreign Secretary issued a draft communiqué on AMDA for consideration by the DOPC at its meeting on 16 October. Clearly the core of his paper, which he termed "not a treaty but a declaration of intention", lay in its fifth paragraph:

> Ministers also declared, in the interests of the external defence of Malaysia and Singapore, that in the event of any form of armed attack, externally organised or supported, or the threat of such attack against Malaysia or Singapore, their Governments would consult together for the purpose of deciding what measures should be taken jointly or separately in relation to such attack or threat.[100]

At the subsequent DOPC meeting, Douglas-Home hoped that all parties would agree to accept the terms of this communiqué as the basis for their official discussions on defence policy in London during the following spring. His confidence in the existence of this mutual support seems to have exceeded the cautious sentiments of the two Southeast Asian states most intimately affected by the loss of AMDA. Noticeably less accommodating than of late, they were both likely to drive a hard bargain when those talks began in 1971.[101]

After Carrington presented the Defence White Paper to Parliament on 28 October, detailed planning for the formation of the five-power defence arrangements reverted back to the Chiefs of Staff (COS) and the relevant ministry officials in Whitehall, as well as the military authorities on the spot in Singapore.[102] Needless to say, working out the interlocking elements of the new system would be both difficult and time consuming. From the outset, the COS favoured the establishment of some form of integrated ANZUK command structure for the external forces, which would operate alongside that of the independent Malaysian and Singaporean military leadership as far as ground forces and naval matters were concerned.[103] If IADS was to be effective, however, it would need a fully integrated five-power command centre.[104]

Senior officials of the five powers gathered at MINDEF in Singapore on 7–8 January 1971, to review the planning that had already been done by the Commander-in-Chief Far East (CINCFE) and his officers at Far East Command for the new defence system that would come into place upon AMDA's demise. By degrees constructive and yet contentious, this two-day meeting was hardly the military equivalent of the Woodstock love-in. Tension between the Malaysians and the Singaporeans was evident and not just over the fate of the Jungle Warfare School, the ownership of which the former claimed in its entirety. Lee Kuan Yew's courtship of the Soviet Union had been looked at askance by both the British and the Malaysians and his government's desire to charge rent for the use of all property and facilities by external troops was divisive to say the least. Despite the acrimonious self interest, progress was made on most of the basic issues for discussion at the five-power ministerial meeting arranged for London in April.[105]

It had also been possible for the three external powers to discuss their role in SEATO and what forces they might commit to it beyond April 1971. In a memo on this subject in mid-February, Carrington put forward his recommendation to the DOPC for an extension of the commitment in the following terms:

> Our decision to retain a military presence in South East Asia has created an expectation that we shall also reverse the Labour Government's plans to cancel the last of our SEATO force declarations on 1ˢᵗ April this year. Moreover, although Malaysia and Singapore are not members of SEATO, it would be difficult, because of the obvious connection between operations in those countries and operations in Thailand, to present a convincing argument to SEATO members for retaining a military presence in the area without participating actively in SEATO. I understand that the Australian and New Zealand Governments intend to maintain their current declarations. I judge, therefore, that renewal of our own declarations will be necessary if we are to reap the full political benefit from the decisions we have already taken.[106]

Pragmatic and designed to curry favour with the Nixon administration in Washington, the renewed British commitment to SEATO, though better than nothing, was still unlikely to bowl over either the State Department or the Pentagon, since the entire force that Carrington proposed offering them was hardly some kind of behemoth and did not include any nuclear bombers for deployment in support of either Plan 4 or Plan 9.[107] While it supported the declaration of ground forces, the DOPC pointed out that the battalion group involved would need three months before it could be operationally inserted into Thailand. Whatever its shortcomings, the British declaration in support of SEATO was seen as a political statement of intent and one that Carrington obviously hoped Nixon and Kissinger might appreciate. He would have done well to remember that all things were relative. His proposals were far better than Healey's, who was abandoning any force declarations to SEATO, but they appeared to be well short of the shock and awe factor that would really gain the attention of those in the White House, Foggy Bottom, and Arlington.[108]

Building on his SEATO declaration, Carrington's guarded largesse found further expression in his Defence White Paper of 17 February in the provision of an additional frigate or destroyer (making six in all) for the British military contribution to the five power defence arrangements in Southeast Asia. He also guaranteed that a submarine, previously expected to roam the seas of the Far East and appear intermittently in the waters off Singapore, would now be deployed on station in Sembawang.[109] These additional naval units represented a modest improvement over the forces promised in the previous October, but, once again, their importance lay more in the spirit of cooperation they engendered than anything else. It was a feeling of supportive benevolence that was sorely needed if the hopes invested in the five-power talks were not to be disappointed. It was clear that problems over several matters — the proposed communiqué, the terminal date for AMDA, jungle warfare training, and real estate issues, to name the most pressing — had arisen between the powers and hard bargaining was distinctly on the cards for the April meeting in London.[110]

Over the course of a two-day session (15–16 April), the ministerial representatives of the five-powers met in Whitehall and thrashed out most of the outstanding issues that had initially divided them. They eventually agreed on the wording of the communiqué — with its singular commitment to immediate consultation among the signatory powers if Malaysia and Singapore were either attacked or threatened with attack from external forces. It was agreed that the Five Power Defence Arrangements (FPDA) would have a Joint Consultative Committee comprising the Permanent Secretaries from Malaysia and Singapore and the High Commissioners from Australia, New Zealand and the UK. This body would meet on a regular basis, alternating between Kuala Lumpur and Singapore, to discuss defence issues of joint concern to all five-powers. It might be a little unfair to describe these worthy servants of the state as low key, but the truth was that no provision was made for regular ministerial-level conferences on defence matters. An Air Defence Council (of a broadly similar composition) was established to oversee the IADS which would be headquartered at the RMAF base at Butterworth in the state of Penang and become operational on 1 September 1971, with Australian Air Vice-Marshal R.T. Susans as its first Commander (CIADS).[111]

Not all was happiness and light, however, and Carrington did not carry the day on all matters. He had vainly hoped to convince Razak that the Jungle Warfare School at Ulu Tiram in Johor could be run as a Commonwealth Jungle Warfare Centre. It was a badly kept secret that the Malaysians were not interested in doing so. It took several months and a number of meetings between CINCFE (Air Chief Marshal Sir Brian Burnett) and the Malaysian Chief of Armed Forces Staff (General Ibrahim) together with some financial "horse trading" to settle the details of ANZUK's use of the training facilities.[112] He also fell a long way short in persuading an aggrieved Dr. Goh Keng Swee, Singapore's Minister of Defence, to modify his strident demand that ANZUK forces pay rent for the use of both the extensive range of facilities and accommodation on the island. Goh was not the most equitable individual at the best of times and he was temperamentally disinclined to yield ground if he thought others were seeking to take advantage of him. If the Malaysians continued to deny the Singaporeans jungle training opportunities and the Australians were not prepared to provide his armed forces with extensive air and ground training facilities, Dr. Goh felt justified in making ANZUK pay. For several months, the linked real estate-training issues lurched from crisis to crisis and looked distinctly capable of disrupting the FPDA before it could begin its official existence. This episodic soap opera — Burnett and Admiral Sir Peter Hill-Norton, Chief of the Defence Staff (CDS), referred to it as "The Forsyte Saga" — was hugely disruptive and aggravating. It did nothing to improve Australian-Singaporean relations and even the usually milder New Zealanders were bitterly upset by Goh's intransigence. Matters were eventually resolved; again the outcome was not entirely satisfactory, but — in the absence of the truculent John Gorton — a settlement that owed as much to compromise as good sense was finally reached.[113]

Ultimately, it was agreed that AMDA and Far East Command would cease to function at the end of October 1971 and be replaced by an integrated ANZUK force that would give effect to the Five Power Defence Arrangements with Malaysia and Singapore from 1 November 1971. If it was still a bitter pill to swallow — and that was by now debatable as Lee Kuan Yew wryly acknowledged — digestion of it was certainly made easier by the attractive sweeteners the British dispensed to their former colonies.[114] Apart from the grants they had already received from the Wilson regime, the Heath government handed over real estate (property and facilities) worth £168m to the Singaporeans alone. Across the border,

the Malaysians had gleefully and more speedily taken possession of the
excellent range of facilities existing at the Terendak, Seremban, Kluang, and
Sungei Patani military camps.[115]

Over time, Far East Command had been progressively reduced in
strength so that by the end of October 1971, only about 4,500 British
service personnel were left on the island of Singapore. A farewell parade
was memorably staged for all forces under Burnett's command at Sembawang in the late afternoon of Friday 29 October. In a display of unmis-
takeable symbolism, the Beating of Retreat and the hauling down of the
three service flags took place once the equatorial sun disappeared over the
skyline. A couple of days later, Far East Command disbanded and AMDA
quietly dissolved. Another vestige of British imperialism had gone into
retirement. Confirmation, if such was needed of this undeniable fact of
life, seamlessly followed. As the FPDA formally came into existence on 1
November 1971, so command of the new modest ANZUK Force, total-
ling roughly 7,000 men, was assumed by Rear-Admiral David C. Wells,
RAN.[116] A headline in Singapore's *New Nation* newspaper captured the
spectacle memorably: "The British Pull Out Causes Scarcely a Ripple".[117]
Times indeed had changed.

So was the outrageous indignation expressed by the Tories in January
1968 in response to the British military withdrawal from East of Suez
the usual knockabout stuff of the everyday parliamentary scene, and in
the end much ado about nothing? Frankly, it looks like it. Time, as we
know, has its way with pomp and circumstance. Opposition rhetoric is
often cheap; in denigrating the government of the day, it plays to the party
faithful, the press in search of a headline or two, and the "swing voters"
who might be persuaded that their new and temporary political allegiance
could lie elsewhere. Opposition leaders can promise a new deal safe in the
knowledge that they do not immediately have to pay the costs of what
they are proposing. When they come into power, those past promises can
come back to haunt them, but the nightmare rarely endures for long as
we have seen.

Ultimately, what the Tories committed themselves to "East of Suez"
was little more than what Healey and the Labour government had tried,
but failed, to arrange. Indeed, one could say that the only real difference
lay in the small number of troops and arms that the Heath government
left in Singapore to form part — and not the largest either — of ANZUK
Force.[118] It is emphatically clear that Carrington did not try to rescue
AMDA or give Far East Command a new lease of life. In establishing the
consultative FPDA framework for the defence of Malaysia and Singapore,

he gave effect to what had essentially become a bi-partisan commitment to render assistance to the two former colonies if such was needed in the future — and everyone hoped it would not be.[119]

Another perspective on this matter was offered by the acerbic diplomat Sir Arthur de la Mare, the British High Commissioner in Singapore (1968–1970). Looking back at Far East Command, the knight of the realm was far from nostalgic about the passing of the "good old days":

> By 1968 our grossly inflated military presence in Singapore had become an anachronism and an embarrassment. The Far East Command had outlived its usefulness. Its senior officers, lacking better employment, were driven to spend their time flitting from each capital of their purported bailiwick to another in a continuous round of 'orientation' and 'courtesy' visits which, by their frequency and lack of purpose, annoyed their foreign hosts and became a burden on Her Majesty's diplomatic representatives. It was not without cause that I wrote in my valedictory despatch from Singapore that the pretentious ostentation of our military establishment there 'provides the sniggers of our enemies and embarrasses our friends' ... If, now freed of the illusion of a military power which we could not sustain, we devote even the merest fraction of the time and money thus saved to the promotion of our commercial interests in East Asia our prestige will suffer no diminution: it will be enhanced.[120]

Notes

1.	Bob Dylan wrote this classic folk hit as an anthem for change and released it to great success in the US in 1964. It subsequently became a top ten hit in the UK in the following year.

2.	A popular aphorism attributed to Harold Wilson and thought to have been used by him during a lobby briefing in late 1964. It has now become a cliché, but like most tired expressions of this sort, there is still an element of truth in it.

3.	Nassim Nicholas Taleb, *The Black Swan: The Impact of the Highly Improbable* (London: Allen Lane, 2008).

4.	Peter Clarke, *A Question of Leadership: From Gladstone to Blair* (London: Penguin, 1999), pp. 235, 255, 258–66.

5.	According to his official biographer, Edward Heath actually hated and despised his gifted, pragmatic, and astonishingly insecure political rival. Philip Ziegler, *Edward Heath: The Authorised Biography* (London: HarperCollins, 2010), pp. 161–4, 174, 455. Lamenting about the manipulation of the media by the distinguished alumnus of Jesus College, Oxford, Heath described Wilson as a "charlatan". Tony Judt, *Postwar: A History of Europe Since 1945*

(New York: Penguin, 2010), p. 346. It was hardly an objective assessment, but it represented a deeply held view of the Labour leader, suggesting that he was a talented but untrustworthy figure — perhaps a Pennine Macchiavelli with a pipe.

6. A complex individual, the aloof and celibate Heath was never able to shed his "Selsdon Man" image in the post-1970 period. He was stuck with the opprobrium of being a "free marketeer" before it became the rage to be so and his U-Turns on Rolls Royce and Upper Clyde Shipbuilders (very un-Selsdon like) when in government ensured that his political rivals would attack him for lacking consistency and decisiveness. John Campbell, *Edward Heath: A Biography* (London: Jonathan Cape, 1993), pp. xviii, 233, 235, 264–8, 391, 539.

7. A closer investigation into the beginning of the end for the "East of Suez" policy will be given in my essay "What's in It For Us? Rethinking the British Defence Commitment to Singapore and Malaysia from Macmillan to Wilson", in *The Cold War in Southeast Asia*, ed. Malcolm H. Murfett (forthcoming).

8. Henry Kissinger, *Years of Upheaval* (Boston: Weidenfeld & Nicolson, 1982), pp. 137, 140–3; Ziegler, pp. 292–3, 331, 374–7, 379, 383–4.

9. Enoch Powell was decidedly unimpressed by Heath's European credentials and his courtship of the EEC. Sadly, like so much about the self-obsessed Powell, his comments were wounding, disrespectful and unfair. See Patrick Cosgrave, *The Lives of Enoch Powell* (London: Bodley Head, 1989), pp. 65, 117–8, 209–10, 266–7, 277–9, 291, 295–6, 305, 308, 310–26. Heath's attachment to the EEC may be followed in Campbell, *Edward Heath*, pp. 74–6, 112–3, 116–33, 246–7, 299–300, 334–6, 352–63, 396–405.

10. Toni Schönenberger, *Der britische Rückzug aus Singapore 1945–1976* (Zurich and Freiburg: Atlantis Verlag, 1981), pp. 27–30.

11. Ibid., p. 29.

12. *The Financial Times*, 21 July 1966; *The Mirror*, 16 May 1966.

13. David Easter, *Britain and the Confrontation with Indonesia 1960–1966* (London: I.B. Taurus, 2004), pp. 110–2.

14. John Darwin, *Britain and Decolonisation: The Retreat from Empire in the Post-War World* (London: Macmillan Education, 1988), p. 291; David Reynolds, *Britannia Overruled: British Policy and World Power in the Twentieth Century* (London: Longman, 1991), pp. 226–31.

15. House of Commons Debates, Vol. 704, 16 December 1964, col. 423ff, cited by Schönenberger, p. 107; *The Times*, 17 December 1964.

16. *The Daily Telegraph*, 16 May 1961.

17. *The Guardian*, 4 June 1966.

18. Kenneth O. Morgan, *Callaghan: A Life* (Oxford: Oxford University Press, 1997), p. 193.

19. Kenneth O. Morgan, *Britain Since 1945: The People's Peace* (Oxford: Oxford University Press, 2001), p. 243.

20. Ibid., pp. 231–6, 311, 402; Ben Pimlott, *Harold Wilson* (London: HarperCollins., 1992), pp. 302–5.

21. Saki Dockrill, *Britain's Retreat from East of Suez: The Choice between Europe and the World?* (Basingstoke: Palgrave Macmillan, 2002), pp. 43–226; Morgan, *Callaghan*, pp. 203–59.

22. Diane B. Kunz, "'Somewhat Mixed Up Together': Anglo-American Defence and Financial Policy during the 1960s", in *The Statecraft of British Imperialism: Essays in Honour of Wm. Roger Louis*, eds. Robert D. King and Robin W. Kilson (London: Frank Cass, 1999), pp. 213–32; Peter Lowe, *Contending with Nationalism and Communism: British Policy Towards Southeast Asia, 1945–65* (London: Palgrave Macmillan, 2009), pp. 82, 153–7, 231; P.L. Pham, *Ending 'East of Suez': The British Decision to Withdraw from Malaysia and Singapore 1964–1968* (Oxford: Oxford University Press, 2010), pp. 34–57.

23. Dockrill, *Britain's Retreat from East of Suez*, pp. 103–4, 134–7.

24. Easter, *Britain and the Confrontation with Indonesia*, pp. 174–92.

25. Morgan, *The People's Peace*, pp. 239, 254–5, 263–6.

26. Dockrill, *Britain's Retreat from East of Suez*, pp. 174–7; NA, CAB129/128, memorandum by George Brown and Denis Healey, *Defence Expenditure Studies*, C(67)40, 31 March 1967.

27. Harold Wilson, *The Labour Government 1964–70* (London: Penguin, 1974), p. 513.

28. Richard Crossman, *Diaries of a Cabinet Minister, Vol. II* (London: Cape, 1976), pp. 406–7.

29. Morgan, *Callaghan*, pp. 268–76.

30. Morgan, *The People's Peace*, p. 275.

31. Roy Jenkins, *A Life at the Centre* (London: Macmillan, 1991), pp. 222–3; Philip Ziegler, *The Authorised Life of Lord Wilson of Rievaulx* (London: HarperCollins, 1993), p. 211.

32. NA, CAB 129/135, telegrams George Thomson to Harold Wilson, No. 26, 8 January, No. 32, 9 January, memorandum by Michael Stewart, C(68)15, 11 January, memorandum by Thomson, C(68)23, 15 January 1968.

33. NA, CAB 129/135, telegram George Brown to Michael Stewart, No. 54, 11 January, attachment to *Singapore and Malaysia: Far East*, C(68)22, 12 January 1968.

34. Lee Kuan Yew, *From Third World to First: The Singapore Story: 1965–2000* (Singapore: Times Editions, Singapore Press Holdings, 2000), p. 58.

35. *The Times*, 18, 19, 25 January 1968.

36. *The Straits Times*, 19 January 1968.

37. When in Cabinet under Macmillan, Macleod had been a leading light in decolonisation and he admitted: "Of course, one day we shall leave. I think it is folly to assume anything else. But we believe it is wrong to name a date even in the mid-70s. However, having done so, to break our word, solemnly pledged and reaffirmed only a few months ago, is shameful and criminal". Schönenberger, p. 115.

38. James H. Willbanks, *The Tet Offensive: A Concise History* (New York: Columbia University Press, 2007); Ang Cheng Guan, *Southeast Asia and the Vietnam War* (New York: Routledge, 2010), pp. 54–78.

39. Schönenberger, p. 115.

40. *The Times*, 18 January 1968.

41. *The Straits Times*, 19 January 1968.

42. *The Times*, 19 January 1968.

43. *The Times*, 25 January 1968.

44. Ibid.

45. Ibid.

46. *The Times*, 26 January 1968.

47. Ibid.

48. Chin Kin Wah, *The Defence of Malaysia and Singapore: The Transformation of a Security System 1957–71* (Cambridge: Cambridge University Press, 1983), pp. 150–1.

49. Among the most important background studies and briefing papers for the British delegation to the Five Power Conference in Kuala Lumpur in June 1968 are the following (all held at NA): Healey to CDS, *Five Power Conference*, 14 March 1968, DEFE 25/251; Healey to CDS, *Brigade Exercise in the Far East*, 1 April 1968, DEFE 25/251; memorandum by F. Cooper (D.U.S.[P]), *Note on Visit to Wellington and Canberra — 27th March to 5th April, 1968*, 10 April 1968, DEFE 25/251; memorandum by Ministry of Defence, *Note of a Meeting at the Ministry of Defence on 22 May 1968*, 24 May 1968, DEFE 25/251; minute by J.F. Mayne, *Five Power Talks — Preliminary Discussions with Australia and New Zealand*, 20 March 1968, and attached memorandum, *The RAF's General Capability and Facilities needed in Malaysia and Singapore*, ETC/43/19/15, (undated), DEFE 25/251; *Ministry of Defence Conference Briefs for UK Delegation, (Nos. 1–25)*, May 1968, DEFE 13/693.

50. NA, PREM 13/2082, memorandum by British Delegation, *Five Power Conference on Far East Defence*, 11 June 1968; CAB148/35, minutes of OPD(68) 12th Mtg., 26 June 1968; Chin, *The Defence of Malaysia and Singapore*, pp. 153–6.

51. *The Guardian*, 10 August 1968.

52. *The Straits Times*, 21 August 1968.

53. Ibid. Such sentiments were exactly in line with the vulnerability felt by the Malaysians amidst the darkening contretemps that had broken out between the Philippines and themselves over the disputed sovereignty of Sabah on the island of Borneo. Would this issue disrupting two founder members of ASEAN (Association of South East Asian Nations) become the new Confrontation in Southeast Asia? It was clear that the jury was out on this issue since another mercurial figure (Ferdinand Marcos) had come into power in Manila, and with him, anything was seen as being possible. Malaysian politicians were not alone in wondering just how far the unpredictable Filipino president was prepared to go in whipping up the Sabah issue into a populist

nationalist movement that might be prepared to launch terrorist attacks on the East Malaysian state from either within or, less likely, without. No one knew for certain, but the Corregidor incident suggested that the days of counter-terrorism on the island of Borneo might not have ended. While the powers were inclined to think Marcos was merely playing to his home audience, none wanted the sovereignty of Sabah to endanger the Commonwealth defence system in Southeast Asia and much time was spent on the issue over the coming months. Chin, *The Defence of Malaysia and Singapore*, pp. 149–74; Michael Carver, *Out of Step: The Memoirs of Field Marshal Lord Carver* (London: Hutchinson, 1989), pp. 382–7.

54. *The Straits Times*, 21 August 1968.

55. *The Times*, 12 September 1968.

56. Enoch Powell, ever controversial, was far from convinced that the UK could afford to be mounting a military presence in Southeast Asia. When he was still responsible for "shadowing" defence matters as part of Heath's front bench team, he wrote a review in *The Spectator* on 3 February 1967 in which he declared: "The 'world role east of Suez' is a piece of humbug". He quickly followed this trenchant criticism with another piece in *The Sunday Times* on 12 February 1967: "We should be strong in our own quarter, in our own island; strong economically and strong militarily to defend ourselves and our neighbours. It is grotesque to imagine us reinvigorating and leading any alliance in Southeast Asia". After being dismissed from the Shadow Cabinet for his infamous "rivers of blood" anti-immigration speech, he returned to the theme of external defence, labelling it: "an exorbitant premium against a risk so remote that it cannot be identified ..." *The Times*, 19 September 1968; Cosgrave, *The Lives of Enoch Powell*, pp. 230–1. See also Jeffrey Pickering, *Britain's Withdrawal from East of Suez: The Politics of Retrenchment* (Basingstoke: St. Martin's Press, 1998), p. 145

57. Heath's position on defence matters "East of Suez" — like so much about the man — remains shrouded in mystery. Interesting insights are offered in Simon Heffer, *Like the Roman: The Life of Enoch Powell* (London: Weidenfeld & Nicolson, 1998), pp. 386–7, 391–4, 396–7, 405–8, 412, 424–5, 432, 441, 477–8; while there is surprisingly little in Ziegler, *Heath*, pp. 197–9, 392–4.

58. NA, DEFE 4/242, Far East Command to CDS, CINCFE 2320/6130/34, Enclosure to COS 5001/8/69, 29 July 1969.

59. *The Straits Times*, 4 January 1969; see also (all held at NA): minute by A. Campbell to Healey, DS 11/6/1/3/1, 31 December 1968, DEFE 25/247; minute by J.M. Stewart, E165, 6 January 1969, DEFE 25/237; memorandum by J.P. Mayne, *Five Power Talks*, MO/3/8/2, 9 January 1969, DEFE 25/247; Ministry of Defence Note of discussion at lunch between Healey, Gorton, Holyoake, and Hasluck on 13 January 1969, MO/3/8/2, DEFE 25/247.

60. Despite the lack of a final withdrawal date, Malaysian suspicions about Gorton remained and were fanned once more by his response to the communal riots that broke out in Kuala Lumpur on 13 May 1969. NA, DEFE

25/237, brief by J.M. Gibbon to Healey, E26/3/1, 28 February 1969; Chin, *The Defence of Malaysia and Singapore*, pp. 158–66.

61. NA, PREM 13/2082, FCO to Certain Missions and Dependent Territories, *Five Power Conference on South East Asia Defence*, Guidance No. 144, 5 June 1969; DEFE 25/248, Brief for Healey, *1969 Conference on Far East Defence*, OPD(69)27, 9 June, Steering Brief for UK Delegation, *Five Power Conference on Far East Defence June 1969*, 9 June 1969.

62. NA, DEFE 25/248, British High Commission (Singapore) [hereafter BHC, Singapore] to FCO, No.437, 24 June 1969.

63. Ibid.

64. NA, DEFE 25/248, note by F. Cooper to Healey, 17 June, telegram from Healey to FCO, No.609, 20 June 1969; DEFE 25/237 minute by Cooper to Healey, *Five-Power Conference, Canberra, June 1969*, 18 June 1969; DEFE 25/245, Defence Advisor, British High Commission, Singapore, Quarterly Report 2/69 (1 April–30 June 1969).

65. Australia had offered an Air Defence Commander for IADS, but the question of who would take the ultimate decision to attack an enemy remained unresolved. Chin, pp. 168–70.

66. Healey certainly was upbeat about the conference proceedings in a statement which he gave to the House of Commons on 2 July 1969. House of Commons Debates, Vol. 786, 2 July 1969, cols. 433–7, cited in Schönenberger, p. 207n31; *The Times*, 3 July 1969; NA, DEFE 25/248, Brief for Healey OPD(69)12th Mtg., *1969 Conference on Far East Defence*, OPD(69)33, 22 July 1969.

67. *The Mirror*, 16 October 1969.

68. Morgan, *The People's Peace*, pp. 289–92, 299–305.

69. Judt, *Postwar*, pp. 409–13, 496–500, 526.

70. NA, CAB129/147, *Draft Statement on the Defence Estimates*, 1970, Annex A, C(70)16, 27 January 1970.

71. Malcolm H. Murfett, John N. Miksic, Brian P. Farrell and Chiang Ming Shun, *Between Two Oceans: A Military History of Singapore from First Settlement to Final British Withdrawal* (Singapore: Marshall Cavendish Academic, 2004 [1999]), p. 402; Rob Williams, "The Australian Army and the Vietnam War 1962–1972", at <http://www.army.gov.au/ahu/docs/The_Australian_Army_and_the_Vietnam_War_Rob_Williams.pdf>

72. *The Straits Times*, 9 January 1970. It was an ambiguous position that Healey wanted Heath to clarify on the basis that the Opposition's defence policy might encourage the Australians and New Zealanders not to commit themselves on "East of Suez" questions until after the British General Election was held in 1970/71. NA, DEFE68/2, memorandum by J.F. Mayne, *Far East Commitments*, MO 3/8, 22 January 1970; Chin, pp. 170–1.

73. *The Straits Times*, 21 January 1970. Ian Orr-Ewing indicated that British investments in Malaysia and Singapore were worth more than £800m. *The Times*, 9 February 1970.

74. NA, DEFE68/2, memorandum by J.M. Gibbon, *Government and Opposition Policies East of Suez*, Hd.DS11/53, 6 February 1970.

75. Ibid.

76. NA, DEFE68/2, John K. Hickman (BHC, Singapore) to David P. Aiers, South West Pacific Dept., FCO, *Visit of Sir Alec Douglas-Home*, 11 March 1970.

77. Ibid.

78. NA, DEFE68/2, Anthony A. Duff (BHC, Kuala Lumpur) to David Aiers, FCO, 16 March 1970. This note needs to be contrasted with one in which a report is made of the Tunku's grave concern expressed over the UK's attitude to Malaysian defence in the post-withdrawal period: DEFE25/238, Richard Clift (BHC, KL) to David Le Breton, South West Pacific Dept, FCO, 8 May 1970.

79. To help reassure the Tunku and Lee that there could be life after AMDA, Exercise *Bersatu Padu* (Complete Unity) was held in Malaysia for several weeks from April 1970 onwards. It involved approximately 27,000 men, 500 transport vehicles, 10 armoured cars, 104 aircraft, 120 helicopters and 50 ships. It cost the UK a total of £2.5M alone. NA, DEFE 13/853, memorandum and brief for Healey, *Exercise Bersatu Padu*, D/DPR/73/2/2, 14 February, Ministry of Defence Press Release, *Exercise Bersatu Padu to be held in Western Malaysia*, 21/70, 23 February 1970; CAB 129/155, note by Carrington, *Statement on the Defence Estimates 1971*, CP(71)8, 26 January 1971; Chin, pp. 171–2.

80. In his final "East of Suez" policy statement made in June before the General Election, Healey gave the other four Commonwealth Powers an undertaking that 3,000 British troops would be trained on an annual basis at the Jungle Warfare Centre in Johor; a small number of RAF technicians would remain based at the Tengah air base in Singapore for help with the fledgling Singapore Air Force; and a warship might be deployed in the region for the entire year. Schönenberger, 42.

81. NA, DEFE68/2, BHC, Singapore to FCO, telegram 516, 23 June 1970; DEFE25/245, BHC, Singapore to FCO, telegram 515, 23 June 1970.

82. Lord Carrington, *Reflect on Things Past: The Memoirs of Lord Carrington* (London: Collins, 1988), pp. 225–7.

83. His instincts that carried him through on Europe, Hong Kong and Zimbabwe let him down over the Vassal case in 1961, and were absent once more at the time of the Falklands.

84. Ibid., p. 218.

85. NA, CAB148/101, memorandum by Sir Alec Douglas-Home, *Foreign Policy Issues*, Defence and Overseas Policy Committee, DOP(70)3, 29 June, memorandum by Carrington, *UK Military Presence in South East Asia after 1971*, DOP(70)10, 17 July 1970.

86. House of Commons Debates, Vol. 803, 2 July 1970, col. 80, cited in Schönenberger, p. 207n40; *The Times*, 3 July 1970.

87. NA, CAB148/101, memoranda by Douglas-Home, *Brunei*, DOP(70)9, 20 July, *Anglo-Malaysian Defence Agreement*, DOP(70)8, 20 July 1970, and *Priorities in our Foreign Policy*, DOP(70)13, 21 July 1970.

88. NA, DEFE 24/568, memorandum by FCO, *Priorities for British Interests Overseas, Country by Country*, (no date but likely post-July 1970).

89. NA, CAB148/101, memorandum by Carrington, *UK Military Presence in South East Asia after 1971*, DOP(70)10, 17 July 1970.

90. Ibid.

91. It is interesting to compare the initial annual cost of £2.5m–£3.5m given in NA, CAB128/47, Cabinet Conclusions CM(70) 8th Mtg., 23 July 1970 with the sum of £5–6m in Carrington's memorandum, *UK Military Presence in South-East Asia after 1971*, DOP(70)26, 1 October 1970.

92. NA, CAB148/101, memorandum by Maurice Macmillan, *U.K. Military Presence in South East Asia*, DOP(70)12, 21 July, DOP(70) 4th Mtg., 22 July 1970; CAB128/47, Cabinet Conclusions CM(70) 8th Mtg., 23 July 1970.

93. NA, DEFE 25/239, note of Carrington's discussions with Lee Kuan Yew at dinner on 26 July 1970, E26/3/1, 27 July, *Record of Official Talks in Singapore on 27th July between Carrington, Lim Kim San and Lee Kuan Yew*, MO25/3/2, 28 July, memorandum by Carrington for Heath, *Five Power Defence Arrangements and British Military Presence in South East Asia*, MO25/2/2, 6 August, memorandum by Carrington to CDS, Five Power Defence Arrangements and British Military Contribution, MO/3/8/2, 6 August 1970.

94. *The Straits Times*, 25, 26, 29, 30 July 1970; NA, DEFE 25/239, Sir Michael Walker (BHC, KL) to FCO, telegram 17, 10 August, FCO to BHC, Singapore, telegram 500, 12 August, BHC Singapore to FCO, telegram 18, 14 August 1970.

95. NA, DEFE 25/239, letter from Douglas-Home to Carrington, *Five Power Defence Arrangements and British Military Presence in South East Asia*, FCS/70/50, 15 August 1970.

96. NA, CAB 148/102, memorandum by Carrington, *UK Military Presence in South-East Asia after 1971*, DOP(70)26, 1 October 1970.

97. NA, CAB 148/101, minutes of DOP(70) 7th Mtg., 5 October 1970.

98. Tony Duff summed up the Malaysian position perfectly: "… it would still be worth pointing out to H.M.G. that a few frigates or destroyers were not a very impressive force; Malaysia would like to see an aircraft carrier stationed in South-East Asia". NA, DEFE 68/3, Anthony A. Duff (BHC, KL) to David Aiers (FCO), *Five Power Defence*, 10/109, 19 October, Sir Michael Walker (BHC, KL) to FCO, telegram 646, 16 October 1970.

99. Carrington admitted to Lee Kuan Yew on 5 October, that working out the Five Power Defence Arrangements was "going well, if somewhat slowly". See the record of their discussion at the Ministry of Defence in Whitehall, NA, DEFE 68/3, MO 25/8, 5 October 1970.

100. NA, CAB 148/102, memorandum by Douglas-Home, *Replacement of Anglo-Malaysian Defence Agreement*, DOP(70)32, 13 October 1970.

101. NA, CAB 148/101, minutes of DOP(70) 8th Mtg., 16 October 1970; DEFE 68/3, John Hickman (BHC, Singapore) to FCO, *British Contribution to Five — Power Defence*, telegram 793, 19 October, Hickman to FCO, telegram 815, *5-Power Defence*, 26 October 1970.
102. NA, CAB 129/153, memorandum by Carrington, *Presentation of Defence Policy*, CP(70)87, 14 October 1970; *Supplementary Statement on Defence Policy 1970*, Cmnd.4521, London, October 1970.
103. An ANZUK Planning Group was formed in Singapore in December 1970 with the aim of considering every aspect of establishing a three-power defence force in Singapore. It did just that. Its report was finalized in March 1971, and was contained in six volumes and spread over 1,500 pages in length. NA, DEFE 69/179, memorandum by Air Chief Marshal Sir Brian K. Burnett to Admiral Sir Peter Hill-Norton (Chief of Defence Staff, UK), *Commander-in-Chief Far East: End of Tour Report — November 1971*, 10 November 1971.
104. NA, DEFE 68/3, telegram FCO-Canberra, No.1093, 6 November 1970.
105. NA, CAB 129/155, note by Carrington, *Statement on the Defence Estimates 1971*, CP(71)8, 26 January 1971; CAB 148/102, note by Sir Burke Trend (Cabinet Secretary), *Interdepartmental Study on Defence Problems in the Indian Ocean*, DOP(70)49, 30 December 1970. Chin, 174–5.
106. NA, CAB 148/116, memorandum by Carrington, *Declaration of Forces to SEATO*, DOP(71)11, 12 February 1971.
107. Carrington proposed that the UK commit forces to Plan 4, which was designed to defend the SEATO area against an attack by China and North Vietnam; Plan 8, which dealt with counterinsurgency in Thailand; and Plan 9, which envisaged a North Vietnamese attack on Thailand. Previously, the Wilson government had declared forces for only Plans 4 and 8.
108. NA, CAB 148/115, minutes of DOP(71) 6th Mtg., 24 February 1971.
109. Chin, p. 175.
110. NA, CAB 148/116, memorandum by Carrington, *Five Power Defence Arrangements in Malaysia and Singapore*, DOP(71)24, 24 March 1971; ANZ, LONB — 106/7, Pt.11, minutes of meeting held between the Australian, British and New Zealand Ministers on 14 April 1971, No.3/8/3, 15 April 1971.
111. Chin, pp. 175–7.
112. Malaysia was not as forthcoming with the Singaporeans who were denied use of these training facilities and had to seek them elsewhere. Ibid., pp. 175, 210–1n110. NA, DEFE 69/179, memorandum by Burnett to Hill-Norton, *Commander-in-Chief Far East: End of Tour Report — November 1971*, 10 November 1971.
113. In the eventual settlement, the Australians and New Zealanders were not charged for any military facilities, but were required to pay rent (at less than market rates) for the accommodation, sporting and educational facilities they

used. For a glimpse at some of the background to this saga: NA, DEFE68/3, FCO to BHC, Canberra, *Five Power Defence*, undated (likely early June 1971); DEFE 5/190/15, note by Air Commodore B.G.T. Stanbridge (Secretary to COS Co.), COB 48/71, 30 June 1971; DEFE 69/179, memorandum by Burnett to Hill-Norton, *Commander-in-Chief Far East: End of Tour Report — November 1971*, 10 November 1971; CAB148/115, minutes of DOP(71) 12th Mtg., 16 June 1971. ANZ, LONB106/7, Pt. 11, telegrams Douglas-Home to BHC, Singapore, No.724, 14 June, Douglas-Home to BHC, Canberra, No. 632, 14 June, D.P. Aiers (FCO) to J.D.L. Richards, (NZHC, London), 17 June 1971; LONB — 106/7 Pt.12, telegram FCO to BHC, Singapore, No. 953, 9 September 1971; Chin, 177.

114. In an interview Lee gave to *The Mirror* on 13 April 1970, he coyly admitted: "… what appeared to be a calamity when the British Government announced that they were to close down their bases in January 1968, has now turned out a blessing, though not altogether unmixed".

115. NA, DEFE 69/179, memorandum by Burnett to Hill-Norton, *Commander-in-Chief Far East: End of Tour Report — November 1971*, 10 November 1971; Murfett *et al.*, *Between Two Oceans*, pp. 404–5.

116. ANZUK Force comprised roughly 3,300 Australians, 2,550 British, and 1,150 New Zealanders. Chin Kin Wah, *The Five Power Defence Arrangements and AMDA* [Occasional Paper No.23] Singapore, 1974; David Stevens, "The British Naval Role East of Suez: An Australian Perspective", in *British Naval Strategy East of Suez 1900–2000: Influences and Actions*, ed. Greg Kennedy (London: Routledge, 2005), p. 239.

117. C.M. Turnbull, *A History of Modern Singapore 1819–2005* (Singapore: NUS Press, 2009), p. 313.

118. Talking up the British military commitment beyond November 1971, Lee Kuan Yew observed: "In terms of numbers, it is a modest force. But because of the experience, expertise and sophistication of the equipment of these forces, they will make a significant contribution to peace and stability in the Malaysia-Singapore area". *The Mirror*, 9 November 1970.

119. While the FPDA remains in existence at the time of publication (2011), ANZUK Force was not so fortunate. It had a brief existence being undermined by political events off stage in Australia and the UK. Gough Whitlam's administration in Canberra decided to withdraw its ground troops from Singapore and they were gone by February 1974, while the Wilson government's decision to end their force declarations to SEATO, CENTO, and the FPDA saw the last of the British servicemen leave the island republic in March 1976. *The Financial Times*, 31 March 1976; Murfett *et al.*, *Between Two Oceans*, pp. 404–6.

120. NA, DEFE69/179, memorandum by Sir Arthur de la Mare (British Ambassador in Bangkok) to Douglas-Home, *The End of Far East Command: Are We Diminished?*, 3 November 1971.

Bibliography

Archival Sources*

*For primary sources available online, please refer to the Notes section in this volume.

Archives New Zealand (ANZ)

London High Commission Records

BBC Archives

BBC Written Archives
Listener Research Department Reports
Listener Survey Department Reports

British Library (BL)

Balfour Papers

Cambridge University Library (CUL)

Crewe Papers
Harding Papers
Jardine Matheson Papers

Library and Archives Canada (Ottawa) (LAC)

W.L. Mackenzie King Diary

Churchill Archives Centre, Churchill College, Cambridge University (CAC)

Leo Amery Papers
Julian Amery Papers
Lawrence Burgis Papers
Winston Churchill Papers
Dennis Kelly Papers
Maurice Hankey Papers
Norwich (Duff Cooper) Papers
British Diplomatic Oral History Programme

Liddell Hart Centre for Military Archives (Kings College London) (LHCMA)

Brooke-Popham Papers

Mass Observation Archive (University of Sussex) (MO)

File Reports

National Archives (United Kingdom), Kew (NA)

Admiralty Records (ADM series)
Cabinet Office Records (CAB series)
Colonial Office Records (CO series)
Ministry of Defence Records (DEFE series)
Prime Minister's Office Records (PREM series)
War Office Records (WO series)
Kitchener Papers

Printed Sources

Addison, Paul. *The Road to 1945*. London: Jonathan Cape, 1975.
_____. *Churchill on the Home Front 1900–1955*. London: Jonathan Cape, 1992.
Allen, Louis. *Singapore 1941–42*. London: Davis-Poynter Ltd, 1977.
Ang, Cheng Guan. *Southeast Asia and the Vietnam War*. New York: Routledge, 2010.
Angell, Norman. "A Re-Interpretation of Empire". *United Empire* 43 (September–October 1952).
Ball, Stuart, ed. *Parliament and Politics in the Age of Churchill and Attlee: The Headlam Diaries, 1935–1951*. London: Cambridge University Press for the Royal Historical Society, 1999.
Barnes, John and David Nicholson. *The Empire at Bay: The Leo Amery Diaries 1929–1945*. London: Hutchinson. 1988.
Niall Barr. *The Pendulum of War: The Three Battles of El Alamein*. London: Pimlico, 2005.
Cabinet Office (UK). *Principal War Telegrams and Memoranda 1940–1943, Vol. 1*. Nandeln, Lichtenstein: KTO Press, 1976.
Bayly, Christopher and Tim Harper. *Forgotten Armies: Britain's Asian Empire and the War with Japan*. London: Allen Lane, 2004.
Bell, Christopher. *The Royal Navy, Seapower and Strategy Between the Wars*. London: Macmillan, 2000.
_____. "The 'Singapore Strategy' and the Deterrence of Japan: Winston Churchill, the Admiralty, and the Dispatch of Force Z". *English Historical Review* 116 (2001).
Best, Geoffrey. *Churchill: A Study in Greatness*. Oxford: Hambledon & London, 2001.

Boberach, Heinz, ed. *Meldungen Aus Dem Reich 1938–1945: Die geheimen Lageberichte des Sicherheitsdienste der SS*, Vol. 9. Berlin: Pawlak Verlag Herrsching, 1984.

Blake, Robert and William Roger Louis, eds. *Churchill: A Major New Reassessment of His Life in Peace and War*. Oxford: Oxford University Press, 1993.

Blunt, W.S. *My Diaries, Vol. II 1900–1914*. London: M. Secker, 1920.

Bramsted, Ernest K. *Goebbels and National Socialist Propaganda 1925–1945*. N.P.: The Cresset Press, 1965.

Brendon, Piers. *Winston Churchill: A Short Life*. New York: Harper & Row, 1984.

————. *The Dark Valley: A Panorama of the 1930s*. New York: Viking Books, 2002 [2000].

————. *The Decline and Fall of the British Empire*. London: Jonathan Cape, 2007.

Brown, J.M. "Gandhi — A Victorian Gentleman: An Essay in Imperial Encounter". *Journal of Imperial and Commonwealth History* XXVII (May 1999).

Buchan, Alastair, ed. *Problems in Modern Strategy*. London: Chatto and Windus, 1970.

Callaghan, John *et al.*, eds. *In Search of Social Democracy: Responses to Crisis and Modernisation*. Manchester: Manchester University Press, 2009.

Callahan, Raymond A. *Churchill: Retreat from Empire*. Wilmington, DE: Scholarly Resources, 1984.

————. *Churchill and His Generals*. Lawrence, KS: University Press of Kansas, 2007.

Campbell, John. *Edward Heath: A Biography*. London: Jonathan Cape, 1993.

Cannadine, David. *In Churchill's Shadow: Confronting the Past in Modern Britain*. London: Allen Lane, 2002.

Carrington, Lord. *Reflect on Things Past: The Memoirs of Lord Carrington*. London: Collins, 1988.

Bonham Carter, Violet. *Winston Churchill As I Knew Him*. New York: Harcourt, Brace & World, 1965.

Carver, Michael. *Out of Step: The Memoirs of Field Marshal Lord Carver*. London: Hutchinson, 1989.

Chadha, Yogesh. *Rediscovering Gandhi*. London: Century, 1997.

Chan, Heng Chee and Obaid ul Haq, eds. *The Prophetic and the Political: Selected Speeches and Writings of S. Rajaratnam*. Singapore: Graham Brash, 1987.

Charteris-Black, Jonathan. *Politicians and Rhetoric: The Persuasive Power of Metaphor*. London: Palgrave Macmillan, 2005.

Chew, Ernest C.T. and Edwin Lee, eds. *Singapore: A History*. Singapore: Oxford University Press, 1991.

Chin, Kin Wah. *The Defence of Malaysia and Singapore: The Transformation of a Security System 1957–71*. Cambridge: Cambridge University Press, 1983.

Churchill, Randolph S. and Martin Gilbert. *Winston S. Churchill*, 8 vols., plus *Companions*. London: Heinemann, 1966–continuing.

Churchill, Winston S. *My African Journey*. London: Icon Books, 1964.

_____. *The Collected Works of Sir Winston Churchill*, 34 vols. London: Library of Imperial History in association with Hamlyn Publishing Group Limited, 1973–1976.

_____. *The Second World War*, 6 vols. London: Cassell, 1948–1954.

_____. *Savrola*. New York: Random House, 1974.

_____. *The Story of the Malakand Field Force*. London: Library of Imperial History, 1974.

_____. *London to Ladysmith via Pretoria*. London: Library of Imperial History, 1974.

_____. *The River War*, I. London: Longmans, Green & Co, 1899.

_____. *The River War*, II. London: Longmans, Green & Co, 1902.

Churchill, Winston S., ed. *Never Give In! The Best of Winston Churchill's Speeches*. London: Hyperion, 2003.

Clarke, Peter. *A Question of Leadership: From Gladstone to Blair*. London: Penguin, 1999.

_____. *The Cripps Version: The Life of Sir Stafford Cripps*. London: Allen Lane, 2002.

Cohen, Michael J. *Churchill and the Jews*. London: Frank Cass, 2003.

Collini, Stefan. *Liberalism and Sociology: L.T. Hobhouse and Political Argument in England 1880–1914*. London: Cambridge University Press, 1979.

Colville, John. *The Fringes of Power: Downing Street Diaries, 1939–1955*. London: Hodder & Stoughton, 1985.

Cooper, Artemis. *Cairo in the War 1939–1945*. London: H. Hamilton, 1989.

Cosgrave, Patrick. *The Lives of Enoch Powell*. London: Bodley Head, 1989.

Crossman, Richard. *Diaries of a Cabinet Minister*, 2 vols. London: Cape, 1976.

Curran, James. "'An Organic Part of the Whole Structure': John Curtin's Empire". *Journal of Imperial and Commonwealth History* 37 (2009): 51–75.

Danchev, Alex. *Very Special Relationship: Field Marshal Sir John Dill and the Anglo-American Alliance 1941–1944*. London: Brasseys, 1986.

Danchev, Alex and Daniel Todman, eds. *War Diaries 1939–1945: Field Marshal Lord Alanbrooke*. London: Weidenfeld & Nicolson, 2001.

Darwin, John. *Britain and Decolonisation: The Retreat from Empire in the Post-War World*. London: Macmillan Education, 1988.

_____. *The Empire Project: The Rise and Fall of the British World-System 1830–1970*. Cambridge: Cambridge University Press, 2009.

Day, David. *The Great Betrayal: Britain, Australia & the Onset of the Pacific War 1939–42*. London: Angus & Robertson, 1988.

_____. *Menzies & Churchill at War*. Melbourne: Oxford University Press, 1993.

_____. *The Politics of War*. Sydney. Pymble, NSW: HarperCollins, 2003.

Dilks, David. *'The Great Dominion': Winston Churchill in Canada, 1900–1954*. Toronto: Thomas Allen, 2005.

Dilks, David, ed. *The Diaries of Sir Alexander Cadogan*. New York: Putnam, 1971.

Dockrill, Saki. *Britain's Retreat from East of Suez: The Choice between Europe and the World?* Basingstoke: Palgrave Macmillan, 2002.

Eade, Charles, ed. *Secret Session Speeches by the Right Hon. Winston S. Churchill O.M., C.H., M.P.* London: Cassell and Co, 1946.

Easter, David. *Britain and the Confrontation with Indonesia 1960–1966.* London: I.B. Taurus, 2004.

Edgerton, David. *England and the Aeroplane: An Essay on a Militant and Technological Nation.* London: Macmillan, 1991.

Edwards, Peter. "Labor's Vice-Regal Appointments: The Case of John Curtin and the Duke of Gloucester, 1943". *Labour History* 34 (May 1978).

Elphick, Peter. *Far Eastern File: The Intelligence War in the Far East 1930–1945.* London: Hodder & Stoughton, 1998.

Emmert, Kirk. *Winston S. Churchill on Empire.* Durham, NC: Carolina Academic Press, 1989.

Farrell, Brian P. *The Basis and Making of British Grand Strategy 1940–1943: Was There a Plan?* Lewiston, NY: Edwin Mellen Press, 1998.

————. *The Defence and Fall of Singapore 1940–1942.* Stroud: Tempus, 2005.

————. *Leadership and Responsibility in the Second World War: Essays in Honour of Robert Vogel.* Montreal: McGill-Queen's University Press, 2004.

Farrell, Brian P. and Sandy Hunter, eds. *Sixty Years On: The Fall of Singapore Revisited.* Singapore: Eastern Universities Press, 2002.

Fay, Peter W. *The Opium War 1840–1842.* Chapel Hill, NC: UNC Press, 1975.

Ferguson, Niall. *Empire: The Rise and Demise of the British World Order and the Lessons for Global Power.* New York: Basic Books, 2004.

Ferris, John R. *Men, Money and Diplomacy: The Evolution of British Strategic Policy 1919–1926.* Ithaca, NY: Cornell University Press, 1989.

Finlayson, Alan and James Martin. "'It Ain't What You Say …': British Political Studies and the Analysis of Speech and Rhetoric". *British Politics* 3 (2008): 445–64.

Foster, Roy F. *Lord Randolph Churchill.* Oxford: Clarendon Press, 1981.

Freeman, Charles W., Jr. *The Diplomat's Dictionary.* Washington, DC: United States Institute of Peace Press, 1997.

Freudenberg, Graham. *Churchill and Australia.* Sydney: Macmillan, 2008.

Frost, Mark R. and Yu-Mei Balasingamchow. *Singapore: A Biography.* Hong Kong: Hong Kong University Press, 2010.

Garfield, Simon, ed. *Private Battles: How The War Almost Defeated Us.* London: Ebury Press, 2007 [2006].

Gelber, H.G. *Nations Out of Empires.* Basingstoke: Palgrave, 2001.

Gilbert, Martin. *Winston S. Churchill*, IV. London: Heineman, 1975.

————. *Winston S. Churchill*, V. London: Heineman, 1979.

————. *Winston S. Churchill*, VI. London: Heineman, 1983.

————. *Churchill: A Life.* London: Pimlico, 2000

Gilbert, Martin, ed. *The Churchill War Papers, Vol. III: The Ever Widening War: 1941.* New York. W.W. Norton & Co., 2000.

Gilmour, D. *The Long Recessional: The Imperial Life of Rudyard Kipling.* New York: Farrar, Strous & Giroux, 2002.

Gilmour, O.W. *With Freedom in Singapore*. London: Ernest Bonn, 1950.

Hack, Karl. *Defence and Decolonisation: Britain, Malaya and Singapore 1941–1967*. London: Routledge, 2001.

Hack, Karl and Kevin Blackburn. *Did Singapore Have to Fall? Churchill and the Impregnable Fortress*. London: Routledge, 2004.

Hamill, Ian. *The Strategic Illusion: The Singapore Strategy and the Defence of Australia and New Zealand 1919–1942*. Singapore: Singapore University Press, 1981.

Halifax, Lord. *Fulness of Days*. London: Collins, 1957.

Halle, Louis J. *American Foreign Policy: Theory and Reality*. London: Bradford & Dickens, 1960.

Herman, Arthur. *Gandhi and Churchill*. London: Arrow Books, 2009.

Hart, B.H. Liddell. *Strategy: The Indirect Approach*. London: Faber and Faber Limited, 1967.

Hastings, Max. *Finest Years: Churchill As Warlord 1940–45*. London: HarperPress, 2009 [also published in New York by Alfred A. Knopf under the title *Winston's War: Churchill, 1940–1945*, 2010].

Heffer, Simon. *Like the Roman: The Life of Enoch Powell*. London: Weidenfeld & Nicolson, 1998.

Horner, David. *High Command: Australia and Allied Strategy 1939–1945*. Sydney: George Allen & Unwin, 1982.

Hudson, W.J. and R.G. Neale, eds. *Documents on Australian Foreign Policy 1937–39*, 16 vols. Canberra: Australian Government Publications Service, 1975–1998.

Huxley, E. *White Man's Country: Lord Delamere and the Making of Kenya*, 2 vols. London: Chatto & Windus, 1935.

Hyam, Ronald. *Understanding the British Empire*. Cambridge: Cambridge University Press, 2010.

————. *Britain's Declining Empire*. Cambridge: Cambridge University Press, 2006.

————. *Elgin and Churchill at the Colonial Office, 1905–1908*. London: Macmillan, 1968.

————. "Winston Churchill Before 1914". *Historical Journal* XII, 1 (1969): 169.

Jackson, Ashley. *The British Empire and the Second World War*. London: Hambledon Continuum, 2006.

James, Lawrence. *The Rise and Fall of the British Empire*. New York: Little, Brown, 1994.

James, Robert Rhodes. *Churchill: A Study in Failure 1900–1939*. London: Penguin, 1981.

Jenkins, Roy. *A Life at the Centre*. London: Macmillan, 1991.

Judd, Dennis. *Empire: The British Imperial Experience from 1765 to the Present*. London: Phoenix Press, 2001.

Judt, Tony. *Postwar: A History of Europe Since 1945*. New York: Penguin, 2010.

Kennedy, Greg, ed. *British Naval Strategy East of Suez 1900–2000: Influences and Actions*. London: Routledge, 2005.

Kimball, Warren F., ed. *Churchill & Roosevelt: The Complete Correspondence*, 3 vols. New York: Collins, 1984.

King, Cecil. *With Malice Toward None: A War Diary*. London: Sidgwick and Jackson, 1970.

King, Robert D. and Robin W. Kilson, eds. *The Statecraft of British Imperialism: Essays in Honour of William Roger Louis*. London: Frank Cass, 1999.

Kimball, Warren F., ed. *Churchill and Roosevelt: The Complete Correspondence*, Vol. 1. Princeton, NJ: Princeton University Press, 1984.

Kissinger, Henry. *Years of Upheaval*. London: Weidenfeld & Nicolson, 1982.

Koebner, Richard and Helmut Dan Schmidt. *Imperialism: The Story and Significance of a Political Word, 1840–1960*. Cambridge: Cambridge University Press, 1964.

Lamb, Richard. *Churchill as War Leader — Right or Wrong*. London: Bloomsbury, 1991.

Lee, Kuan Yew. *The Singapore Story: Memoirs of Lee Kuan Yew*. Singapore: Singapore Press Holdings, 1998.

————. *From Third World to First: The Singapore Story: 1965–2000*. Singapore: Times Editions, Singapore Press Holdings, 2000.

Leifer, Michael. *Singapore's Foreign Policy: Coping with Vulnerability*. London: Routledge, 2000.

Leslie, A. *Jennie: The Life of Lady Randolph Churchill*. London: Hutchinson, 1969.

Lindquist, S. *Exterminate All the Brutes*. London: Granta, 1997.

Low, David. *Low's Autobiography*. London: Michael Joseph, 1956.

Lowe, Peter. *Contending with Nationalism and Communism: British Policy Towards Southeast Asia, 1945–65*. London: Palgrave Macmillan, 2009.

Lukacs, John. *Blood, Toil, Tears & Sweat: The Dire Warning*. New York: Basic Books, 2008.

Louis, William Roger. *Ends of British Imperialism*. London: I.B. Tauris, 2006.

————. *Imperialism at Bay: The United States and the Decolonization of the British Empire, 1941–1945*. Oxford: Oxford University Press, 1977.

————. *The British Empire in the Middle East*. London: Oxford University Press, 1984.

————. *In the Name of God, Go! Leo Amery and the British Empire in the Age of Churchill*. New York. W.W. Norton, 1992.

Macmillan, Harold. *Tides of Fortune 1945–1955*. London: Macmillan, 1969.

Mallaby, George. *From My Level: Unwritten Minutes*. London: Hutchinson of London, 1965.

Manchester, William. *The Last Lion: Winston Spencer Churchill: Alone, 1932–1940*. New York: Bantam, 1989.

Marder, Arthur J. *From the Dreadnought to Scapa Flow*, Vol. I. Oxford: Oxford University Press, 1961.

Mars, Alastair. *British Submarines at War*. London: William Kimber, 1971.

Marwick, Arthur. *The Nature of History*. London: Macmillan Education Limited, 1987.

Maurer, John H., ed. *Churchill and Strategic Dilemmas Before the World Wars*. London: Frank Cass, 2003.

MacKenzie, John M. "'Comfort' and Conviction: A Response to Bernard Porter". *Journal of Imperial and Commonwealth History* 36 (2008).

Mansergh, Nicholas *et al.*, eds. *The Transfer of Power 1942–47*, 12 vols. London: HMSO, 1970–1983.

McCarthy, John. *Australia and Imperial Defence 1918–39: A Study in Air and Sea Power*. St Lucia, Queensland: University of Queensland Press, 1976.

McIntyre, David. *The Rise and Fall of the Singapore Naval Base 1919–1942*. London: Macmillan, 1979.

Menzies, Robert. *Afternoon Light*. London: Cassell, 1967.

Millgate, Helen D., ed. *Mr. Brown's War: A Diary of the Second World War*. Stroud: Sutton Publishing, 2003 [1998].

Moon, Penderel, ed. *Wavell: The Viceroy's Journal*. London: Oxford University Press, 1973.

Moran, Lord. *Winston Churchill: The Struggle for Survival, 1940–1965*. London: Constable, 1966.

Morgan, Kenneth O. *Callaghan: A Life*. Oxford: Oxford University Press, 1997.

————. *Britain Since 1945: The People's Peace*. Oxford: Oxford University Press, 2001.

Morgan, T. *Churchill 1874–1915*. London: Triad/Panthe, 1983.

Murfett, Malcolm H. *et al. Between Two Oceans: A Military History of Singapore from First Settlement to Final British Withdrawal*. Singapore: Marshall Cavendish Academic, 2004 [1999].

Myers, Frank. "Harold Macmillan's 'Winds of Change' Speech: A Case Study in the Rhetoric of Policy Change". *Rhetoric & Public Affairs* 3 (2000).

Neidpath, James. *The Singapore Naval Base and the Defence of Britain's Eastern Empire 1918–1941*. Oxford: Clarendon Press, 1981.

Nicholas, H.G., ed. *Washington Despatches 1941–1945: Weekly Reports from the British Embassy*. Chicago: University of Chicago Press, 1981.

Nicolson, Nigel, ed. *Harold Nicolson: Diaries and Letters 1939–1945*. London: Collins, 1967.

Nixon, Richard M. *Leaders*. London: Sidgwick & Jackson, 1982.

Observer, The, eds., *Churchill by His Contemporaries: An Observer Appreciation*. London: Hodder and Stoughton, 1965.

Ong, Chit Chung. *Operation Matador: Britain's War Plans Against the Japanese 1918–1941*. Singapore: Times Academic Press, 1997.

Orwell, Sonia and Ian Angus, eds. *The Collected Essays, Journalism and Letters of George Orwell Vol. 2: My Country Right or Left, 1940–1943*. London: Penguin, 1970 [1968].

[Various authors]. *Oxford Dictionary of National Biography*. Oxford: Oxford University Press, 2004.

Paterson, T. *A Seat for Life*. Dundee: David Winter, 1981.

Pelling, Henry. *Winston Churchill*. London: Macmillan, 1974.

Pham, P.L. *Ending 'East of Suez': The British Decision to Withdraw from Malaysia and Singapore 1964–1968*. Oxford: Oxford University Press, 2010.

Pickering, Jeffrey. *Britain's Withdrawal from East of Suez: The Politics of Retrenchment*. Basingstoke: St. Martin's Press, 1998.

Pickersgill, J.W. *The Mackenzie King Record*, 3 vols. Toronto: Toronto University Press, 1960–1970.

Pimlott, Ben. *Harold Wilson*. London: HarperCollins, 1992.

Porter, Bernard. *The Absent-Minded Imperialists: Empire, Society, and Culture in Britain*. Oxford: Oxford University Press, 2004.

_____. "Further Thoughts on Imperial Absent-Mindedness". *Journal of Imperial and Commonwealth History* 36 (2008).

Pottle, Mark, ed. *Champion Redoubtable: The Diaries and Letters of Violet Bonham Carter, 1914–1945*. London: Weidenfeld & Nicholson, 1998.

Probert, Henry. *The Forgotten Air Force: The Royal Air Force in the War Against Japan 1941–1945*. London: Brasseys, 1995.

Ramsden, John. *Man of the Century: Winston Churchill and His Legend since 1945*. New York: Columbia University Press, 2003.

Reynolds, David. *Britannia Overruled: British Policy and World Power in the Twentieth Century*. London: Longman, 2000 [1991].

_____. *In Command of History: Churchill Fighting and Writing the Second World War*. London: Allen Lane, 2004.

James, Robert Rhodes, ed. *Winston S. Churchill: His Complete Speeches, 1897–1963*, 8 vols. New York: Chelsea House, 1974.

_____. *Churchill Speaks 1897–1963: Collected Speeches in Peace and War*. Leicester: Windward, 1981.

_____. *'Chips': The Diaries of Sir Henry Channon*. London: Weidenfeld and Nicolson, 1993 [1967].

Roskill, Stephen W. *Naval Policy Between the Wars*, 2 vols. London: Collins, 1968, 1976.

Ryan, Henry B. "A New Look at Churchill's 'Iron Curtain' Speech". *The Historical Journal* 22 (1979).

Sarantakes, Nicholas Evan. *Allies Against the Rising Sun: The United States, the British Nations and the Defeat of Imperial Japan*. Lawrence, KS: University Press of Kansas, 2009.

Schönenberger, Toni. *Der britische Rückzug aus Singapore 1945–1976*. Zurich and Freiburg: Atlantis Verlag, 1981.

Schuckburgh, Evelyn. *Descent to Suez: Diaries 1951–56*. London: Weidenfeld & Nicolson, 1986.

Sherwood, Robert E. *The White House Papers of Harry L. Hopkins*, 2 vols. London: Eyre & Spottiswoode, 1949.

Seldon, A. *Churchill's Indian Summer*. London: Faber & Faber Limited, 1981.

Slim, Field Marshal Viscount. *Defeat into Victory: Battling Japan in Burma and India, 1942–1945*. New York: Cooper Square Press, 2000.

Spurr, David. *The Rhetoric of Empire: Colonial Intercourse in Journalism, Travel Writing, and Imperial Administration*. Durham, NC: Duke University Press, 1993.

Stafford, David. *Churchill and Secret Service*. London: John Murray, 1997.

Stern, Fritz, ed. *The Varieties of History from Voltaire to the Present*. New York: Vintage Books, 1972.

Stewart, Andrew. *Empire Lost: Britain, the Dominions and the Second World War*. London: Continuum, 2008.

Taleb, Nassim Nicholas. *The Black Swan: The Impact of the Highly Improbable*. London: Allen Lane, 2008.

Tarling, Nicholas. *The Fall of Imperial Britain in Southeast Asia*. Oxford: Oxford University Press, 1993.

Taylor, A.J.P. *et al. Churchill: Four Faces and the Man*. London: Allen Lane, 1967.

Thompson, Andrew S. "The Language of Imperialism and the Meanings of Empire: Imperial Discourse in British Politics, 1895–1914". *Journal of British Studies* 36 (1997).

Thompson, R.W. *The Yankee Marlborough*. London: Allen & Unwin, 1963.

Thorne, Christopher. *Allies of a Kind: The United States, Britain, and the War Against Japan 1941–45*. New York: Oxford University Press, 1978.

Tohmatsu, Haruo and H.P. Willmott. *A Gathering Darkness: The Coming of War to the Far East and the Pacific, 1921–42*. Lanham, MD: SR Books, 2004.

Toye, Richard. *Churchill's Empire: The World That Made Him and the World He Made*. London: Macmillan, 2010.

Tulis, Jeffrey K. *The Rhetorical Presidency*. Princeton, NJ: Princeton University Press, 1987.

Turnbull, C.M. *A History of Modern Singapore 1819–2005*. Singapore: NUS Press, 2009 [1977].

von Clausewitz, Carl. *On War*, Book I, "On the Nature of War". London: N. Trübner, 1873.

Waller, P.J., ed. *Politics and Social Change in Modern Britain*. Brighton: Harvester, 1987.

Warren, Alan. *Singapore 1942: Britain's Greatest Defeat*. London: Talisman, 2002.

Webster, Wendy. *Englishness and Empire 1939–1965*. Oxford: Oxford University Press, 2005.

Weidhorn, Manfred. "Churchill the Phrase Forger". *Quarterly Journal of Speech* 58 (1972).

West, Mrs George Cornwallis. *The Reminiscences of Lady Randolph Churchill*. London: Edward Arnold, 1908.

Willbanks, James H. *The Tet Offensive: A Concise History*. New York: Columbia University Press, 2007.

Williams, John. "ANZUS: A Blow to Britain's Self-Esteem". *Review of International Studies* 13, 4 (October 1987).

Williamson, Philip. *Stanley Baldwin: Conservative Leadership and National Values*. New York: Cambridge University Press, 1999.

Willmott, H.P. *Grave of a Dozen Schemes: British Naval Planning and the War Against Japan, 1943–1945*. Annapolis, MD: Naval Institute Press, 1996.

Wilson, Harold. *The Labour Government 1964–70*. London: Penguin, 1974.

Wing, Sandra Koa, ed. *Our Longest Days: A People's History of the Second World War*. London: Profile Books, 2008 [2007].

Wood, Ian S. *Churchill*. London: Macmillan, 2000.

Woods, Philip. "From Shaw to Shantaram: The Film Advisory Board and the Making of British Propaganda Films in India, 1940–1943". *Historical Journal of Film, Radio and Television* 21 (2001).

Yap, Sonny *et al. Men in White: The Untold Story of Singapore's Ruling Political Party*. Singapore: Singapore Press Holdings Limited, 2009.

Young, Marilyn B. *The Vietnam Wars 1945–1990*. New York: HarperCollins, 1991.

Ziegler, Philip. *Mountbatten: The Official Biography*. London: Collins, 1985.

————. *The Authorised Life of Lord Wilson of Rievaulx*. London: HarperCollins, 1993.

————. *Edward Heath: The Authorised Biography*. London: HarperCollins, 2010.

Newspapers and Broadcast Media

British Pathe Newsreel

Canberra Times (Canberra)

Daily Mail (London)

The Daily Telegraph (London)

The Evening Independent (St. Petersburg, FL)

Evening Standard (London)

The Financial Times (London)

The Guardian (Manchester, London)

London Illustrated News (London)

Melbourne Herald (Melbourne)

The Mirror (London)

Montreal Gazette (Montreal)

News of the World (London)

Pictorial Weekly (London)

The Spectator (London)

The Straits Times (Singapore)

Sunday Dispatch (London)

Sydney Morning Herald (Sydney)

The Times (London)

CONTRIBUTORS

Piers BRENDON is a British historian. He was Keeper of the Archives at The Churchill Archives Centre, Churchill College, Cambridge from 1995 to 2001, taking over from Correlli Barnett. His major published works include *Winston Churchill: A Brief Life* (1984); *Ike: His Life and Times* (1986); *The Dark Valley: A Panorama of the 1930s* (2000); and *The Decline and Fall of the British Empire* (2007).

Peter EDWARDS is a consultant Australian historian, who has published on Australian defence and foreign policies for over 30 years. He is the Official Historian of Australia's involvement in Southeast Asian conflicts 1948–1975 (Malaya, Borneo and Vietnam), the nine-volume series for which he wrote the volumes dealing with strategy and diplomacy: *Crises and Commitments* (1992) and *A Nation at War* (1997). His other key publications include *Facing North: A Century of Australian Engagement with Asia* (2003); and *Arthur Tange: Last of the Mandarins* (2006).

Brian P. FARRELL (editor) is a Canadian historian, who has been teaching military history at the National University of Singapore since 1993. His research interests include the defence of the British Empire, and coalition warfare. His published works include *The Basis and Making of British Grand Strategy 1940–1943: Was There a Plan?* (1998); *Between Two Oceans: A Military History of Singapore* (1999); *The Defence and Fall of Singapore 1940–1942* (2005); and *Malaya 1942* (2010).

Malcolm H. MURFETT is a British historian, who has been teaching European history at the National University of Singapore since 1980. His research interests comprise naval history and the history of international relations and his publications consist of *Fool Proof Relations: The Search for Anglo-American Naval Cooperation during the Chamberlain Years* (1984); *In Jeopardy: The Royal Navy and British Far Eastern Defence Policy 1945–1951* (1995); *Between Two Oceans: A Military History of Singapore* (1999); and *Naval Warfare 1919–1945: An Operational History of the Volatile War at Sea* (2008).

Allen PACKWOOD has been Director of the Churchill Archives Centre since 2002, its first full-time Director. His major works include *Forging an Alliance for Freedom* (2004) and *Churchill and the Great Republic* (2004).

Geoffrey TILL is a British naval historian and Professor of Maritime Studies in the Defence Studies Department of King's College London. His key publications are *Air Power and the Royal Navy, 1914–1945: A Historical Survey* (1979); *Maritime Strategy and the Nuclear Age* (1984); *Modern Sea Power: An Introduction* (1987); and *Seapower: A Guide for the Twenty-First Century* (2004).

Richard TOYE is a British historian, Senior Lecturer in the Department of History, University of Exeter, UK. His book *Lloyd George and Churchill: Rivals for Greatness* was the winner of the Times Higher Young Academic Author of the Year Award in 2007. Other major publications consist of *The Labour Party and the Planned Economy 1931–1951* (2003); *Making Reputations: Power, Persuasion and the Individual in Modern British Politics* (2005); and *Churchill and Empire: The World That Made Him and The World He Made* (2010).

INDEX